BARRON'S

ENGLISH

Fourth Edition

THE
EASY
WAY

Harriet Diamond, M.A.
President, Diamond Associates,
Multi-Faceted Training & Consulting
Westfield, New Jersey

and

Phyllis Dutwin, M.A.
President, Dutwin Associates,
Training and Development Programs
Wickford, Rhode Island

BARRON'S

This book is dedicated to those adults committed to lifelong
learning: the students and their teachers.

ACKNOWLEDGMENTS

The authors are grateful to Linda Diamond, Diamond Associates project manager,
for outstanding contributions—refreshing additions and revisions, both in content
and concept, to the fourth edition.

Portion of material adapted from Russell Baker's "Backwards Wheels the Mind," *The
New York Times*, July 1, 1973. © 1973 by the New York Times Company. Reprinted
by permission.

Quote from Richard Bach's *Jonathan Livingston Seagull*. © 1970, Macmillan Publishing Co., Inc. Reprinted by permission.

Paragraph from *A Civil Tongue* by Edwin Newman. © 1976 by Edwin Newman.

Portions of Chapter 22 adapted from *Writing the Easy Way* by Harriet Diamond and
Phyllis Dutwin. © 1991 by Barron's Educational Series, Inc.

Quote from Leo Rosen's "Even Bobby Fischer Would Have His Hands Full," *The New
York Times*, July 25, 1972.

All inquiries should be addressed to:
Barron's Educational Series, Inc.
250 Wireless Boulevard
Hauppauge, NY 11788
www.barronseduc.com

International Standard Book No. 0-7641-1975-3
Library of Congress Catalog Card No. 2002033215

Library of Congress Cataloging-in-Publication Data

Diamond, Harriet.
  English the easy way / Harriet Diamond and Phyllis Dutwin.—
4th ed.
    p. cm.
  ISBN 0-7641-1975-3
  1. English language—Grammar—Problems, exercises, etc.
2. English language—Usage—Problems, exercises, etc.
I. Dutwin, Phyllis. II. Title.

PE1112 .D47 2003
428.2—dc21

                                            2002033215

PRINTED IN THE UNITED STATES OF AMERICA
9 8 7 6 5 4 3 2 1

CONTENTS

INTRODUCTION

In traditional grammar programs, students are often baffled by the necessity of memorizing numerous definitions of grammatical terminology, none of which has any practical meaning in terms of day-to-day speech and writing. The confusion that results is often detrimental; the student's frustration ultimately overcomes his or her desire to learn.

English The Easy Way is designed to encourage, not frustrate, the student. Written specifically for adult students who want an all-inclusive self-help program in grammar, *English The Easy Way* also serves as an invaluable tool for all English language improvement programs.

Its main feature is a common-sense approach to language study. Recognizing that traditional grammar is not easy for everyone to master, *English The Easy Way* emphasizes language structure. Thus, the main purpose of this format is to motivate by showing how much the student already knows about the language.

English The Easy Way builds upon the student's basic understanding in an organized way. Beginning with the basic sentence pattern—performer-action—the book continues until all essential elements are introduced. Ample practice material follows each newly introduced concept. Because of the manner of presentation of the instructional material, *English The Easy Way* lends itself easily either to group or individualized classroom instruction or to independent study.

New for the Fourth Edition

For those who are comfortable with basic terms or who are looking to understand them, we have added sections that explain the basic grammar terms relevant to each section. We find that students who use the book appreciate being able to dive in and learn to improve their grammar without having to master the technical jargon. On the other hand, we find that some people appreciate having a basic understanding of terms.

In order to satisfy everyone, we added optional Grammar Connection sections. These are very brief sections that provide basic grammar terms and their definitions. In keeping with the *English the Easy Way* tradition, we do not use these terms throughout the chapters, but we provide these terms immediately after the lessons that best demonstrate their uses. So, by the time you see the new term, you already understand what it means. Once again, by the time you reach these sections, you will find that you know more than you think you know.

Getting the Most from *English the Easy Way*

Because *English The Easy Way* is a cumulative study, we recommend beginning with Chapter 1 and continuing consecutively. There are three chapters that do not fit into the consecutive pattern of the book: "Spelling," "Building Vocabulary," and "Word Usage." Spelling rules can be summarized in one chapter, but they cannot be learned in one lesson. The same is true of word usage and vocabulary. The authors, therefore, recommend that students begin studying these chapters early in their program and continue on a regular basis.

Guard against skimming over instructional material. Skipping instructional material, in order to complete practices quickly, will result in unnecessary errors and time lost. Before attempting a Cumulative Review, the authors recommend reviewing the major concepts presented in the chapters that precede it.

> **Consistent use of the *Answer Key* is essential to proper study.** The authors recommend that students check each practice exercise with the *Answer Key* before going on to the next section. By checking answers after each exercise, students can avoid repeating errors. Cumulative Reviews should be considered tests and should be taken in their entirety before checking answers. Students should note the kinds of errors made in Cumulative Reviews (these answers have been keyed to the applicable review chapters) and return to the appropriate chapters for reinforcement of the correct concepts.

Chapter 1

THE SIMPLEST COMPLETE THOUGHT

"Twas brillig and the slithy toves
Did gyre and gimble in the wabe;
All mimsy were the borogroves,
All the mome raths outgrabe.

"Beware the Jabberwock, my son!
The jaws that bite, the claws that catch!
Beware the Jubjub bird, and shun
The frumious Bandersnatch!"

—Lewis Carroll
from "Jabberwocky"

A Word With You ...

"Jabberwocky," the most famous nonsense poem ever written, can be enjoyed on several levels. Literary detectives have tried to find hidden meanings in the made-up words, while others have been amused by the poet's cleverness with sounds and rhythms.

Although Lewis Carroll never heard of "the flink glopped," it is a phrase he might have approved of—especially in the way it is used in the chapter you are about to read.

What You've Always Known

The flink glopped.

What is the above sentence about? What action is taking place in this sentence? Who is performing this action? You are able to understand the nonsense sentence because you are familiar with that sentence pattern: a person or thing performing an action.

Performer Action
| |
(The) flink glopped.

You frequently see this pattern written, and you hear it spoken.

1

Another clue in this sentence is a clue to time. Is the action past, present, or future? What was the clue? Yes, the _–ed_ ending is the clue to time. The action occurred in the past.

This sentence offers a clue to number (how many flinks) as well. Notice the word endings in the following sentences:

The flin<u>k</u> glopp<u>ed</u>. (one flink)
The flink<u>s</u> glopp<u>ed</u>. (more than one flink)

What about in present tense? That can seem confusing at first.

The flin<u>k</u> glop<u>s</u>. (one flink)
The flink<u>s</u> glo<u>p</u>. (more than one flink)

"The" could refer to one or more. The <u>s</u> is added to flink tells you there is more than one flink. Notice that in the present tense, when the performer (_flink_) is <u>singular</u>, an s is added to the action. When the performer (_flinks_) is <u>plural</u> (more than one), no <u>s</u> is added to the action.

Another example of this sentence pattern using more than one performer is:

The _flink and his brother glop_.

There may be one performer and more than one action:

The _flink glops and glarks_.

There may also be more than one performer and more than one action:

The _flink and his brother glop and glark_.

Now, let's examine some real sentences that use the same pattern: a person or thing performing an action and then the action. As you read the following sentences, think about who or what is performing the action, what the action is, and when the action occurs (present, past, or future). Next, write the performer, the action, and the times in the spaces provided. The first sentence is done for you.

	Performer	Action (s)	(present, past, future) Time
1. The plane raced across the sky.			
2. They will speak at the November meeting.			
3. The interviewer listened attentively.			
4. The waitress took our order.			
5. Star Cleaners picks up and delivers cleaning.			
6. The woman and her children crossed the street.			

	Performer	Action (s)	(present, past, future) Time
7. The gardener rakes the leaves and cuts the grass.			
8. Diane and Joe ate at their favorite restaurant and went to a concert.			

Practice I

Directions: Complete the pattern in each of the following sentences by adding either the person or thing performing the action or the action.

1. The children _____ into the street.
2. _____ barked at the mailman.
3. _____ will signal at the light.
4. The choir _____ last Sunday.
5. _____ hesitated in the doorway.

Practice II

Directions: Draw a line from the people or things in the left column to the actions in the right column to make complete sentences.

Performers	Actions
The jury	travel.
An accident	will attend.
A salesman and his assistant	occurred.
A motorcycle	convened and concurred.
We	backfires.

Practice III

Directions: Write three sentences of your own using the sentence pattern you have just studied: a person or thing performing an action and an action.

Performer	Action
1. _____	_____
2. _____	_____
3. _____	_____

Practice IV

Directions: In each of the following sentences, one word is underlined. If the underlined word is the person or thing performing the action, blacken number 1. If the underlined word is the action word, blacken number 2.

1. The *manager* shouted at the salesman.   ① ②
2. A large delivery *truck* approached the intersection.   ① ②
3. We *celebrated* her graduation.   ① ②
4. The *mayor* proclaimed a clean-up week.   ① ②
5. The members *contributed* large sums of money.   ① ②
6. The huge *machine* sputtered menacingly.   ① ②
7. A committee *will convene* within the week.   ① ②
8. The *union* struck after much negotiation.   ① ②
9. The checkbook *balances* for the first time.   ① ②
10. A soprano *will sing* this part of the opera.   ① ②

Practice V

Directions: Blacken number 1 if a sentence has one performer and one action; blacken number 2 if a sentence has more than one performer and one action; blacken number 3 if a sentence has one performer and two actions; blacken number 4 if a sentence has more than one performer and two actions.

1. This candidate addresses the issues.   ① ② ③ ④
2. His opponent evades difficult questions.   ① ② ③ ④
3. Meditation relaxes many people.   ① ② ③ ④
4. Mr. Valdez proposed several good ideas.   ① ② ③ ④
5. Six team members shouted at the coach.   ① ② ③ ④
6. Maria and Julia sold their pottery.   ① ② ③ ④
7. The electrician and his assistant stopped and rested. ① ② ③ ④
8. The audience cheered and applauded.   ① ② ③ ④
9. Batman always wins.   ① ② ③ ④
10. I asked a technical question.   ① ② ③ ④

Recognizing Complete and Incomplete Thoughts

You are ready now to add another element to your understanding of complete thoughts.

EXAMPLE:

When you arrive.

The example above has a performer *(you)* and an action *(arrive)*; yet, it is not a complete thought. Because the example begins with the word *when,* the thought is not complete as it stands.

> Any sentence that begins with such words as *when, after, because, as soon as, before,* or *since* needs to have a completing thought.

Possible thought completions for *When you arrive* are:

a. When you arrive, *relax.*
b. When you arrive, *call me.*
c. When you arrive, *I will leave.*

EXAMPLE:

The tall figure walking hurriedly through the park.

The above example has a performer *(figure),* but the action *(walking)* is incomplete. It would be correct to say the figure *was walking* or the figure *is walking.*

Possible thought completions for *The tall figure walking hurriedly through the park* are:

a. The tall figure *is walking hurriedly through the park.*
b. The tall figure *was walking hurriedly through the park.*
c. The tall figure *walked hurriedly through the park.*
d. The tall figure *walking hurriedly through the park* turned out to be a short man on stilts.

Practice VI

Directions: Blacken the circle that corresponds to the number of the incomplete sentence in each group. If there is no error, blacken number 5.

1. (1) After the mayor's defeat, he retired from public office.   ① ② ③ ④ ⑤
    (2) Bring me a cup of coffee, please.
    (3) When Richard called his office.
    (4) The two truckers arrived at the delivery depot at the same time.
    (5) No error
2. (1) The man in the blue suit and the lady in the tan coat walking.   ① ② ③ ④ ⑤
    (2) The legislature meets daily.
    (3) I did not buy enough yarn for the sweater.
    (4) A large delivery truck reached the intersection.
    (5) No error
3. (1) The nervous waitress spilled the coffee in the celebrity's lap.   ① ② ③ ④ ⑤
    (2) The fumbling, bumbling clown dancing.
    (3) The county official faced the angry crowd.
    (4) The women in the community organized a boycott against Sam's Market.
    (5) No error

4. (1) A favorite history question involves the causative factors of   ① ② ③ ④ ⑤
       the Civil War.
   (2) Federal spending cuts will cause much discussion.
   (3) The winning pitcher threw a fast ball.
   (4) Her considerate husband brought a dozen roses for their
       anniversary.
   (5) No error

5. (1) The students studied and reviewed.   ① ② ③ ④ ⑤
   (2) Flour, sugar, and three eggs blending.
   (3) The book fell suddenly from the shelf.
   (4) The mayor proclaimed a clean-up week.
   (5) No error

Action Words: Special Problems

Many action words undergo simple changes to show changes in time. *For example:*

Present	Past	Action words used with helping words, such as has, had, have, is, etc.
kick	kicked	kicked
plan	planned	planned
cheer	cheered	cheered

The simplest change is the addition of an *-ed* ending.

1. I _kick_ the ball 200 yards each time. (Present)
2. The tenants' association _planned_ a victory party. (Past)
3. The overzealous Viking fans _had_ _cheered_ before they realized that the Eagle quarter-back was really injured. (Past with helping word, _had_)

Many action words use entirely different forms to show these same changes. *For example:*

Present	Past	Action words used with helping words, such as has, had, have, is, etc.
break	broke	broken

1. Anna never _breaks_ a promise.
2. Rosemary _broke_ several promises to Anna.
3. Rosemary _has_ _broken_ her last promise.

Following is a list of commonly used action words that change their forms to show time changes.

Present	Past	Action words used with helping words, such as has, had, have, is, etc.
begin	began	begun
blow	blew	blown
break	broke	broken
bring	brought	brought
build	built	built
burst	burst	burst
choose	chose	chosen
dive	dived *or* dove	dived
do	did	done
draw	drew	drawn
drink	drank	drunk
drive	drove	driven
eat	ate	eaten
fall	fell	fallen
flee	fled	fled
fly	flew	flown
forbid	forbade	forbidden
freeze	froze	frozen
get	got	gotten *or* got
give	gave	given
go	went	gone
grow	grew	grown
have, has	had	had
know	knew	known
lay (place)	laid	laid
lead	led	led
leave (depart)	left	left
lie (recline)	lay	lain
pay	paid	paid
raise (elevate)	raised	raised
ride	rode	ridden
ring	rang	rung
rise (ascend)	rose	risen
run	ran	run
see	saw	seen
shake	shook	shaken
shine	shone, shined	shone, shined
shoot	shot	shot
shrink	shrank, shrunk	shrunk
sing	sang	sung
sit	sat	sat
slay	slew	slain
speak	spoke	spoken
spring	sprang	sprung
steal	stole	stolen
sting	stung	stung
swear	swore	sworn
swing	swung	swung
swim	swam	swum

Present	Past	Action words used with helping words, such as has, had, have, is, etc.
take	took	taken
tear	tore	torn
throw	threw	thrown
wake	waked *or* woke	waked
wear	wore	worn
write	wrote	written

Practice VII

Directions: Choose an action word in the parentheses to complete each sentence. Find the correct form of the word in the list above.

1. The employee entered the correct code and the gate (rose, rise). (Hint: Choose the word that means *goes up*, or, *ascends*.)
2. I bought new running shoes because the heels had (worn, wore) down in the old ones.
3. If we had (knew, known) how long the movie was, we wouldn't have rented it.
4. The laundry had (shrinked, shrunk) my only good shirt just before the awards dinner.
5. The children have always (lain, laid) the money on the counter when they arrived, but today it was not there. (Hint: Choose the word that means *to place*.)

Practice VIII

Directions: Blacken the circle that corresponds to the number of the sentence with the incorrect action word in each group. If there is no error, blacken number 5. (Note: Refer to the preceding list to find the correct form of the action word.)

1. (1) Marigolds always have _grown_ well in that sunny spot.   ① ② ③ ④ ⑤
   (2) I have _rang_ her doorbell several times today.
   (3) After we had _set_ the bowl of flowers on the table, the room looked complete.
   (4) Having _ridden_ for hours, the sightseers were ready to check into a motel.
   (5) No error
2. (1) Angela _led_ the church choir.   ① ② ③ ④ ⑤
   (2) Last year, Marlene _lead_ the church choir.
   (3) I never _have_ _led_ a church choir.
   (4) Have you ever _led_ a church choir?
   (5) No error
3. (1) I _swear_ that I told the truth.   ① ② ③ ④ ⑤
   (2) The defendant _swore_ to tell the truth.
   (3) The plaintiff _swore_ to tell the truth.
   (4) All of the witnesses have been _sworn_ in.
   (5) No error

4. (1) Venus Williams has _swung_ many tennis rackets in her time.   ① ② ③ ④ ⑤
   (2) I, on the other hand, have never _swung_ a tennis racket quite like she did during that decisive game.
   (3) I wonder if Joani _swings_ a golf club incorrectly.
   (4) He _swinged_ a tennis racket fairly well.
   (5) No error

5. (1) The opinionated Mr. Dobbs never had _run_ for office himself.   ① ② ③ ④ ⑤
   (2) Colonel Adams has _run_ for mayor several times.
   (3) I have _ran_ for public office once.
   (4) Carla Diaz plans to _run_ next year.
   (5) No error

Practice IX

Directions: Blacken the circle that corresponds to the number of the incorrect word in each sentence. If there is no error, blacken number 5.

1. The injured bird _flew_ to the ground, _letting_ his _broken_ wing   ① ② ③ ④ ⑤
               1   2   3

   lay at his side. _No error_
    4   5

2. Upon seeing the young child _fall_ into the lake, Eric _sprung_ to   ① ② ③ ④ ⑤
                      1   2

   his feet, _ran_, and _dived_. _No error_
        3   4   5

3. Because Teddy had frequently _fallen_ asleep on the job, he was   ① ② ③ ④ ⑤
                       1

   not _payed_ the full _amount_ that had been _written_ into his
        2   3   4

   contract. _No error_
        5

4. If you _choose_ to _rise_ within the company, you _must_ _raise_ your   ① ② ③ ④ ⑤
        1   2   3   4

   level of work. _No error_
        5

5. The guest _arrived_ unexpectedly, _shaked_ everyone's hand, _ate_,   ① ② ③ ④ ⑤
        1   2   3

   and _left_ as unexpectedly as he had arrived. _No error_
      4   5

6. We _seen_ the lights that _shined_ in the distance, and we _began_   ① ② ③ ④ ⑤
      1   2   3

   to _walk_ toward them. _No error_
      4   5

7. Because I had *forgotten* my driver's license, the policeman   ① ② ③ ④ ⑤
                     1

   forbidded me to *drive* any *farther*. *No error*
      2   3   4   5

8. Once the cult leader had *fallen*, the young followers did not   ① ② ③ ④ ⑤
                     1

   know how to continue, so they *fleed* in many directions and
    2   3

   many were *seen* returning home. *No error*
         4   5

9. James Bond *says* he *likes* his martinis *shaken*, not *stirred*.   ① ② ③ ④ ⑤
             1   2   3   4
   No error
    5

10. Maxine *waked* me early this morning, and I *ate* my eggs,   ① ② ③ ④ ⑤
        1   2

   drunk my juice, and *left*. *No error*
    3   4   5

Grammar Connection: Nouns and Verbs

Sentence subjects, or performers, are nouns, but the subject is not the only noun in the sentence.

Nouns

A noun is a person, place, or thing. Performers are nouns that act as the *subject* of the sentence. By using the word *performer*, the authors hinted at the word's job. That is true of all words; they have names (noun) and jobs (subject).

You now know that a noun is a person, place, or thing. However, what does a noun *do*? In the following sentences, the italicized nouns have the job of subject.

noun (person) / subject
|
Bob plays the guitar.

noun (place) / subject
|
Kentucky hosts the Derby.

noun (thing) / subject
\
The *ball* hit the fence.

In addition to being the subject, nouns have other jobs in sentences. Look at the other italicized nouns in the same sentences.

direct object
|
Bob plays the *guitar*.

direct object
|
Kentucky hosts the *Derby*.

direct object
|
The ball hit the *fence*.

In these sentences, the italicized nouns do not act as subjects. They are *direct objects*. *Direct objects* do not do anything. Instead, something is done to them. *Bob* (the subject) does the playing. The *guitar* (the object) receives the playing.

Verbs

The action words in the sentences in this chapter are all verbs. All action words are verbs, but all verbs are not action words. For now, think of verbs as action words.

EXAMPLES:

Bob *plays* the guitar. (*Plays*, an action word, is a verb.)
Kentucky *hosts* the Derby. (*Hosts*, an action word, is a verb.)
The ball *hit* the fence. (*Hit*, an action word, is a verb.)

In this chapter, you learned about nouns and verbs and how they interact. In the next chapter, you will learn more about how to make nouns and verbs agree in time and number. What does that mean, you ask? Do not worry, it will all be clear in the next chapter.

Chapter 1   The Simplest Complete Thought

Performer	Action	Time
1. plane	raced	past
2. they	will speak	future
3. interviewer	listened	past
4. waitress	took	past
5. Star Cleaners	picks up, delivers	present
6. woman, children	crossed	past
7. gardener	rakes, cuts	present
8. Diane, Joe	ate went	past

Practice I *Page 3.*
Answers will vary. *Sample* answers:
1. The children *ran* into the street.
2. *The dog* barked at the mailman.
3. *Henry* will signal at the light.
4. The choir *sang* last Sunday.
5. *Susan* hesitated in the doorway.

Practice II *Page 3.*
1. The jury convened and concurred.
2. An accident occurred.
3. A salesman and his assistant travel.
4. A motorcycle backfires.
5. We will attend.

Practice III *Page 3.*
Answers will vary. *Sample* answers:
1. *John cashed* a check at the bank.
2. The *roses bloomed* early this year.
3. My *mother-in-law calls* every Friday.

Practice IV *Page 3.*

Performer	Action
1. **(1)** manager	
2. **(1)** truck	
3. **(2)**	celebrated
4. **(1)** mayor	
5. **(2)**	contributed
6. **(1)** machine	
7. **(2)**	will convene
8. **(1)** union	
9. **(2)**	balances
10. **(2)**	will sing

Practice V *Page 4.*

Performer	Action
1. **(1)** candidate	addresses
2. **(1)** opponent	evades
3. **(1)** meditation	relaxes
4. **(1)** Mr. Valdez	proposed
5. **(2)** members	shouted
6. **(2)** Maria and Julia	sold
7. **(4)** electrician and assistant	stopped and rested
8. **(3)** audience	cheered and applauded
9. **(1)** Batman	wins
10. **(1)** I	asked

Practice VI *Page 5.*

Possible Corrections:

1. **(3)** a. When Richard called his office, the phone rang unanswered.
   b. Richard called his office.
2. **(1)** a. The man in the blue suit and the lady in the tan coat walk.
   b. The man in the blue suit and the lady in the tan coat, walking along the street, were stopped by a stranger.
3. **(2)** a. The fumbling, bumbling clown danced.
   b. The fumbling, bumbling clown dancing makes the children laugh.
4. **(5)** No error
5. **(2)** a. Blend flour, sugar, and three eggs.
   b. Flour, sugar, and three eggs blending completes the recipe.

Practice VII *Page 8.*

1. Use *rose* (the past form of the action word that means *to ascend*).
2. Use *worn* with the helping word *had*.
3. Use *known* with the helping word *had*.
4. Use *shrunk* with the helping word *had*.
5. Use *laid* (the action word that means *to place*) with the helping word *have*.

Practice VIII *Page 8.*

1. **(2)** have *rung*
   Use *rung* with the helping word *have*.

2. **(2)** *led*
   Lead is present; *led* is past.
3. **(5)** No error
   Swear is present; *swore* is past; *sworn* is used with *have been*.
4. **(4)** *swung*
   Swinged is not a word.
5. **(3)** have *run*
   Use *run* with the helping word *have*.

Practice IX *Page 9.*

1. **(5)** No error
2. **(2)** sprang
   Sprung is used only with helping words such as *has*, *have*, or *had*.
3. **(2)** paid
   Payed is not a word.
4. **(5)** No error
5. **(2)** shook
   Shaked is not a word.
6. **(1)** saw
   Seen is used only with helping words such as *has*, *have*, or *had*.
7. **(2)** forbade
   Forbidded is not a word.
8. **(3)** fled
   Fleed is not a word.
9. **(5)** No error
10. **(3)** drank
    Drunk is used only with helping words such as *has*, *have*, or *had*.

Chapter 2

PERFORMER AND ACTION: UNDERSTANDING TIME AND NUMBER

Every so often, Mr. Spector called on Vinnie to answer, and that was when English 117 really came to life.

"So I says to Angie . . ."

"No, Vinnie," interjected Mr. Spector, "you didn't '*says*' to Angie, you '*said*' to him."

"That's right," continued Vinnie, "I *says* to Angie . . ."

"Go on," Mr. Spector replied wearily; "You *says* to Angie . . ."

"That's what I *said*, man," snorted Vinnie. "Can't a guy tell a story without bein' interrupted?"

—Roger Talifiero
Our Little Red Schoolhouse

A Word With You . . .

Mr. Spector's English class was a lively place because the teacher encouraged free and open discussion. At times, however, Mr. Spector's classical training set his teeth on edge when he saw a misspelling or a failure to capitalize.

In this excerpt, his student, Vinnie, was confused about different forms of the action word *to say*. After you read Chapter 2, you should know why Mr. Spector often needed an aspirin after English 117.

14

Understanding Time

As you learned in Chapter 1, the action word changes form to give a sense of time.

John walks. (*present*)
John walked. (*past*)
John will walk. (*future*)

Practice I

Directions: Use *work, worked,* or *will work* in each of the following sentences.

1. Willie Farris _____ overtime last week.
2. We must _____ a certain number of hours each day.
3. Four employees _____ overtime next week.

The action word in the first sentence sets the time for the paragraph. If the paragraph begins in the past tense, it should remain in the past; if it begins in the present, it should remain in the present. The exception is when a word or phrase triggers a change in tense (for example: before that, after that, yesterday, today). However, tense should not shift without a very clear clue that you were referring to one time and now you are referring to another.

Remember, the action word in the first sentence sets the time for the paragraph.

INCORRECT: John *entered* the library. He *speaks* to the librarian. He *walked* from stack to stack looking for something in particular. Finally, John *chooses* a book.
CORRECT: John *entered* the library. He *spoke* to the librarian. He *walked* from stack to stack looking for something in particular. Finally, John *chose* a book.

Because *entered* is in the past, *spoke, walked,* and *chose* must be in the past, too.

Practice II

Directions: For each underlined action word, blacken circle number 1 if the time is correct and circle number 2 if the time is incorrect. Remember that the action word *filed* sets the time for the other action words in the paragraph.

The crowd filed into the meeting room. The chairman <u>raps</u> his gavel.   (1) ① ②
                                 1

An angry murmur <u>continued</u> in the room. The chairman <u>will rap</u> his   (2) ① ②
                    2   3

gavel a second time. Quiet finally <u>settles</u> over the room. The chairman   (3) ① ②
                                 4

<u>began</u> his report.   (4) ① ②
  5   (5) ① ②

Understanding Number

When we talk about a performer's *number*, we are talking about whether it is singular or plural.

EXAMPLE:

performer (singular)
|
Sometimes the <u>*appliance*</u> works.

EXAMPLE:

performer (plural)
|
Sometimes the <u>*appliances*</u> don't work.

A plural performer is most commonly expressed in one word that ends in *s*, such as girls. However, irregular plurals, such as children, do not end in *s*.

EXAMPLE:

performer (plural)
/
The *children* are playing outside.

A plural performer may also be expressed in more than one word. A number of singular performers acting together may be plural.

EXAMPLES:

performer (singular)
/
Exercise keeps weight off.

performer (plural)
/   \
Diet and *exercise* keep weight off.

performer (singular)
/
A *computer* is essential office equipment.

performer (plural)
/ | \
A *computer*, a *printer*, and *a fax machine* are essential office equipment.

Practice III

Directions: In each of the following sentences, underline the performer or performers. Write an *S* over the word if the performer is singular. Write a *P* over the word or words if the performer is plural.

EXAMPLE:

S
Mr. Warner knows everyone in town.

1. The women work well together.

2. Mr. Smith and his son address the Cub Scouts.

3. Flour, sugar, and milk complete this recipe.

4. Connie Martine understands community relations.

5. Mr. Luchner's grandchildren often visit him.

As you are beginning to see, the performer and action words *work together* (grammarians say they *agree*) to show that they are singular or plural.

EXAMPLE:

singular   singular
performer   action word

Our *aunt comes* to dinner every Sunday.

EXAMPLE:

plural   plural
performer   action word

Our *relatives come* to dinner every Sunday.

Did you notice anything surprising? You are probably saying to yourself, as you did when you read Chapter 1, "Why is there an *s* at the end of a singular action word (come*s*)? An *s* means the word is plural, doesn't it?" Well, yes—and no. An *s* at the end of the performer (relative*s*) shows that it is plural. On the other hand, an *s* at the end of an action word (come*s*) shows that the action word is singular and should be used with a singular performer.

EXAMPLE:

singular   singular
performer   action word

That *car travels* at top speed.

EXAMPLE:

plural   plural
performer   action word
| |
Those <u>*cars*</u> <u>*travel*</u> at top speed.

EXAMPLE:

singular performer
|
The <u>*house*</u> stand<u>s</u> on a hill.

EXAMPLE:

plural performer
|
The <u>*houses*</u> stan<u>d</u> on a hill.

Practice IV

Directions: Correct the number error in each underlined action word.

1. Today, companies *focuses* on their customers._____
2. The machine *make* 300 gallons of pure water._____
3. Beautifully wrapped presents *does* not stay that way for very long._____
4. Today, many businesses *manages* offices all over the world._____
5. That agency *give* the kind of advice I need._____

You have been working with performers in the present time: *comes, travels, stands,* etc. Now we've come to the easier part—performers in past time. Why easier? You will see that even when the performer changes from a singular to a plural performer, the action word does not change. For example, we can select the action word *ride* and use it in its past form, *rode.* Now, when we change the performer in every sentence below so that there are both singular and plural performers, what happens to the word *rode*? Nothing. *Rode* remains the same.

I *rode* the subway.
You *rode* the subway.

(He)	David *rode* the subway.
(She)	Pam *rode* the subway.
	Who *rode* the subway?
(We)	David and I *rode* the subway.
	You and Pam *rode* the subway.
(They)	Ellen and Linda *rode* the subway.

In the following sentences, the time is present. Notice that the form of the action word changes for singular and plural performers. You see that an *s* is added to the action word when the performer is *singular*—except when the performer is *I* or *you.*

EXAMPLE:

The studen*t* ride*s* the subway.
The student*s* rid*e* the subway.

I *ride* the subway.
You *ride* the subway.
(He)   David *rides* the subway.
(She)   Pam *rides* the subway.
Who *rides* the subway?
(We)   David and I *ride* the subway.
You and Pam *ride* the subway.
(They)   Ellen and Linda *ride* the subway.

Practice V

Directions: Blacken the circle that corresponds to the number of the incorrect action word in each group of sentences. If there is no error, blacken number 5.

1. A shopping trip *makes* me angry. Prices *soar* each week. Meat   ① ② ③ ④ ⑤
         1   2

   prices *changes* almost daily. Oranges, apples, and bananas
            3

   cost more than ever. A shopper needs more and more money
    4

   each week. *No error*
          5

2. Tom *jogs* each morning. Macon and Gary *join* him on Mondays   ① ② ③ ④ ⑤
       1   2

   and Thursdays. The Robinson twins *likes* jogging too. Jogging
                                3

   now *replaces* basketball as the neighborhood pastime. *No error*
        4   5

3. Each year local artists *participate* in an art show. The   ① ② ③ ④ ⑤
                        1

   Community Center *offers* a perfect gallery. One artist *wins* in
                    2   3

   each of five categories. The winning artists *displays* their
                                            4

   works in the Town Hall. *No error*
          5

The above paragraphs had errors in *number*. In the following exercise, look for errors in *time* and *number*.

Practice VI

Directions: Blacken the circle that corresponds to the number of the incorrect word in each group of sentences. If there is no error, blacken number 5.

1. In the spring, the honeysuckle *droops* over the hillside. Its   ① ② ③ ④ ⑤
                                    1

   sweet *smell* *hangs* heavily in the air outside. It floats into the
         2   3

   room when the doors *are open*. *No error*
                        4   5

2. A hummingbird *dives* daily in and out of the honeysuckle.   ① ② ③ ④ ⑤
                 1

   He *bombs* *past* the doors with his heavy load and *balanced* on
      2   3   4

   a branch of the little olive tree. *No error*
                                       5

3. Distractions, such as cell phone use, *causes* car accidents. A   ① ② ③ ④ ⑤
                                          1

   five-year study concluded that 284,000 drivers annually *are*
                                                            2

   involved in serious crashes caused by distractions. These
   distractions also *include* adjusting the radio, eating, men
                     3

   using electric razors, and women putting on mascara. *No error*
   4   5

4. The farmer and his hired men *gathers* the corn. The farmer,   ① ② ③ ④ ⑤
                                1

   along with his hired men, *harvests* the wheat. Neither the
                             2

   corn nor the wheat is *neglected*. The farmer's wife and
                         3

   daughter *argue* a great deal. *No error*
            4   5

Chapter 2 Performer and Action: Understanding Time and Number

Practice I *Page 15.*
1. Willie Farris *worked* overtime last week.
2. We must *work* a certain number of hours each day.
3. Four employees *will work* overtime next week.

Practice II *Page 15.*
Remember *filed* set the time (past) for the other action words in the paragraph. The crowd *filed* into the meeting room.
1. **(2)** The chairman *rapped* his gavel.
   1
2. **(1)** An angry murmur *continued* in the
   2
3. **(2)** room. The chairman *rapped* his
   3
   gavel a second time. Quiet finally
4. **(2)** *settled* over the room. The chairman
   4
5. **(1)** *began* his report.
   5

Practice III *Page 17.*
   P
1. women
      P
2. Mr. Smith and his son
      P
3. Flour, sugar, and milk
   S
4. Connie Martine
   P
5. grandchildren

Practice IV *Page 18.*
1. focus   Use the plural form of the action word *(focus)* when the performer is plural *(companies)*.
2. makes   Use the singular form of the action word *(makes)* when the performer is singular *(machine)*.
3. do   Use the plural form of the action word *(do)* when the performer is plural *(presents)*.
4. manage Use the plural form of the action word *(manage)* when the performer is plural *(businesses)*.
5. gives   Use the singular form of the action word *(gives)* when the performer is singular *(agency)*.

Practice V *Page 19.*
1. **(3)** change
   Change is the plural form of the action word that agrees in number with the performer, *prices*.
2. **(3)** like
   Like is the plural form of the action word that agrees in number with the performer, *twins*.
3. **(4)** display
   Display is the plural form of the action word that agrees in number with the performer, *artists*.

Practice VI *Page 20.*

1. **(5)** No error

   All of the action words in the paragraph are in the *present time*.

2. **(4)** balances

   All of the action words in the paragraph are in the *present time*.

3. **(1)** cause

   Cause is the plural form of the action word that agrees with *distractions*.

4. **(1)** gather

   Gather is the plural form of the action word that agrees with *farmer and his hired men*.

Chapter 3

ADDING DESCRIPTIVE WORDS

Vic:	We have to advertise, Charley. No wonder no one comes into our store.
Charley:	I hate all those phoney ads where they hit you in the head with one lie after another.
Vic:	We don't have to lie. The truth will bring the suckers in.
Charley:	This is a fruit store—that's it, a fruit store. What else can we say about it?
Vic:	Use your head, Charles, my boy. Our fruit isn't just fruit, it's *delectable* fruit; we've got *golden* bananas, our cherries are *heavenly delicious*, the *sugar-sweet* pears would kill a diabetic.
Charley:	I dunno, to me fruit is fruit.

—L. I. Meyers
A Lovely Bunch of Coconuts

A Word With You . . .

Vic and Charley, the owners of Plaza Fruit, appear in a one-act play called *A Lovely Bunch of Coconuts*. As you can see, their personalities are different. Charley lacks romance—to him an apple is an apple. But Vic has the Madison Avenue approach to glamorizing his product.

Actually, what Vic did in this brief slice from the play is to add meaning by the use of descriptive words. You'll learn more about the technique in the next few pages.

Descriptive Words: Adding Meaning

You know that an English sentence must have a person or thing performing an action and the action itself. You might say that these words are the core of every sentence. But we don't speak in such simple sentences: *He ran. She jumped.* Other words are added to the core to make a sentence more meaningful and interesting. These words may tell you more about the performer, or they may tell you more about the action. Look at the following example:

performer action

The beautiful swan swam quickly.

The performer is *swan* and the action is *swam*. Note the words *the*, *beautiful*, and *quickly*. These are descriptive words. *The* tells which *swan*; *beautiful* tells you more about the performer, *swan*, and *quickly* tells you more about *swam*, the action.

performer action

The beautiful swan swam quickly.

descriptive words

Now study the two sentences below. Label the performer, action, and descriptive words in each sentence.

A large apple fell suddenly.

Large describes *apple*.   *Suddenly* describes *fell*.

The decaying tooth throbbed painfully.

Decaying describes *tooth*.   *Painfully* describes *throbbed*.

Practice I

Directions: Complete the pattern in each of the following sentences by adding a descriptive word.

1. A _____ man entered the store.
2. _____ music annoys me.
3. The cat jumped _____.
4. The _____ book slipped to the floor.
5. Dolores Bremmer walked _____ from the room.

Practice II

Directions: Write five sentences of your own. Use descriptive words to tell more about the performer, the action, or both.

1. _____
2. _____
3. _____
4. _____
5. _____

Practice III

Directions: In each of the following sentences, one word is underlined. If the underlined word is the performer, blacken number 1. If the underlined word is the action, blacken number 2. If the underlined word describes the performer, blacken number 3. If the underlined word describes the action, blacken number 4.

1. The <u>gooey</u> candy stuck to the seat of the unsuspecting moviegoer's pants. ① ② ③ ④
2. Mr. McCarthy strode <u>away</u> angrily. ① ② ③ ④
3. The sweet old man <u>winked</u>. ① ② ③ ④
4. My <u>friend</u> cooks well. ① ② ③ ④
5. Ricardo <u>gave</u> me a good suggestion. ① ② ③ ④
6. We <u>sat</u> down beneath some trees. ① ② ③ ④
7. Four hungry <u>children</u> arrived for lunch. ① ② ③ ④
8. <u>Northern</u> merchants paid little for raw materials. ① ② ③ ④
9. Rita came <u>directly</u> home after work. ① ② ③ ④
10. A <u>violent</u> storm of controversy raged at our council meeting. ① ② ③ ④

Practice IV

Directions: The descriptive words in the following sentences are underlined. In each sentence, draw an arrow from the descriptive word to the word that it describes.

EXAMPLE:

The subway lurched *wildly*.

1. The telephone rang <u>unexpectedly</u>.
2. A <u>heavy</u> rain ruined our picnic.
3. The <u>talented</u> fingers knit the sweater.
4. The speeding truck swerved <u>abruptly</u>.
5. The <u>soft</u> snow fell <u>gently</u>.

Practice V

Directions: Blacken the circle that corresponds to the number of the action word in each sentence.

1. <u>Celine Dion</u> <u>sings</u> <u>emotionally</u> charged <u>songs</u>. ① ② ③ ④
       1   2   3   4
2. The <u>rumbling</u> truck <u>sped</u> <u>down</u> the <u>highway</u>. ① ② ③ ④
       1   2 3   4
3. A <u>monotonous</u> <u>tapping</u> <u>annoyed</u> the <u>students</u>. ① ② ③ ④
       1   2   3   4
4. My foreman, Roy, <u>bought</u> beer for <u>all</u> the men <u>on</u> the <u>shift</u>. ① ② ③ ④
       1   2   3 4
5. The <u>President of the United States</u> <u>walked</u> <u>slowly</u> <u>toward</u> ① ② ③ ④
       1   2 3 4

the microphone.

Practice VI

Directions: Draw an arrow from each descriptive word to the word that it describes.

1. Mr. Hudson displays a cheerful disposition.
2. The dull day passed slowly.
3. The fast car raced quickly.
4. The cool, clear water shimmered.
5. A hungry seagull greedily grabbed the fish.

Descriptive Words: Special Problems

Many words that are used to describe performers must add *-ly* in order to describe actions. *For example:*

The <u>*nice*</u> woman spoke at the meeting.
The woman spoke <u>nice*ly*</u> at the meeting.

In the above sentences, *nice* and *nicely* do two very different jobs. *Nice* describes the performer, *woman*. *Nicely* describes the action, *spoke*. You would never say, "The *nicely* woman spoke at the meeting." However, a common error is, "The woman spoke *nice*." You can avoid that common error by recognizing that most words that describe actions end in *-ly*.

The gauge dipped *suddenly*.
The *sudden* dip in the gauge alarmed us.
INCORRECT: The gauge dipped *sudden*.

Leach passed the test *satisfactorily*.
Leah's *satisfactory* test scores placed her in the program.
INCORRECT: Leah passed the test *satisfactory*.

- *Well* describes actions, unless referring to a state of health. *Good* never describes an action.

My neighbor paints *well*.
My neighbor is a *good* painter.
I don't feel *well* today.

- *Real* describes a person, place, or thing.

The shoes were made of *real* leather.
I prefer *real* butter to imitation.
His loyalty makes him a *real* friend.

- *Really* describes another descriptive word.

Many of the events in our history are *really* exciting.
His story was not *really* believable.
Jan's shoes were *really* too small.

- *Very* describes another descriptive word.

> The basketball game was *very* exciting.
> The members of this community work *very* well together.
> The guitarist played *very* quickly.

Practice VII

Directions: Choose the word that best completes each sentence and draw an arrow from this word to the word it describes.

1. My brother adds (quick, quickly).
2. That neighbor's (loud, loudly) radio annoys me.
3. He behaved (polite, politely) toward me.
4. The old dog walked (lazy, lazily) down the street.
5. I'll give you a (quick, quickly) call when I need you.
6. He plays the piano too (loud, loudly).
7. I don't like (soft, softly) music.
8. The (delicate, delicately) bird hovered in the sky.
9. Maria (sincere, sincerely) apologized for her error in bookkeeping.
10. The dancer balanced (delicate, delicately) on one foot.
11. You have my (sincere, sincerely) apology.
12. Stanley answered (immediate, immediately).
13. This problem requires your (immediate, immediately) attention.
14. Rosemary sings (good, well).
15. A (good, well) singer remains calm.

Grammar Connection: Adjectives, Adverbs, and Articles

Adjectives, adverbs, and articles are all descriptive words.

Adjectives

An adjective describes a noun (person, place, or thing).

EXAMPLE:

The *new* car rode smoothly. (*New* is an adjective describing a noun, *car*.)

If you hear the term *adjective phrase*, all that means is a phrase (group of words) that describes a noun. You will see examples of adjective phrases later.

Adverbs

An adverb describes a verb (action word), an adjective, or another adverb.

EXAMPLES:

The new car rode *smoothly*. (*Smoothly* is an adverb describing a verb, *rode*.)
Alicia is a *pretty* tall woman. (*Pretty* is an adverb that describes the adjective *tall*.)
The train sped by *very* quickly. (*Very* is an adverb that describes the adverb *quickly*.)

If you hear the term *adverbial phrase*, all that means is a phrase (group of words) that begins with an adverb and describes a verb, an adjective, or another adverb. You will see examples of adverbial phrases later.

Articles

The words *a*, *an*, and *the* are articles. Articles add meaning to nouns. As you know, *the* is more specific than *a* or *an*.

I am working on *a* project. (any project)
I am working on *the* project. (the one we were talking about; the one you know I am working on)

Chapter 3   Adding Descriptive Words

Page 24.

performer action

A large apple fell suddenly.

descriptive words

performer   action

The decaying tooth throbbed painfully.

descriptive words

Practice I *Page 24.*
Answers may vary.
   Sample answers:
1. A *tall* man entered the store.
2. *Loud* music annoys me.
3. The cat jumped *suddenly*.
4. The *heavy* book slipped to the floor.
5. Dolores Bremmer walked *quickly* from the room.

Practice II *Page 24.*
Answers may vary.
   Sample answers:
The shy girl spoke softly.
The bright daffodils announced spring.

Practice III *Page 25.*
1. (3) *gooey* describes candy, the performer.
2. (4) *away* describes strode, the action.
3. (2) *winked* is the action.
4. (1) *friend* is the performer.
5. (2) *gave* is the action.
6. (2) *sat* is the action.
7. (1) *children* is the performer.

8. (3) *northern* describes merchants, the performers.
9. (4) *directly* describes came, the action.
10. (3) *violent* describes storm, the performer.

Practice IV *Page 25.*
1. rang   *unexpectedly* describes rang.
2. rain   *heavy* describes rain.
3. fingers   *talented* describes fingers.
4. swerved   *abruptly* describes swerved.
5. snow, fell *soft* describes snow, *gently* describes fell.

Practice V *Page 25.*
1. (2) sings
2. (2) sped
3. (3) annoyed
4. (1) bought
5. (2) walked

Practice VI *Page 26.*
1. *cheerful* describes disposition.
2. *dull* describes day, *slowly* describes passed.
3. *fast* describes car, *quickly* describes raced.
4. *cool* describes water, *clear* describes water.
5. *hungry* describes seagull, *greedily* describes grabbed.

Practice VII *Page 27.*

1. My brother adds *quickly*.

2. That neighbor's *loud* radio annoys me.

3. He behaved *politely* toward me.

4. The old dog walked *lazily* down the street.

5. I'll give you a *quick* call when I need you.

6. He plays the piano too *loudly*.

7. I don't like *soft* music.

8. The *delicate* bird hovered in the sky.

9. Maria *sincerely* apologized for her error in bookkeeping.

10. The dancer balanced *delicately* on one foot.

11. You have my *sincere* apology.

12. Stanley answered *immediately*.

13. The problem requires your *immediate* attention.

14. Rosemary *sings* well.

15. A *good* singer remains calm.

Chapter 4

USING DESCRIPTIVE WORDS CORRECTLY

Maury Wills has described a player as having good running speed. "I knew it was hit good," said Mike Schmidt of the Philadelphia Phillies, "but the ball doesn't carry good in the Astrodome." It carries bad. When James J. Braddock died, there were stories about the fight in which he lost his heavyweight championship to Joe Louis. In the first round, Braddock knocked Louis down. Louis got up. Braddock: "I thought if I hit him good, he'll stay down." It did not work out that way. Braddock was a brave man, a light-heavyweight, really, who returned to fighting when he was unemployed and on relief and went on to win the heavyweight championship. He was a longshoreman and uneducated. Tom Seaver of the New York Mets is a college graduate: "Cedeno hit the ball pretty good." Budd Schulberg is a novelist. Said he, after the Ali-Foreman fight, "The fight turned out pretty good."

—Edwin Newman
A Civil Tongue

A Word With You . . .

Obviously, many people's use of *good* isn't their *best* grammar. The notables quoted by Edwin Newman are not alone in their misuse of that common adjective. Remember, no matter how *good* a player you are, you *play well*. This chapter will help you *use* descriptive words *well*.

Descriptive Words: Using Comparison

Many descriptive words follow this pattern:

Avery built a _tall_ fence.
Anita built a _taller_ fence.
Dwayne built the _tallest_ fence _of the three_.

Why is the fence in sentence 1 described as _tall_, the fence in sentence 2 described as _taller_, and the fence in sentence 3 described as _tallest? Tall_ is a descriptive word that describes _fence. Taller_ is a descriptive word that describes and compares _two fences. Tallest_ is a descriptive word that compares _more than two fences_.

As you have seen in the above sentences, _-er_ is added to a descriptive word to show a comparison between two people or things; _-est_ is added to a descriptive word to show a comparison among more than two people or things. This is the general rule for comparison of descriptive words. _Study the examples below:_

Description	Comparison of Two	Comparison of More than Two
pretty	prettier	prettiest
small	smaller	smallest
fast	faster	fastest
near	nearer	nearest
soon	sooner	soonest
rude	ruder	rudest
shrewd	shrewder	shrewdest
spicy	spicier	spiciest
green	greener	greenest
stout	stouter	stoutest

Many descriptive words sound awkward when _-er_ or _-est_ is added. These words use _more_ instead of _-er_ and _most_ instead of _-est_ when making a comparison. _Study the examples below:_

Description	Comparison of Two	Comparison of More than Two
beautiful	more beautiful	most beautiful
tenacious	more tenacious	most tenacious
enormous	more enormous	most enormous
quickly	more quickly	most quickly
torrid	more torrid	most torrid
valuable	more valuable	most valuable
legible	more legible	most legible
difficult	more difficult	most difficult
wonderful	more wonderful	most wonderful
sympathetic	more sympathetic	most sympathetic

Some descriptive words have entirely different forms to express different degrees of comparison. _Study the examples below:_

Description	Comparison of Two	Comparison of More than Two
good	better	best
bad	worse	worst

Practice I

Directions: Complete the pattern in each of the following sentences by adding the *proper form* of one of the descriptive words below.

boring   magnificent   long   high   good

1. This is the _____ meeting I've ever attended.
2. We chose the _____ day of the summer for our office picnic.
3. Amanda Valdez is one of the _____ people I know.
4. Ricky works _____ hours than anyone else in the plant.
5. Our plants grew _____ this year than last year.

Practice II

Directions: Blacken the circle that corresponds to the number of the incorrect sentence in each group.

1. (1) This week's show was more funnier than last week's show.   ① ② ③
   (2) A tiny, delicate bird flew quietly away.
   (3) That loud noise is very irritating.
2. (1) The nervous woman seemed very impatient.   ① ② ③
   (2) Only close relatives visited the very old man.
   (3) John received the job because he was the efficientest competitor.
3. (1) Seven of the candidates competed vigorously for the local mayoralty.   ① ② ③
   (2) This dinner is the most delicious I've ever had.
   (3) Willie is the better basketball player of the three.
4. (1) Harry Truman read continually.   ① ② ③
   (2) Of the two, Freddie runs quicker.
   (3) The delightful aroma drifted across the room.
5. (1) Ed suggests a better solution.   ① ② ③
   (2) This coffee pot makes the baddest coffee I've ever had.
   (3) He handled the bus more skillfully than any other driver.
6. (1) The worst damage occurred in the rear.   ① ② ③
   (2) Of the two books I like this one most.
   (3) This is the shortest of the three books.
7. (1) I like Indian sand paintings better than modern art.   ① ② ③
   (2) The corner market always has the best cheese.
   (3) I chose the evergreen because it is the beautifulest of the three.

8. (1) Navajo artwork is more elaborate than Pueblo artwork.   ① ② ③
   (2) The morning trains are slower than the afternoon trains.
   (3) This horse wins frequentlyer than any other.

9. (1) We liked this movie more better than any other.   ① ② ③
   (2) Our team was the best in the league.
   (3) Professor Ito was a better listener than any other teacher in
       the department.

10. (1) Victor said this was the worse job he has ever had.   ① ② ③
    (2) The science teacher carefully explained that this was the
        best technique.
    (3) The record showed that their team was stronger than any
        other in the conference.

Practice III

Directions: The following paragraph has four descriptive words or phrases. On the lines below, correct those that are incorrect.

The department meeting this month was the <u>boringest</u> one yet. Each speaker was
                                              1

<u>most difficult</u> to understand than the next. The meeting notes were <u>difficult</u> to read, and
     2   3

the refreshments were <u>the worse</u> I've ever had.
                          4

1. _____

2. _____

3. _____

4. _____

Chapter 4   Using Descriptive Words Correctly

Practice I *Page 33.*
Answers may vary.
   Sample answers:
1. longest
   most boring
   best
2. best
   longest
   most magnificent
3. most boring
   most magnificent
   best
4. longer
5. higher
   better

Practice II *Page 33.*
1. **(1)** This week's show was _funnier_ than last week's show. Do not use *more* with a descriptive word that ends in *-er*.
2. **(3)** John received the job because he was the _most efficient_ competitor. Use *most* rather than *-est* with *efficient*.
3. **(3)** Willie is the _best_ basketball player of the three. Use *best* when comparing three or more.
4. **(2)** Of the two, Freddie runs _more quickly_. Quickly describes *run*; therefore, *more quickly* compares how *two* people run.

5. **(2)** This coffee pot makes the _worst_ coffee I've ever had. *Worst* is the form of *bad* used when comparing three or more.
6. **(2)** Of the two books, I like this one _more_. Use *more* to compare two items.
7. **(3)** I chose the evergreen because it is the _most beautiful_ of the three. Use *most* rather than *-est* with _beautiful_.
8. **(3)** This horse wins _more frequently_ than any other. Use *more* with *frequently* rather than *-er*.
9. **(1)** We liked this movie _better_ than any other. Do not use _more_ with better.
10. **(1)** Victor said this was the _worst_ job he has ever had. *Worst* is the form of *bad* used when comparing three or more.

Practice III *Page 34.*
1. most boring
2. more difficult
3. correct as is
4. the worst

Chapter 5

ADDING DESCRIPTIVE PHRASES

> "I spoke to Jerry at the office party about his need to
> get more education," said Mr. Grogan.
> "You mean that there was an office party just to
> consider Jerry's lack of education," Mrs. Grogan
> sweetly replied. "Maybe Jerry should ask you to go
> back to school if you use sentences like that."
> Mrs. Grogan ducked as the pillow came sailing at her
> head. Lions don't like to have their tails tugged.
>
> —Les Camhi
> *V.I.P. at I.B.M.*

A Word With You . . .

Mrs. Grogan was having some fun at her husband's expense because he had been tarred with his own brush. Instead of coming across as the friendly vice-president who points out a weakness to his employee, he had the tables turned on him by the clever Mrs. Grogan, who spotted an error in her husband's sentence structure.

Do you see the mistake? In Chapter 5 you will learn how to avoid it.

Descriptive Phrases: Adding Meaning

You have just been working with descriptive words that help to make the sentence more meaningful and interesting. Frequently, one descriptive word is not enough. We need a group of words (a phrase) to expand the meaning.

EXAMPLE:

The coffee cup fell *on the floor*.

The entire phrase, *on the floor*, describes the action word, *fell*. Before you look for descriptive phrases, you must be sure that you understand the core of the sentence. Ask yourself these questions:

1. What is the action word in the sentence?
   fell
2. What is performing the action?
   cup
3. What do *the* and *coffee* describe?
   cup
4. Finally, what does *on the floor* describe?
   fell

EXAMPLE:

The Rocky Horror Picture Show, a cult film at our local theater, attracts a fun crowd.

1. What is the action word in the sentence?
   attracts
2. Who or what is performing the action?
   The Rocky Horror Picture Show
3. What does *cult film* describe?
   The Rocky Horror Picture Show
4. Finally, what does *at our local theater* describe (or relate to in the sentence)?
   cult film

Prepositions

The phrases in this chapter all begin with the following small connecting words, called prepositions. The preposition boxes below will help you understand how prepositions are used.

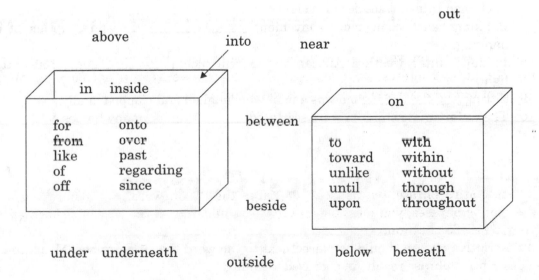

Practice I

Directions: Each of the sentences below contains at least one descriptive phrase. Draw an arrow from each descriptive phrase to the word it describes. The first one is done for you.

1. The company solved its financial problems <u>through efficiency techniques</u>.
2. The musicians <u>at the club</u> played <u>into the night</u>.
3. The dentist's ultrasonic cleaner sped <u>along the surfaces</u> of his patient's teeth.
4. Maria put a wallpaper border <u>around the kitchen</u>.
5. A contestant <u>with an electric guitar</u> won the talent competition.
6. The cable installer drilled a hole <u>through the closet</u>.
7. A lonely figure waited <u>on the bridge</u>.
8. Everyone <u>except him</u> cheered.
9. The dealer divided the cards <u>among the four players</u>.
10. An argument raged <u>between the two teams</u>.

Practice II

Directions: These words frequently begin descriptive phrases. Choose from among them to complete the following sentences. More than one answer may be correct.

of	at	between	after	under	on
in	from	through	beside	over	before
to	into	around	except	off	along
for	among	by	alongside	up	with

1. A brief summary of World War I is _____ the first chapter.
2. A large crowd walked _____ the stairs in the historic building.
3. Surprised by the house owner's return, the intruder hurried _____ the door.
4. Fiona posted her resumé _____ the Internet.
5. The book _____ the top shelf belongs _____ Ada.
6. _____ Akeem lost his connection for the fourth time in a month, he decided to change Internet service providers.
7. Banking has become more convenient _____ the added option of online banking.
8. In dull winter weather, African violets will bloom _____ 100-watt grow lights.
9. Sitting _____ me was a man who laughed and clapped loudly.
10. The unfortunate children were scattered _____ many homes.

Descriptive Phrases: Correct Placement

A descriptive phrase should be placed next to the word that it describes. Misplacement of a descriptive phrase results in confused meaning.

EXAMPLE 1:

The congressman made an unfavorable comment at a White House reception *about rising prices*.

The reception was not *about rising prices*; the congressman's comment was *about rising prices*. The sentence should read:

At a White House reception, the congressman made an unfavorable comment *about rising prices*.

EXAMPLE 2:

After completing his report, Jerry's laptop computer shut down automatically.

The computer did not complete his report, Jerry did. The sentence should read:

After Jerry completed his report, his laptop computer shut down automatically.

Practice III

Directions: The underlined descriptive phrase in each of the following sentences is correctly placed. Draw an arrow from each descriptive phrase to the word that it describes. The first one is done for you.

1. The American way *of life* changes constantly.
2. The speaker inspired us to believe that we can make it *through these difficult times*.
3. This course *of action* is questionable.
4. The prosecutor spoke *to Steve*.
5. The Dalai Lama writes *about peace*.
6. Several angry commuters walked *to the bus stop* together every morning.
7. President Bush spoke *at length*.
8. The actors dine *after the show*.
9. The panelist *at the end* *of the table* spoke decisively.
10. Mr. Simmons sleeps *like a log*.

Notice that each descriptive phrase is next to the word that it describes. In the following exercise, each descriptive phrase is incorrectly placed.

Practice IV

Directions: On the line provided, rewrite each sentence so that each descriptive phrase is next to the word that it describes.

1. The man ran down the stairs in a blue coat.

_____

2. Standing out in the rain, my umbrella blew inside out.

_____

3. Tom did not see across the street the accident.

_____

4. Show Ella in the baggy pants the clown.

_____

5. That boy runs around the track in the sweatsuit each day.

_____

6. The dog belongs to that child with the brown spots.

_____

All of the above sentences had simple placement errors. Each incorrectly placed phrase began with a clue word such as: of, in, to, at, from, with, across, etc.

Practice V

Directions: One sentence in each group has a placement error in it. Blacken the circle that corresponds to the number of the incorrect sentence.

1. (1) The man in the tweed suit ran toward the departing bus.   ① ② ③
   (2) A woman in a raincoat hailed a passing taxi.
   (3) The man in the drawer found his handkerchief.
2. (1) The grateful veteran relaxed after years of battle in his living room.   ① ② ③
   (2) The battery in my car died.
   (3) The woman on the park bench smiled warmly.
3. (1) Cher sang as she sauntered across the stage.   ① ② ③
   (2) Michael Jordan will play in next Tuesday's game.
   (3) Katelin hung on the wall her favorite painting.
4. (1) The car drove 7,000 miles in the driveway.   ① ② ③
   (2) The new sports car in the parking lot was stolen.
   (3) The man in the moon winked at the astronauts.
5. (1) The registration desk was located in the gymnasium.   ① ② ③
   (2) Voter registration took place at three o'clock.
   (3) The voters on the table completed the forms.

Frequently, a descriptive phrase separates the performer and the action. You must remember that _the action agrees in number with the performer._

EXAMPLES:

The _man walks_ slowly.
The _man_ in the blue coat _walks_ slowly.
The _man_ in the blue boots _walks_ slowly.

Notice that the action word remains _walks_ in each sentence. The number of that word is not affected by any word in the descriptive phrase. The action word, _walks_, agrees with _man_ in each sentence. It does not, for example, change to agree with _boots_.

Practice VI

Directions: For each sentence below, blacken circle number 1 if the performer and action agree. If the performer and action do not agree, blacken number 2.

1. Steven King writes popular horror stories.   ① ②
2. The woman in the blue overalls builds skyscrapers.   ① ②
3. The clouds in the sky drifts by.   ① ②
4. The problem of too many cooks create chaos.   ① ②
5. One of the men in our office works late every night.   ① ②
6. The newest watches in the catalog track heart rate and calorie intake.   ① ②
7. Some of the most unusual animals lives at the Bronx Zoo.   ① ②
8. The instant messages from her friends distract Meredith from her   ① ②
   work.
9. One out of three employees stays with the company after the first   ① ②
   year.
10. A catalog of publications arrive at our office monthly.   ① ②

Grammar Connection

As you know, the small connecting words described in the chapter are all *prepositions*.

More details:

You learned in the Grammar Connection in Chapter 4 that words that describe nouns—people, places, things—are called adjectives and words that describe actions (verbs) are called adverbs.

Descriptive phrases that act as adjectives are adjective phrases: The woman *in the raincoat* lost her umbrella. *In the raincoat* is an adjective phrase that describes *the woman*.

Those that describe actions (verbs) are called adverbial phrases: A truck rumbled *down the quiet street at 50 miles an hour*. Both *down the street* and *at 50 miles an hour* describe how the truck rumbled.

Tying it all together:

Both *adjective* and *adverbial phrases* can be *prepositional phrases*.

Chapter 5   Adding Descriptive Phrases

Practice I *Page 38.*

1. *through efficiency techniques* describes solved.
2. *at the club* describes musicians. *into the night* describes played.
3. *along the surfaces* describes sped.
4. *around the kitchen* describes wallpaper border.
5. *with an electric guitar* describes contestant.
6. *through the closet* describes where the hole was drilled.
7. *on the bridge* describes waited.
8. *except him* describes everyone.
9. *among the four players* describes divided.
10. *between the two teams* describes raged.

Practice II *Page 38.*

Answers will vary.
Sample answers:

1. in, after, before
2. up
3. through, to, from
4. on
5. on, to
6. After
7. with
8. under
9. beside
10. among

Practice III *Page 39.*

1. *of life* describes way.
2. *through these difficult times* describes can make it.

3. *of action* describes course.
4. *to Steve* describes spoke.
5. *about peace* describes writes.
6. *to the bus stop* describes walked.
7. *at length* describes spoke.
8. *after the show* describes dine.
9. *at the end* describes panelist; *of the table* describes end.
10. *at length* describes spoke.

Practice IV *Page 39.*

1. The man in a blue coat ran down the stairs.
2. My umbrella blew inside out while I was standing out in the rain.
3. Tom did not see the accident across the street.
4. Show Ella the clown in the baggy pants.
5. That boy in the sweatsuit runs around the track each day.
6. The dog with the brown spots belongs to that child.

Practice V *Page 40.*

1. **(3)** The man found his handkerchief in the drawer.
2. **(1)** The grateful veteran relaxed in his living room after years of battle.
3. **(3)** Katelin hung her favorite painting on the wall.
4. **(1)** The car in the driveway drove 7,000 miles.
5. **(3)** The voters completed the forms on the table.

Practice VI *Page 41.*

The descriptive phrases in these sentences have been set off with parentheses so that you can clearly see the *performer* and *action* in each sentence.

1. **(1)** Steven King writes
2. **(1)** woman (in the blue overalls) builds
3. **(2)** clouds (in the sky) drift
4. **(2)** problem (of too many cooks) creates
5. **(1)** one (of the men in our office) works
6. **(1)** watches (in the catalog) track
7. **(2)** some (of the most unusual animals) live
8. **(2)** instant messages (from her friends) distract
9. **(1)** one (out of three employees) stays
10. **(2)** catalog (of publications) arrives

Chapter 6

CUMULATIVE REVIEW

This review covers:

- Performer and Action: Agreement in Number
- Action Words: Agreement in Time
- Correct Use of Descriptive Words

After completing the Cumulative Review exercises, evaluate your ability using the SUMMARY OF RESULTS chart on page 49. Acceptable scores for each practice are given.

To learn your areas for skill improvement, find the question numbers you answered incorrectly on the SKILLS ANALYSIS table. The table will show which of your skills need improvement and the necessary chapters to review.

Practice Exercises

Practice I

Directions: Blacken the circle that corresponds to the number of the error in each sentence. If there is no error, blacken number 5.

1. The delegate and _his_ alternate _votes_ at _each_ _monthly_   ① ② ③ ④ ⑤

                1   2   3   4

    meeting. _No error_

             5

2. If a person _maintains_ a _good_ historical perspective, he   ① ② ③ ④ ⑤

               1   2

    understands the present and _predicted_ the future. _No error_

      3   4   5

3. Although I _cannot_ _see_ you, I can _hear_ you _good_. _No error_   ① ② ③ ④ ⑤

            1   2   3   4   5

4. The _plumbers_ union, along with _several_ other unions in the   ① ② ③ ④ ⑤

      1   2

    area, _choose_ not to _work_ on Saturdays. _No error_

      3   4   5

5. We *spent* a perfect day at the beach because the ocean was   ① ② ③ ④ ⑤
      1

   real calm and the sun *wasn't* *too* hot. *No error*
     2   3   4   5

6. Before anyone *makes* a decision, he *weighs* all of the   ① ② ③ ④ ⑤
              1   2

   alternatives and *chose* the *best*. *No error*
                  3   4   5

7. Because *she* *enjoys* the exercise, Patricia, *along* with several   ① ② ③ ④ ⑤
          1 2   3

   of her friends, *skates* every Friday evening. *No error*
                 4   5

8. Because *less* money is available, we are *faced* with the   ① ② ③ ④ ⑤
          1   2

   problem of providing *better* education at *lower* cost. *No error*
                 3   4   5

9. The *more* they *grapple* with the problem, the *less* the   ① ② ③ ④ ⑤
        1   2   3

   members of the legislature *understands* it. *No error*
                       4   5

10. Of *all* the *downtown* merchants, I *like* Mr. Mitchell *more*.   ① ② ③ ④ ⑤
        1   2   3   4

    No error
     5

Practice II

Directions: Blacken the circle that corresponds to the number of the error in each sentence. If there is no error, blacken number 5.

1. The electrician and his assistant *always* *shuts* off the   ① ② ③ ④ ⑤
                                      1   2

   electricity *before* beginning *work*. *No error*
             3   4   5

2. The late Louis Braille, *inventor* of the Braille alphabet,   ① ② ③ ④ ⑤
                        1

   pioneered in his own right and *contributes* to *aids* for the
      2   3   4

   handicapped. *No error*
          5

3. As food prices continue to _rise_, more and _more_ people turn
                               1   2
     to farming and _most_ of them _enjoy_ it. _No error_
                       3   4   5 ① ② ③ ④ ⑤

4. Some of the finest modern artists cannot _sketch_ _accurate_ or
                                     1   2
     reproduce a likeness _well_. _No error_
         3   4   5 ① ② ③ ④ ⑤

5. Robert Pace _designed_ a unique method of piano instruction
                 1
     that _combines_ _classical_, _romantic_, and contemporary music.
                2   3   4
     No error
       5 ① ② ③ ④ ⑤

6. During the _recent_ blackout, _many_ refrigerators _defrosted_
                1   2   3
     and the food _spoils_. _No error_
                4   5 ① ② ③ ④ ⑤

7. Maria and her _best_ friend, Lucy, _goes_ to _adult_ school twice
                 1   2   3
     each week and _study_ together. _No error_
               4   5 ① ② ③ ④ ⑤

8. The tools _in_ the storage chest _accomplishes_ _most_ of the
            1   2   3
     necessary tasks. _No error_
         4   5 ① ② ③ ④ ⑤

9. The _tiles_ in the bathroom _shows_ _signs_ of _wear_. _No error_
       1   2   3   4   5 ① ② ③ ④ ⑤

10. Of all the people I _know_, Manuel _works_ _most_ _efficient_.
                  1   2   3   4
     No error
       5 ① ② ③ ④ ⑤

Practice III

Directions: Blacken the circle that corresponds to the number of the error in each sentence. If there is no error, blacken number 5.

1. Martin and his brother _walks_ to _work_ _each_ morning and _take_
                    1   2 3   4

   the bus home each evening. _No error_
                           5

   ① ② ③ ④ ⑤

2. _One_ of those packages _belong_ to the _tall_ man at the end of the
    1   2   3

   long line. _No error_
    4   5

   ① ② ③ ④ ⑤

3. A book of food _stamps_ _fell_ _onto_ the counter in the supermarket
                   1   2 3

   and several people _reached_ for it. _No error_
                  4   5

   ① ② ③ ④ ⑤

4. The superintendent and his wife _argues_ _frequently_ and the
                          1   2

   neighbors _listen_ _attentively._ _No error_
          3   4   5

   ① ② ③ ④ ⑤

5. The team _played_ _clumsy_ and, therefore, _lost_ the _game_.
            1   2   3   4

   No error
    5

   ① ② ③ ④ ⑤

6. Perry _enters_ the _crowded_ movie theater, _buys_ popcorn,
          1   2   3

   and _looked_ for a seat. _No error_
       4   5

   ① ② ③ ④ ⑤

7. Don't _raise_ your hand at the meeting unless you _plan_ to
         1   2

   speak in _favor_ of the proposal. _No error_
    3   4   5

   ① ② ③ ④ ⑤

8. _Please_ _bring_ the _tape_ recorder with you and tape the evening's
    1   2   3

   discussion. _No error_
      4   5

   ① ② ③ ④ ⑤

9. A carton of eggs _smash_ on the floor at _least_ _once_ a week in
              1   2   3

   that store. _No error_
    4   5

   ① ② ③ ④ ⑤

10. The radio and the TV _play_ so _loud_ that I _have_ trouble _reading_.
                    1   2   3   4

    No error
     5

    ① ② ③ ④ ⑤

11. I would not *have rang* your doorbell if I didn't *have* an   ① ② ③ ④ ⑤
                    1   2   3

     important message. *No error*
          4   5

12. Carmine *played* basketball *so good* that the men *asked* him   ① ② ③ ④ ⑤
                    1   2   3   4

     to be the center on the neighborhood team. *No error*
                                                     5

13. Several doses of that medicine *makes* me *feel* tired and *react*   ① ② ③ ④ ⑤
                                       1   2   3

     slowly. *No error*
          4   5

14. Buddy *listens* to instructions *attentively*, but cannot *remember*   ① ② ③ ④ ⑤
               1   2   3

     them *clear*. *No error*
              4   5

15. One of the women *on* the bus *talk incessantly* and *annoys* the   ① ② ③ ④ ⑤
                         1   2   3   4

     driver. *No error*
                  5

After reviewing the Answer Key on page 50, chart your scores below for each practice exercise.

SUMMARY OF RESULTS

Practice Number	Number Correct	Number Incorrect (Including Omissions)	Acceptable Score
I			7 correct
II			7 correct
III			11 correct

To identify your areas for skill improvement, locate the questions you answered incorrectly and circle the numbers on this Skills Analysis chart. Wherever you have circled errors, review the chapters listed in the last column.

SKILLS ANALYSIS

Skill	Question Number	Review Chapter
Practice I		
Performer and Action: Agreement in Number	1, 4, 7, 9	2
Action Words: Agreement in Time	2, 6	2
Correct Use of Descriptive Words	3, 5, 8	3
Correct Use of Descriptive Words: Comparison	10	4
Practice II		
Performer and Action: Agreement in Number	1, 7, 8, 9	2
Action Words: Agreement in Time	2, 5, 6	2
Correct Use of Descriptive Words	3, 4, 10	2
Practice III		
Performer and Action: Agreement in Number	1, 2, 4, 9, 13, 15	2
Correct Use of Descriptive Words	5, 10, 12, 14	3
Performer and Action: Agreement in Time	6	2
Action Words: Special Problems	7, 11	1

Chapter 6 Cumulative Review

Practice I *Page 44.*

1. **(2)** *Vote* agrees with the plural performer, *The delegate and his alternate.*

2. **(4)** *Predicts* agrees in time with the action words, *maintains* and *understands.*

3. **(4)** *Well* describes the action word, *hear.*

4. **(3)** *Chooses* agrees with the singular performer, *union.*

5. **(2)** *Really* describes the descriptive word, *calm.*

6. **(3)** *Chooses* agrees in time with the action words, *makes* and *weighs.*

7. **(5)** No error. *Enjoys* and *skates* agree.

8. **(5)** No error. *Faced* and *is* agree in time.

9. **(4)** *Understand* agrees in number with the plural performer, *members.*

10. **(4)** Use *most* to compare three or more groups of people, as indicated in "Of *all* the downtown *merchants* . . ."

Practice II *Page 45.*

1. **(2)** *Shut* agrees with the plural performer, *the electrician and his assistant.*

2. **(3)** *Contributed* agrees in time with the action word, *pioneered.*

3. **(5)** No error

4. **(2)** *Accurately* describes the action word, *sketch.*

5. **(5)** No error

6. **(4)** *Spoiled* agrees in time with the action word, *defrosted.*

7. **(2)** *Go* agrees with the plural performer, *Maria and her best friend, Lucy.*

8. **(2)** *Accomplish* agrees with the plural performer, *tools.*

9. **(2)** *Show* agrees with the plural performer, *tiles.*

10. **(4)** *Efficiently* describes the action word, *works.*

Practice III *Page 46.*

1. **(1)** *Walk* agrees with the plural performer, *Martin and his brother.*

2. **(2)** *Belongs* agrees with the singular performer, *one* (*of those packages* describes one).

3. **(5)** No error

4. **(1)** *Argue* agrees with the plural performer, *superintendent and his wife.*

5. **(2)** *Clumsily* describes the action, *played.* Clumsy would describe a person or thing.

6. **(4)** *Looks* agrees in time with *enters* and *buys.*

7. **(5)** No error

8. **(5)** No error

9. **(1)** *Smashes* agrees with the singular performer, *carton.*

10. **(2)** *Loudly* describes the action, *play.* Loud would describe a person or thing.

11. **(2)** *Rung* is used with the helping word, *have.*

12. **(3)** *Well* describes the action, *played*. Good would describe a person or thing.

13. **(1)** *Make* agrees with the plural performer, *doses*.

14. **(4)** *Clearly* describes the action, *remember*. Clear would describe a person or thing.

15. **(2)** *Talks* agrees with the singular performer, *one*.

Chapter 7

LINKING VERBS

> "The murderer is . . ."
> "Yes, yes," exclaimed Colonel Van Raalte, speaking
> for everyone in the living room. "Tell us who it is."
> Detective Ling went on: "The murderer is . . . a real villain."
> "We don't need any genius of a Chinese detective to
> tell us that," sneered the Colonel. "You might just twist
> that sentence around and tell us that 'the real villain is
> . . . a murderer.' It makes just as much sense—or stupidity!"
> "Patience, my friend, patience," said Ling. "Before
> the evening is much older, I will point my finger in the
> direction of the killer."
>
> —Stillwell Kee
> *The Inscrutable Detective Ling*

A Word With You . . .
The murderer is a villain.

A villain is the murderer.

Colonel Van Raalte was right in that he didn't learn anything from Detective Ling's statement.

You, however, are going to learn what a *linking verb* is, why certain sentences can be reversed without changing their meanings—and you might even discover who killed Mrs. Van Raalte.

What Are Linking Verbs?

In most chapters, we do not use grammatical terms for explanations. However, here it is helpful to use the term *verbs* to understand the two types better: *linking verbs* and *action verbs*.

In Chapter 1, you were introduced to action words. As explained in the Chapter 1 Grammar Connection, all action words are verbs, but not all verbs are action words. The verb's job in the sentence is either to show the *action* of the subject or to *link* a subject to a descriptive word.

EXAMPLE:

The van is huge.

As you see, the word *van* in this sentence cannot be called the performer since it is not performing any action (swerving, speeding, stopping). It is actually being described (huge). *Huge* describes *van*. *Is* links the descriptive word *huge* to the subject *van*. The subject is the word *van*, which the sentence is about.

EXAMPLE:

<pre>
                              linking verb
                                   |
                    The van is huge.
                         | |
                    subject descriptive word
</pre>

The word *is* is not an action word; it is a *linking verb*. Study these examples of linking verbs:

<pre>
                              linking verb
                                  /
               The proposal sounds good.
                      /   \
                 subject   descriptive word
</pre>

<pre>
                    linking verb
                        /
          Alex seems happy in his new job.
           /   \
      subject   descriptive word
</pre>

<pre>
                    linking verb
                        /
            I feel wonderful.
            \   \
          subject   descriptive word
</pre>

Sometimes *is* links the subject with another word which equals the subject.

EXAMPLE:

<pre>
                    linking verb
                        |
          Columbo is a detective.
            | |
         subject   subject
</pre>

It is interesting to note that whenever the word linked with the subject *equals* the subject, the sentence can be reversed without changing its meaning. The reversed sentences may sound awkward; however, the meaning remains clear.

EXAMPLES:

linking verb
|
A detective is Columbo.
| |
subject   subject

linking verb
|
Columbo is a detective.
| |
subject   subject

linking verb
|
Gerald Ford was the United States' first nonelected president.
/   \
subject   subject

linking verb
|
The United States' first nonelected president was Gerald Ford.
\   /
subject   subject

linking verb
|
The Statue of Liberty is a remarkable sight.
\   /
subject   subject

linking verb
|
The remarkable sight is the Statue of Liberty.
\   /
subject   subject

Sometimes an action word takes a break from the action and becomes a linking verb. In other words, the way a word is used in the sentence can change it from an action word to a linking verb. Consider the action word *tasted*:

action verb
/
Lucas tasted the new flavored coffee.
\
subject

Tasting is an action performed by Lucas. Now, here is the same word, *tasted*, used as a linking verb:

linking verb
/
The new coffee tasted like caramel.
/   \
subject   descriptive word

Can the coffee be considered a performer in this sentence? Did the coffee actually do anything or perform the action of tasting itself? Of course not; it just *is* something that *tastes* like caramel. Consider the word *smell*.

action verb
/
Emily smelled the flowers in the garden.
/
subject

linking verb
/
The flowers smelled like spring.
/   \
subject   descriptive word

Another example:

action verb
/
Juan grows tomatoes.
/
subject

linking verb
/
Pat grows weary of eating Juan's tomatoes.
/
subject

Linking Verbs

appear	remain	become	seem
feel	smell	grow	sound
look	taste	be	is
are	am	was	were

Practice I

Directions: Complete each sentence using the correct form of a linking verb from the list on page 55. Several words may be appropriate. Choose one.

1. After the Knicks game, the players _____ tired.
2. The labor representative _____ angry during the extensive negotiations.
3. The late Dwight Eisenhower _____ once a general.
4. The watchman _____ restless.
5. While shooting hoops, the teens never _____ exhausted.

Practice II

Directions: Locate the subject in each sentence, and label it. Then underline the linking verb that connects the subject and the descriptive word. Draw an arrow from the descriptive word to the subject.

EXAMPLE:

An extensive renovation *seems* wasteful.

1. The entire class felt more ambitious after the coffee break.
2. The lilacs in the park are breathtaking.
3. Seven noisy children suddenly grew still.
4. Bill Clinton was president of the United States for eight years.
5. The smoke in the kitchen became unbearable.

Practice III

Directions: Each of the sentences below contains either an action word or a linking verb. If the sentence contains an action word, blacken circle 1. If the sentence contains a linking verb, blacken circle 2.

1. The snowmobile raced down the hill.   ① ②
2. The tone of the meeting became threatening.   ① ②
3. That candidate was our favorite.   ① ②
4. We eat only organic foods.   ① ②
5. Our day at the lake was pleasant.   ① ②
6. Maximum individual choice is the democratic ideal.   ① ②
7. Alvin Toffler, author of *Future Shock,* conjures up a bleak   ① ②
    picture of the future.
8. People turn to a variety of experts.   ① ②
9. The situation appeared uncomfortable.   ① ②
10. Most people do not consider their own lives as typical of particular life styles. ① ②
11. It was Pam at the door.   ① ②

Use the descriptive word correctly in the *Subject — Linking Word — Descriptive Word* pattern.

> Never use a descriptive word that ends in *-ly* to describe the subject of the sentence. Descriptive words that end in *-ly* are reserved for describing actions.

CORRECT: The child *is* adorable. (linking verb)
INCORRECT: The child is adorably.
CORRECT: She *speaks* too softly. (action)
INCORRECT: She speaks too soft.

Practice IV

Directions: Blacken the circle that corresponds to the number of the incorrect sentence in each group. If all the sentences in a group are correct, blacken number 5.

1. (1) The delicate bird is graceful.   ① ② ③ ④ ⑤
   (2) The graceful bird seems delicate.
   (3) The bird is graceful and delicate.
   (4) The bird flies graceful.
   (5) No error
2. (1) Mr. Jackson plays piano loud.   ① ② ③ ④ ⑤
   (2) Mr. Jackson's piano is loud.
   (3) Mr. Jackson, along with his piano, is loud.
   (4) Mr. Jackson plays piano loudly.
   (5) No error
3. (1) Floyd reads quickly.   ① ② ③ ④ ⑤
   (2) Angelo is the quickest sorter in the mailroom.
   (3) Floyd reads more quick than Harvey.
   (4) Alex seems very quick.
   (5) No error
4. (1) Annemarie seems nicely.   ① ② ③ ④ ⑤
   (2) Carmen seems nice.
   (3) Annemarie seems nicer than Cathy.
   (4) Raymond's nice sister is Georgia.
   (5) No error
5. (1) Good butter tastes sweet.   ① ② ③ ④ ⑤
   (2) Taste the good butter.
   (3) The butter tastes well.
   (4) This butter tastes good!
   (5) No error
6. (1) Rudy feels badly about the argument.   ① ② ③ ④ ⑤
   (2) That dress looks bad on Vera.
   (3) That was a bad choice.
   (4) Since she had the flu, Carla has felt bad.
   (5) No error

Subject and Linking Verb: Agreement in Number

You have already studied agreement of performer and action in number. The same concept applies to the subject and the linking verb. For example, look at the following incorrect sentences:

1. *All* of our relatives *is* coming to dinner.
2. Those *cars appears* fast.
3. The *house are* on a hill.

Of course, these sentences sound awkward. Look at the same sentences written correctly. What changes have been made?

1. *All* of our relatives *are* coming to dinner.
2. Those *cars appear* fast.
3. The *house is* on a hill.

You see that a singular subject needs a singular linking verb, and a plural subject needs a plural linking verb.

Every linking verb must agree with its subject in time and number.

Notice that agreement in the past is easier to achieve than agreement in the present. For example:

Linking Verb: *Appear*

Present Time, *Singular and Plural*

	I appear nervous.
	You appear confident.
(He)	Andy appears belligerent.
(She)	Jodi appears calm.
(It)	The dog appears ill.
	Who appears contented?
(We)	Michael and I appear relaxed.
(You)	You and Marcel appear tired.
(They)	Holly and Nilijah appear friendly.

Past Time, *Singular and Plural*

	I appeared nervous.
	You appeared confident.
(He)	Andy appeared belligerent.
(She)	Jodi appeared calm.

(It)	The dog appeared ill.
	Who appeared contented?
(We)	Michael and I appeared relaxed.
(You)	You and Marcel appeared tired.
(They)	Holly and Nilijah appeared friendly.

Linking Verb: *Be*

Be is a difficult word to understand. *Be* is used when preceded by *to, will, can, could, would,* or *should. Examples:*

The policeman wants *to be* helpful.
Next time, I *will be* more thoughtful.
Crowded supermarkets *can be* annoying.
This *could be* one chance in a lifetime.
The supervisor *would be* grateful if you could work late.
World peace *should be* everyone's goal.

Other forms of *be* are used in sentences that do not have the helping words *to, will, can, could, would,* or *should.* You are already familiar with these forms: *am, is, are, was, were.* The following lists show you the proper use of these words.

Present Time, Singular and Plural

	I am a nurse.
	You are a policeman.
(He)	Rubin is a crossing guard.
(She)	Asha is a teacher.
(It)	The dog is a collie.
	Who is that lady?
(We)	Bill and I are co-chairmen.
(You)	You and your brother are partners.
	Who are those ladies?
(They)	Samantha and Ariel are sisters.

Past Time, Singular and Plural

	I was a nurse.
	You were a policeman.
(He)	Rubin was a crossing guard.
(She)	Asha was a teacher.
(It)	The dog was a collie.
	Who was that lady?
(We)	Bill and I were co-chairmen.
(You)	You and your brother were partners.
	Who were those ladies?
(They)	Samantha and Ariel were sisters.

Practice V

Directions: Use *is, are, was,* or *were* in each of the following sentences.

1. Fritz _____ always late.
2. The Murphys _____ home from their vacation.
3. The woman and her child _____ in the park.
4. The books _____ interesting.
5. He _____ a member of the group when it was first formed.

Practice VI

Directions: Use the *correct form* of one of the following linking verbs to complete each of the following sentences. Use at least one form of each word.

   be   grow   become   appear   feel

1. The soldiers _____ weary after the long march.
2. The crowd _____ angry.
3. The child quickly _____ tired of his new toy.
4. The Toglias _____ elated after winning the lottery.
5. The football players _____ traded.

Practice VII

Directions: Blacken the circle that corresponds to the number of the error in each passage. If there is no error, blacken number 5.

1. Cloning *is* a hotly *debated* topic. The ethics and safety of cloning *is* *questioned* by
        1   2   3   4
   many. *No error*.
        5

2. Sheep, goats, mice, and cows *has been* cloned and *are being* studied to determine
                                 1 2   3   4
   whether the health of cloned animals is affected. *No error*.
                                           5

3. Now, as scientists *are getting* closer to human cloning, these studies *are being* closely
                        1 2   3   4
   examined. *No error*.
        5

4. People's *belief* that they should *control* nature *are* *reaching* new heights. *No error*.
        1   2   3   4   5

5. The possibility of human cloning *have been seen* as inevitable since 1997, when a
                                       1   2   3
   Scottish scientist *created* a sheep named Dolly. *No error*.
                     4   5

6. Many people <u>*believe*</u> that Frankenstein, written in 1816, <u>*is*</u> a perfect illustration of

             1   2

what happens when a person <u>*plays*</u> the role of God. The story <u>*is*</u> timeless in its

                         3   4

examination of human nature. <u>*No error*</u>.

                     5

The Missing Link(ing Verb)

Often, a linking verb is combined with another word. In combining, the initial letters of the linking verb are dropped and replaced by an apostrophe.

EXAMPLE:

There is one answer to that question.
There's one answer to that question.

There is = There's

Common Missing Link(ing Verb) Combinations

he is = he's	*He's* the most forward-looking senator.
she is = she's	*She's* the strongest voice in Congress.
we are = we're	*We're* eager to hear your proposal.
you are = you're	*You're* one of the few people I trust.
they are = they're	*They're* determined to interfere.
here is = here's	*Here's* your hat.
it is = it's	*It's* an active committee.

NOTE: *Its* without the apostrophe indicates possession.

EXAMPLE:

The committee concluded *its* hearing.

Missing Link Combinations with *Not*

is not = isn't	Destruction *isn't* my idea of fun.
are not = aren't	The striking workers *aren't* going to settle for less pay.
were not = weren't	Lou and Toby *weren't* on the train.
was not = wasn't	I *wasn't* prepared for the crowd at the bus stop.

Practice VIII

Directions: In each of the following sentences, there is an underlined phrase. Make a missing link combination from each underlined phrase and write it on the line provided.

EXAMPLE:

If <u>it</u> <u>is</u> convenient for Lucy, the bowling team will meet at 6 P.M. <u>it's</u>

1. <u>They</u> <u>are</u> the best approaches to the problem. _____
2. If you can understand management-labor relations, <u>you</u> <u>are</u> a better businessperson than I. _____
3. Agreement <u>is</u> <u>not</u> as important as understanding. _____
4. We <u>did</u> <u>not</u> realize that the job action had ended. _____
5. <u>Here</u> <u>is</u> the name of an excellent mechanic. _____
6. The legislators <u>were</u> <u>not</u> expecting such a strong consumer lobby. _____
7. <u>He</u> <u>is</u> the least competent programmer in the company. _____
8. <u>There</u> <u>is</u> only one best product in each line of merchandise. _____

Chapter 7   Linking Verbs

Practice I *Page 56.*
Answers may vary.
  Sample answers:
1. appeared, felt, looked
2. seemed, became, grew
3. was
4. became, grew, is, was
5. were, seemed

Practice II *Page 56.*

subject

1. The entire class *felt* more ambitious after the coffee break.

subject

2. The lilacs in the park *are* breathtaking.

subject

3. Seven noisy children suddenly *grew* still.

subject

4. Bill Clinton *was* president of the United States for eight years.

subject

5. The smoke in the kitchen *became* unbearable.

Practice III *Page 56.*
1. **(1)** raced
2. **(2)** became
3. **(2)** was
4. **(1)** eat
5. **(2)** was

6. **(2)** is
7. **(1)** conjures
8. **(1)** turn
9. **(2)** appeared
10. **(1)** consider
11. **(2)** was

Practice IV *Page 57.*
1. **(4)** The bird flies gracefully.
2. **(1)** Mr. Jackson plays piano loudly.
3. **(3)** Floyd reads more quickly than Harvey.
4. **(1)** Annemarie seems nice.
5. **(3)** The butter tastes good.
6. **(1)** Rudy feels bad about the argument.

Practice V *Page 60.*
Answers may vary.
  Sample answers:
1. is, was
2. are, were
3. are, were
4. are, were
5. was

Practice VI *Page 60.*
Answers may vary.
  Sample answers:
1. were, grew, became, appeared, felt, are, become, grow, appear, feel
2. was, grew, became, appeared, appears, becomes, grows, is
3. grew, became, is, grows, becomes
4. were, appeared, felt, are, appear, feel
5. were, are

Practice VII *Page 60.*

1. **(3)** Cloning is a hotly debated topic. The *ethics and safety* of cloning *are* questioned by many. *Are* agrees in number with the plural subject, *ethics and safety*.

2. **(1)** *Sheep, goats, mice,* and *cows have been* cloned and are being studied to determine whether the health of cloned animals is affected. *Have* agrees in number with the plural subject, *sheep, goats, mice,* and *cows.*

3. **(5)** No error

4. **(3)** People's *belief* that they should control nature *is* reaching new heights. *Is* agrees in number with the singular subject, *belief.*

5. **(1)** The *possibility* of human cloning *has* been seen as inevitable since 1997, when a Scottish scientist created a sheep named Dolly. *Has* agrees in number with the singular subject, *possibility.*

6. **(5)** No error

Practice VIII *Page 62.*

1. They're
2. you're
3. isn't
4. didn't
5. Here's
6. weren't
7. He's
8. There's

Chapter 8

AGREEMENT: SPECIAL PROBLEMS

> *Each* of the veterinary surgeons gathered around
> Ruffian knew *his* job. *Neither* the doctors *nor* Mr.
> Janney *was* willing to give up on the magnificent
> filly, but despite *everyone's* desire to do *his* best,
> it became necessary to put the horse to sleep.

> —Murray Bromberg
> *The Great Match Race*

A Word With You . . .

The scene from the book took place in the early hours of Monday morning, July 7, 1975, as the veterinarians tried to save the life of a great horse whose leg had been shattered.

Our chief interest, however, is in the italicized words.

> each—his
> neither . . . nor—was
> everyone's—his

Some people might not see the reason for using these word combinations. Their relationships will be made clear in the following pages.

You know that an action word must *agree* with its performer in number, and with the sentence or paragraph in time.

> The jury *enters* the courtroom. A hush *falls* over the crowd.
> The judge *asks* for the verdict.

You know that a linking verb must agree with its subject in number and with the sentence or paragraph in time.

> Court *is* in session. Please *remain* silent.
> The defendant *seems* apprehensive. The prosecutor *appears* angry.

Rules Concerning Special Problems of Agreement

Each

Each is singular when it is the performer or subject of the sentence.

EXAMPLE:

Performer Action
| |
Each shows promise.

Practice I

Directions: Underline either the singular or plural action word or linking verb that correctly completes each sentence.

1. Each (gives, give) a lecture.
2. Each of the teachers (gives, give) a lecture.
3. They each (gives, give) a lecture.
4. Each (is, are) a good candidate.

Either-Or

When using *either-or*, you are choosing *one* or the *other*. The action or linking verb is *singular* if the performer or subject closest to it is singular.

EXAMPLE:

Either Tom *or* Bill drives to school.
Drives agrees with the singular performer, *Bill*.
The action or linking verb is *plural* if the performer or subject closest to it is plural.

EXAMPLE:

Either Tom *or* his friends drive to school.
Drive agrees with the plural performer, *friends*.

Practice II

Directions: Underline either the singular or plural linking verb that correctly completes each sentence.

1. Either the coach or the captain (is, are) late.
2. Either the coach or the players (is, are) late.

3. Either the players or the coach (is, are) late.
4. Either these players or those players (is, are) late.

Any

Any is singular. It is used when a choice involves *three* or more. *Either* is used for a choice between *two*.

EXAMPLE:

> *Any* of the *three* movies suits me.

Practice III

Directions: Underline either the singular or plural action or linking verb that correctly completes each sentence.

1. Any of the sandwiches (is, are) fine.
2. Any of the four records (sounds, sound) good.
3. (Any, either) of the three books (serves, serve) well.

Here and There

In sentences that begin with *here* or *there*, the action or linking verb must agree with the performer or subject. *Here* and *there* are never performers or subjects.

EXAMPLE:

> There *is* my coat.
> Here *are* my gloves.

What is there? My *coat*. Coat is the subject. Coat is *singular*; therefore, the singular linking verb *is* correctly completes the first sentence.

What is here? My *gloves*. *Gloves* is the subject. *Gloves* is *plural*; therefore, the plural linking verb *are* correctly completes the second sentence.

Practice IV

Directions: Locate the performer or subject in each sentence. Underline the action or linking verb that correctly completes each sentence.

1. There (is, are) my boots.
2. There (is, are) two sides to the argument.
3. Here (goes, go) my last chance.
4. There (is, are) no way out.

Who and That

You are familiar with the following sentence structures:

performer   action

The woman attends every meeting.
Woman is singular; *attends* agrees with *woman*.

performer   action

One (of those women) attends every meeting.
One is singular; *attends* agrees with *one*.

The following example is significantly different from the above.
One (of those women) *who* ATTEND every meeting seldom SPEAKS.
Ready?

performer   action

"One seldom speaks" is the *core* of the sentence.
One is singular: *speaks* agrees with *one*.

"Of those women who attend every meeting" describes or tells more about *one*.

Who might be singular or plural. How do we decide? We look at the word to which *who* refers. In this case, that word is *women*. *Women* is plural; therefore, *who* is plural. Within the descriptive group of words, "of those women who attend every meeting," *attend* must agree with *who*. *Who* is plural; *attend* agrees with *who*.

This rule also applies to *that*.

EXAMPLES:

performer   action

The *ruler belongs* to me.
One (of those rulers) belongs to me.

One (of those rulers) *that* ARE on the desk BELONGS to me.

Practice V

Directions: Underline either the singular or plural action or linking verb that correctly completes each sentence.

1. One of the musicians (plays, play) better than the others.
2. Several of those companies (e-mail, e-mails) regular updates.
3. John Kennedy was one of those leaders who (has, have) charisma.
4. One of those underdeveloped nations that (counts, count) upon outside sources for food will inevitably be disappointed.
5. One of those vocations that (has, have) always appealed to me (is, are) radio announcing.

Surprisingly Singular Subjects

Some words seem to refer to more than one person when, in fact, they do not. Others refer to more than one person, but they are acting as a group or a single unit. Even though these words refer to more than one person, they act as a singular subject. Surprisingly singular subjects include:

Everybody	means every *single* body.
Somebody	means some *one* body.
Anybody	means any *one* body.
Everyone	means every *one*.

Some Plural Subjects

Six words that take plural action or linking verbs are:

all   few   several   both   many   some

Practice VI

Directions: Underline the action word that correctly completes each sentence.

1. Everybody (hear, hears) a different drummer.
2. Somebody (call, calls) our office at 5:05 each day.
3. Anybody who (want, wants) to can join our cooperative supermarket.
4. None of the children (eat, eats) meat.

To Do	
I do	we do
you do	you do
he, she, it does	they do

Review Exercises

Practice VII

Directions: Underline the action or linking verb that agrees with the performer or subject in each of the following sentences.

EXAMPLE:

The coat (<u>is</u>, are) too large.

1. The books (is, are) on the shelf.
2. Each (selects, select) his own menu.
3. Each of the students (is, are) registered for ten weeks.

4. Any of the six choices (is, are) suitable.
5. Everybody (does, do) his job.
6. This kind of movie (is, are) boring.
7. Those kinds of flowers (seems, seem) delicate.
8. None of the candidates (speaks, speak) well.
9. There (was, were) several good items on the menu.
10. Neither the meats nor the vegetables (is, are) fresh.
11. Either the children or the baby-sitter (drinks, drink) the soy milk.
12. He (doesn't, don't) speak well.
13. She is one of those women who never (says, say) what they mean.
14. One of those tractors (is, are) broken.

To Do Statements

She works with Allen.
> *Works* agrees with *she*.

She does work with Allen.
> *Does* agrees with *she*; *work* is used in the "to work" form.
> (*Does* would be used in this sentence for emphasis or clarification.)

They work with Allen.
> *Works* agrees with *they*.

They do work with Allen.
> *Do* agrees with *they*; *work* is used in the "to work" form.

To Do Questions

Does she work with Allen?
> *Does* agrees with *she*; *work* is used in the "to work" form.
> In a typical question, the subject (*she*) follows *does*.

Do they work with Allen?
> When using a negative, *not* follows *do* or *does*:

Doesn't she work with Allen?

Don't they work with Allen?

Practice VIII

Directions: If the action or linking verb in each sentence agrees with the subject, blacken circle 1. If the action or linking verb does not agree with the subject, blacken circle 2.

1. There were two planes outside the hangar.   ① ②
2. Macaroni or potatoes go with this dinner.   ① ②
3. Any of these dips are great with crackers.   ① ②
4. Ten minutes of my time is all that I can offer.   ① ②
5. Don't she know your address?   ① ②
6. My son or my daughter are coming for me.   ① ②
7. There's two new e-mails.   ① ②

8. One of the most recent discoveries are in regard to aging.   ① ②
9. Doesn't any famous rock star ever arrive on time?   ① ②
10. Here's Joanna's friends.   ① ②
11. One of those library books is lost.   ① ②
12. Either Pat's boss or her coworkers will pick up a cake for her birthday.   ① ②
13. Oprah Winfrey is one of those people who says what she means.   ① ②

Practice IX

Directions: Blacken the circle that corresponds to the number of the incorrect sentence in each group. If there is no error, blacken number 5.

1. (1) Each of the projects is interesting.   ① ② ③ ④ ⑤
   (2) There's my two favorite magazines.
   (3) Here's the best seat in the house.
   (4) Any of those concerts would please me.
   (5) No error
2. (1) Neither of us is really qualified for that job.   ① ② ③ ④ ⑤
   (2) Those kinds of personalities are most difficult to live with.
   (3) Everybody shirks their responsibility occasionally.
   (4) Nelson Mandela is one of the most interesting people I know about.
   (5) No error
3. (1) Any of those arrangements is a suitable centerpiece.   ① ② ③ ④ ⑤
   (2) Either Mr. Hanns or his assistants write the weekly reports.
   (3) The men each take a turn nailing the paneling.
   (4) Either of the two plants enhances that corner.
   (5) No error
4. (1) The Jones sisters are among those people who always have time to listen.   ① ② ③ ④ ⑤
   (2) One of those books is mine.
   (3) Each of those buildings have to be painted.
   (4) Here are my choices.
   (5) No error
5. (1) Don't he ever get to work on time?   ① ② ③ ④ ⑤
   (2) One of these DVDs belongs to Dante.
   (3) There's the only gifted writer I know.
   (4) Carmen is one of those people who speak constantly.
   (5) No error
6. (1) Every day seems busier than the day before.   ① ② ③ ④ ⑤
   (2) Either the stewardesses or their captain make the necessary announcements.
   (3) Neither the lemons nor the oranges were fresh.
   (4) Several of his poems are very good.
   (5) No error

7. (1) Any of these coats or dresses suits you well. ① ② ③ ④ ⑤
   (2) Here's the most authoritative book about the Civil War.
   (3) Doesn't he seem right for the job?
   (4) Each participant is expected to follow the rules.
   (5) No error

8. (1) They each sings in the community choir. ① ② ③ ④ ⑤
   (2) There's no time to waste.
   (3) Colonel Adams or Major Niles is planning to attend.
   (4) Here's the last of those CDs you ordered.
   (5) No error

9. (1) Doesn't he ever take a day off? ① ② ③ ④ ⑤
   (2) Each of my children visits during the holidays.
   (3) Any of these shirts are a bargain.
   (4) Either the grass or the shrubs need tending.
   (5) No error

10. (1) Any one of those mountain trails is the same as the others. ① ② ③ ④ ⑤
    (2) Don't Angie look pretty?
    (3) Four days is long enough for this type of project.
    (4) One of the biggest problems is a lack of honesty.
    (5) No error

Do you remember the paragraph that introduced this chapter?

> *Each* of the veterinary surgeons gathered around
> Ruffian knew *his* job. *Neither* the doctors *nor* Mr.
> Janney *was* willing to give up on the magnificent filly,
> but despite *everyone's* desire to do *his* best, it became
> necessary to put the horse to sleep.

Look at these agreement examples:

1. *Each* of the veterinary surgeons gathered around Ruffian knew *his* job.
2. Neither the doctors nor *Mr. Janney was* willing . . .
3. . . . but despite *everyone's* desire to do *his* best, . . .

These relationships should be clear to you after studying Chapter 8.

Chapter 8   Agreement: Special Problems

Practice I *Page 66.*

1. Each *gives*
    Gives agrees with the singular performer, *each*.

2. Each *gives*
    Gives agrees with the singular performer, *each*.

3. They *give*
    Give agrees with the plural performer, *they*.

4. Each *is*
    Is agrees with the singular subject, *each*.

Practice II *Page 66.*

1. captain *is*
    Is agrees with the singular subject, *captain*.

2. players *are*
    Are agrees with the plural subject, *players*.

3. coach *is*
    Is agrees with the singular subject, *coach*.

4. players *are*
    Are agrees with the plural subject, *players*.

Practice III *Page 67.*

linking verb

1. Any (of the sandwiches) *is* fine.
    Is agrees with the singular subject, *any*.

linking verb

2. Any (of the four records) *sounds* good.
    Sounds agrees with the singular subject, *any*.

action verb

3. Any (of the three books) *serves* well.
    Serves agrees with the singular performer, *any*.

Practice IV *Page 67.*

1. There *are* my boots.
    Are agrees with the plural subject *boots*.

2. There *are* two sides to the argument.
    Are agrees with the plural subject *sides*.

3. Here *goes* my last chance.
    Goes agrees with the singular performer *chance*.

4. There *is* no way out.
    Is agrees with the singular subject *way*.

Practice V *Page 68.*

1. One of the musicians *plays* . . .
    Plays agrees with the singular subject *One*.

2. Several of those companies *e-mail* . . .
    E-mail agrees with the plural subject *several*.

3. John Kennedy was one of those leaders who *have* charisma.
    Have agrees with its subject, *who*, which refers to the plural word *leaders*.

4. One of those underdeveloped nations that *count* . . .
    Count agrees with its subject *that*, which refers to the plural word *nations*.

5. One of those vocations that *have* . . . always appealed to me *is* . . .
    Have agrees with its subject *that*, which refers to the plural word *vocations*; *is* agrees with the singular subject *One*.

Practice VI *Page 69.*
1. Everybody *hears* a different drummer.
2. Somebody *calls* our office at 5:05 each day.
3. Anybody who *wants* to can join our co-operative supermarket.
4. None of the children *eats* meat.

The performer in each sentence is singular and requires a singular action word.

Practice VII *Page 69.*
The correct action or linking verb in each sentence is underlined twice. The subject in each sentence is underlined once.

1. The <u>books</u> <u>are</u> on the shelf.
2. <u>Each</u> <u>selects</u> his own menu.
3. <u>Each</u> (of the students) <u>is</u> registered for ten weeks.
4. <u>Any</u> (of the six choices) <u>is</u> suitable.
5. <u>Everybody</u> <u>does</u> his job.
6. This <u>kind</u> (of movie) <u>is</u> boring.
7. Those <u>kinds</u> (of flowers) <u>seem</u> delicate.
8. <u>None</u> (of the candidates) <u>speaks</u> well.
9. There <u>were</u> several good <u>items</u> on the menu.
10. Neither the <u>meats</u> nor the <u>vegetables</u> <u>are</u> fresh.
11. Either the <u>children</u> or the <u>baby-sitter</u> <u>drinks</u> the milk.
12. He <u>doesn't</u> speak well.
13. She is one of those women <u>who</u> never <u>say</u> what they mean.
14. <u>One</u> (of those tractors) <u>is</u> broken.

Practice VIII *Page 70.*
1. **(1)** planes were there
   Were agrees with the plural subject, *planes*.

2. **(1)** potatoes go
   Go agrees with the plural subject, *potatoes*.

3. **(2)** any (of these dips) is
   Is agrees with the singular subject, *any*.

4. **(1)** ten minutes (as a *unit* of time) is
   Is agrees with the singular subject, *ten minutes*.

5. **(2)** doesn't she know
   Doesn't agrees with the singular performer, *she*.

6. **(2)** my daughter is
   Is agrees with the singular subject, *daughter*.

7. **(2)** there are two
   Are agrees with the plural subject, *e-mails*.

8. **(2)** one (of the most recent discoveries) is
   Is agrees with the singular subject, *one*.

9. **(1)** doesn't any famous rock star ever arrive
   Doesn't agrees with the singular performer, *any*.

10. **(2)** Joanna's friends are here
    Are agrees with the plural subject, *friends*.

11. **(1)** One (of those library books) is
    Is agrees with the singular subject, *one*.

12. **(1)** players argue
    Argue agrees with the plural performer, *players*.

13. **(2)** people who say what they mean.
Who must agree with the plural *people*. *Say* agrees with the plural performer, *who*. *They* agrees with the plural performer, *who*. *Mean* agrees with *they*.

Practice IX *Page 71.*

1. **(2)** There *are* my two favorite magazines.
The plural linking verb *are* agrees with the plural *subject*, magazines.

2. **(3)** Everybody shirks *his* or *her* responsibility occasionally.
The singular word *his* or *her* agrees with the singular performer, *everybody*.

3. **(5)** No error. (1) any . . . is, (2) assistants write, (3) men . . . take, (4) each . . . enhances

4. **(3)** Each of those buildings *has* to be painted.
The singular action word *has* agrees with the singular performer, *each*.

5. **(1)** *Doesn't* he ever get to work on time?
The singular helping word *does* (not) agrees with the singular performer, *he*.

6. **(2)** Either the stewardesses or their captain *makes* the necessary announcements.
The action word *makes* is singular because the performer that is closest to it, *captain*, is singular.

7. **(5)** No error. (1) any . . . suits, (2) here is, (3) he does(n't), (4) participant is

8. **(1)** They each *sing* in the community choir.
The plural action word, *sing*, agrees with the plural performer, *they*.

9. **(3)** Any of these shirts *is* a bargain.
The singular linking verb *is* agrees with the singular subject, *any*.

10. **(2)** *Doesn't* Angie look pretty?
The singular helping word *does* (not) agrees with the singular subject, *Angie*.

Chapter 9

TIME: SPECIAL PROBLEMS

> Eddie's father insisted that he pay attention. If Dad
> was going to give up a half hour of Archie Bunker in
> order to help Eddie with his homework, he wanted to
> make sure that Eddie was all ears.
> "Now, there are the *present perfect*, the *past perfect*, and
> the *future perfect*," explained Eddie's father. "Why can't
> you understand that?"
> "Well, nobody's perfect, Dad," quipped Eddie.
> "Okay, wise guy," his father said. "Just listen to this
> example of the *future perfect tense*: 'By next week, you
> *will have discovered* a decrease in your allowance.'"
>
> —Carol Lehrer
> *Tenting Out in the Suburbs*

A Word With You ...

It might not be fair to cut a youngster's allowance because he had trouble with tenses (time), but Eddie's father seemed to know what he was doing in grammar, as well as in child rearing.

The hapless Eddie was not concentrating—but you will, we are sure. Fortunately, you won't have to grapple with the "perfect" terms.

You know that sentences express time. For instance,

PRESENT ACTION: I commute to work each day.
PAST ACTION: I commuted to work each day.
FUTURE ACTION: I will commute to work each day.

Occasionally, time is more complicated than the simple expression of past or future. Sometimes an action that began in the past continues into the present.

EXAMPLES:

I *have commuted* to work for six years.
Marie *has commuted* to work for five years.

The addition of the helping word *have* or *has* expresses the idea of an action that began in the past, but is continuing into the present. In the above examples, the helping words *have* and *has* are in the present and the action word *commuted* is in the past.

Common Misuses of *Has* and *Have*

a. I *commuted* to work for six years and I am tired of commuting.
b. I *commuted* to work for six years and I have been tired of commuting.

The only correct use of the helping word *have* in this sentence:

I *have commuted* to work for six years and I am tired of commuting.

Practice I

Directions: Blacken the circle that corresponds to the number of the incorrect sentence in each group.

1. (1) I have lived in this community for ten years.   ① ② ③ ④
   (2) Ellen has been climbing trees since she was six years old.
   (3) Eric was the last in line since he began school.
   (4) Liz and Paula have known each other for six years.
2. (1) You and she have worked together for years.   ① ② ③ ④
   (2) Shirley has spoken highly of you always.
   (3) Andrea did not visit us for the past several days.
   (4) Wendy and Karen have babysat for us since we moved here.

Sometimes a past action has occurred before another past action.

EXAMPLE:

I *had commuted* for two hours each way before I *moved* to the city.

Even though both actions occurred in the past (*commuted, moved*), one happened before the other. You need to make clear which past action occurred first (further in the past). The addition of the helping word *had* shows that the *commuting* occurred in the past before the *moving* occurred (also in the past).

EXAMPLE:

William had *resisted* working on a team before he *attended* the training seminar.

The addition of the helping word *had* shows that William *resisted* even before he *attended* the training session (also in the past).

Common Misuses of *Had*

a. I *had commuted* two hours each way before I *had moved* to the city.
b. I *commuted* two hours each way before I *had moved* to the city.

The only correct use of the helping word *had* in this sentence:

I *had commuted* two hours each way before I *moved* to the city.

Practice II

Directions: Blacken the circle that corresponds to the number of the incorrect sentence in each group.

1. (1) John Milton had become immortalized before Ernest Hemingway was born.
   (2) Jean had driven fifteen miles before she had realized that she was going north instead of south.
   (3) Prior to our purchasing a new one, our old refrigerator had needed repair every six to eight weeks.
   (4) Since environmental care has become a public concern, paper and glass recycling are common in many communities.

   ① ② ③ ④

2. (1) If I had known I could have a paying job, I never would have volunteered my services.
   (2) If you had planned a thorough outline earlier, you would not be so rushed to complete your report now.
   (3) I had suffered the pain of a sore throat for three days before I had called a doctor.
   (4) After we had bought the oak table, we saw the glaring imperfection in it.

   ① ② ③ ④

Sometimes a future action can occur before another future action.

EXAMPLE:

I *will have commuted* four million miles by the time I retire.

The addition of the helping words *will have* shows that the commuting will be completed before the retiring. Notice that when you use the words *will have*, you are talking about an action that will be completed in the future *before* another action.

EXAMPLE:

Before the meeting begins, I will have written and circulated the agenda.

All actions will occur in the future, but the *writing* and *circulating* will occur *before* the meeting *begins*.

Common Misuses of *Will Have*

    a. I *will have commuted* four million miles by the time I *will have retired*.
    b. I *will commute* four million miles by the time I *will have retired*.

The only correct use of *will have* in this sentence:

I *will have commuted* four million miles by the time I *retire*.

Practice III

Directions: Blacken the circle that corresponds to the number of the incorrect sentence in each group.

1. (1) By the time your plane lands in Cleveland, I will   ① ② ③ ④
          have left for Colorado.
    (2) By the time you call for me, I will have typed our report.
    (3) Before they leave, Mary and Agnes will have instructed the
          children to go to bed at nine.
    (4) Martin will complete high school by the time his brother
          begins.
2. (1) Jeannie will have graduated from high school before David enters.   ① ② ③ ④
    (2) By next summer, I will retire from public office.
    (3) By this time next week, I will have seen Paris.
    (4) The meeting will have adjourned before you leave your office.

When two actions occur simultaneously, their time must be the same.

EXAMPLE:

    As the curtain rises, the audience *applauds*.
    As the curtain *rose*, the audience *applauded*.

Common Errors Regarding Simultaneous Actions

    a. As the curtain *rose* to reveal the elaborate set, the enthusiastic audience *had applauded*.
    b. As the curtain *had risen* to reveal the elaborate set, the enthusiastic audience *applauded*.

    In sentences a and b, the audience applauded *as* the curtain rose. Since both actions occurred *at the same time*, neither action word should be accompanied by *had*.

The correct sentence:

As the curtain *rose* to reveal the elaborate set, the enthusiastic audience *applauded*.

Practice IV

Directions: Blacken the circle that corresponds to the number of the incorrect sentence in each group.

1. (1) As the class filed out of the room, David noticed the trampled book on the floor.   ① ② ③ ④
   (2) When the power failed, all of our food was ruined.
   (3) As soon as you finish your Web page, please give me the address.
   (4) As the fish bit the worm, he had realized his error.
2. (1) As we began our trip in our brand new convertible, gray clouds hovered threateningly above.   ① ② ③ ④
   (2) When the automobile industry's strike ended, our car was delivered.
   (3) When I lifted the papers, I had found Ellen's missing glasses.
   (4) As soon as you gave me your requirements, I shipped the order.

Linking words express time, also. *Has*, *have*, and *had* are used with linking verbs in order to clarify time.

EXAMPLES:

Tom *has been* irritable all morning.
Tom *had been* irritable before he received his promotion.
Tom *will have been* president for two years, by the time he retires.

Practice V

Directions: Blacken the circle that corresponds to the number of the incorrect sentence in each group.

1. (1) I have felt tired since my illness.   ① ② ③ ④
   (2) Jules always has been a good sport.
   (3) Before she began working full-time, Erica seemed more relaxed.
   (4) By the time this very long documentary ends, I will have grown bored.
2. (1) The amplifier had sounded distorted for several hours before it stopped working.   ① ② ③ ④
   (2) The court claimed that the children had been neglected.
   (3) For the past three days, your socks have been in the same place on the floor.
   (4) As I looked across the room at the woman who bore an uncanny resemblance to me, I had felt as though I were looking into a mirror.

Review Exercises

Practice VI

Directions: Blacken the circle that corresponds to the number of the incorrect sentence. If there is no error, blacken number 5.

1. (1) Lady Bird Johnson had shown an interest in conservation long before she became the First Lady.
   (2) The CIA had overstepped its bounds long before Watergate publicized its far-reaching arm.
   (3) As I spoke, I realized my error.
   (4) Prior to the election, the candidate promised law and order.
   (5) No error

   ① ② ③ ④ ⑤

2. (1) I am teaching for twenty years.
   (2) Betty Friedan has been a pioneer in the women's movement.
   (3) The Thompsons have owned the drug store since 1947.
   (4) Before he spoke, he had carefully prepared his speech.
   (5) No error

   ① ② ③ ④ ⑤

3. (1) In 1974, Richard Nixon resigned.
   (2) John had changed jobs. Then the family followed him.
   (3) Over the past several years, elections have become a blood sport.
   (4) We had seen Laura last night.
   (5) No error

   ① ② ③ ④ ⑤

4. (1) As the car pulled to the curb, a man jumped out.
   (2) Before the phone stopped ringing, Mary had answered it.
   (3) Before the music had started, fans rushed the stage.
   (4) When you arrive, we will begin the discussion.
   (5) No error

   ① ② ③ ④ ⑤

5. (1) By next week, the price of lettuce will have doubled.
   (2) Before the doorbell rang, Ida seemed nervous.
   (3) Because he had known the temper of the crowd, he spoke calmly and clearly.
   (4) By the time the repairman arrives, I will have left.
   (5) No error

   ① ② ③ ④ ⑤

6. (1) By this time tomorrow, I will have taken the test.
   (2) If you studied, you might have known the answer.
   (3) The historian carefully studied his subject.
   (4) Before boarding the plane, Tom had expressed a fear of flying.
   (5) No error

   ① ② ③ ④ ⑤

7. (1) These sentences have been difficult.
   (2) Last week, they would have been impossible.
   (3) By next week, you will have mastered the problem.
   (4) Before he passed the test, the man studied for many hours.
   (5) No error

   ① ② ③ ④ ⑤

Practice VII

Directions: Blacken the circle that corresponds to the correct rewriting of the underlined portion of the sentence. Choice 1 is always the same as the underlined portion and is sometimes the right answer.

1. I signed the letter several days after <u>I wrote it.</u>   ① ② ③ ④ ⑤
   - (1) I wrote it.
   - (2) I writed it.
   - (3) it was written.
   - (4) I had written it.
   - (5) I have written it.

2. By the time the sun comes out, the pool <u>will close</u> for the day.   ① ② ③ ④ ⑤
   - (1) will close
   - (2) will have closed
   - (3) has closed
   - (4) will be closed
   - (5) would close

3. The telephone <u>rang as my guest entered</u> the room.   ① ② ③ ④ ⑤
   - (1) rang as my guest entered
   - (2) rang as my guest had entered
   - (3) had rung as my guest entered
   - (4) had rung as my guest had entered
   - (5) rang as my guest has entered

4. Since I began to study music appreciation, I <u>had enjoyed</u> Beethoven.   ① ② ③ ④ ⑤
   - (1) had enjoyed
   - (2) always had enjoyed
   - (3) have enjoyed
   - (4) will enjoy
   - (5) enjoy

5. On this, his anniversary, Simpson <u>was with the bank</u> for forty years.   ① ② ③ ④ ⑤
   - (1) was with the bank
   - (2) had been with the bank
   - (3) is with the bank
   - (4) has been with the bank
   - (5) will be with the bank

6. I <u>received a ticket because I parked</u> in a no parking zone.   ① ② ③ ④ ⑤
   - (1) received a ticket because I parked
   - (2) received a ticket because I had parked
   - (3) had received a ticket because I parked
   - (4) had received a ticket because I had parked
   - (5) received a ticket because parking

7. If you arrive after 10, the kitchen <u>will have closed</u>.   ① ② ③ ④ ⑤
   - (1) will have closed.
   - (2) closes.
   - (3) will close.
   - (4) should close.
   - (5) has closed.

8. As soon as the bell rings, the horses <u>will begin</u> to run. ① ② ③ ④ ⑤
   (1) will begin
   (2) shall begin
   (3) have begun
   (4) began
   (5) begin

9. He <u>made the appointment</u> before he consulted me. ① ② ③ ④ ⑤
   (1) made the appointment
   (2) made that appointment
   (3) had made the appointment
   (4) has made the appointment
   (5) have made the appointment

10. I <u>was unusually busy</u> for the past two weeks. ① ② ③ ④ ⑤
    (1) was unusually busy
    (2) will have been unusually busy
    (3) am unusually busy
    (4) have been unusually busy
    (5) had been unusually busy

Practice VIII

Directions: Blacken the circle that corresponds to the number of the error in each sentence. If there is no error, blacken number 5.

1. We *had traveled* extensively *before* we *had* *bought* our summer ① ② ③ ④ ⑤
      1   2   3   4
   home. *No error*
         5

2. We *traveled* in Europe and Asia *before* we *went* to *South* ① ② ③ ④ ⑤
      1   2   3   4
   America. *No error*
            5

3. For the past year, *however,* we *were* *inclined* *to stay home*. ① ② ③ ④ ⑤
                      1   2   3   4
   No error
   5

4. Family travel *became* so expensive over the *past* few years ① ② ③ ④ ⑤
                 1   2
   that we *can* no longer *afford* it. *No error*
           3   4   5

5. Perhaps _by the time_ our children _are grown_, _we will have decided_   ① ② ③ ④ ⑤
                    1   2   3

   to _travel_ again. _No error_
           4   5

6. As soon as they _become_ independent of us, _we will_ _have_ _become_   ① ② ③ ④ ⑤
                        1   2   3   4

   independent of them. _No error_
                          5

7. During the _past_ _several_ years, the children's _increasing_ activities   ① ② ③ ④ ⑤
              1   2   3

   hampered our independence. _No error_
       4   5

8. Before we _started_ a family, we _did not_ _travel_ as much as we   ① ② ③ ④ ⑤
                1   2   3

   should have. _No error_
        4   5

Chapter 9   Time: Special Problems

Practice I *Page 77.*

1. **(3)** Eric *has been* the last in line since he began school.

   The addition of the helping word *has* expresses the idea of an action that began in the past but is continuing into the present.

2. **(3)** Andrea *has not visited* us for the past several days.

   See explanation above.

Practice II *Page 78.*

1. **(2)** Jean *had driven* fifteen miles before she *realized* that she was going north instead of south.

   When a sentence contains two past actions, the action that occurred first is accompanied by the helping word *had*.

2. **(3)** I *had suffered* the pain of a sore throat for three days before I *called* a doctor.

   See explanation above.

Practice III *Page 79.*

1. **(4)** Martin *will have completed* high school by the time his brother *begins*.

   When a sentence contains two future actions, the action that will occur first is accompanied by the helping words *will have*.

2. **(2)** By next summer, I *will have retired* from public office.

   See explanation above.

Practice IV *Page 80.*

1. **(4)** As the fish *bit* the worm, he *realized* his error.

   When two actions occur simultaneously, their forms must be the same. Omit *had* before *realized*.

2. **(3)** When I *lifted* the papers, I *found* Ellen's missing glasses.

   See explanation above. Omit *had* before *found*.

Practice V *Page 80.*

1. **(3)** Before she *had begun* working full-time, Erica seemed more relaxed.

   Addition of the helping word *had* shows that *begun* occurred in the past before *seemed*.

2. **(4)** As I looked across the room at the woman who bore an uncanny resemblance to me, I *felt* as though I were looking into a mirror.

   Eliminate *had* before *felt*. *Looked* and *felt* are simultaneous actions.

REVIEW

Practice VI *Page 81.*

1. **(4)** Prior to the election, the candidate *had promised* law and order.

   The addition of the helping word *had* shows that the promising occurred in the past *before* the election.

2. **(1)** I *have been teaching* for twenty years.

The helping words *have been* show that the teaching began in the past and continues into the present.

3. **(4)** We *saw* Laura last night.

Eliminate the helping word *had* since the seeing did not occur in the past before another action.

4. **(3)** Before the music started, fans *had rushed the stage*.

The helping word *had* shows that *rushed* occurred in the past before the music started.

5. **(2)** Before the doorbell rang, Ida *had seemed* nervous.

The helping word *had* shows that *seemed* occurred before the doorbell rang.

6. **(2)** If you *had studied*, you might have known the answer.

The helping word *had* shows that *studied* began in the past before the knowing.

7. **(4)** Before he passed the test, the man *had studied* for many hours.

The helping word *had* shows that *studied* began in the past before *passed*.

Practice VII *Page 82.*

1. **(4)** I signed the letter several days after *I had written it*.

The helping word *had* shows that the writing occurred in the past *before* the signing.

2. **(2)** By the time the sun comes out, the pool *will have closed* for the day.

The helping words *will have* show that the closing will be completed *before* the sun comes out.

3. **(1)** The telephone *rang as my guest entered* the room.

Since both actions occurred at *the same time*, the same form (past) is used for both action words.

4. **(3)** Since I began to study music appreciation, I *have enjoyed* Beethoven.

The helping word *have* shows that *enjoyed* began in the past and is continuing into the present.

5. **(4)** On this, his anniversary, Simpson *has been with the bank* for forty years.

The helping word *has* shows that Simpson *has been* with the bank in the past and is continuing into the present.

6. **(2)** I *received a ticket because I had parked* in a no parking zone.

The helping word *had* shows that the parking occurred in the past *before* the receiving.

7. **(1)** If you arrive after 10, the kitchen *will have closed*.

The helping words *will have* show that the closing will be completed *before* the arrival.

8. **(5)** As soon as the bell rings, the horses *begin* to run.

Since both actions occur at the *same time*, the *same form* (present) is used for both action words.

9. **(3)** He *had made the appointment* before he consulted me.

The helping word *had* shows that the appointment was made *before* the consulting took place.

10. **(4)** *I have been unusually busy* for the past two weeks.

The helping word *have* shows that I *have been* busy in the past and am continuing into the present.

Practice VIII *Page 83.*

1. **(3)** We had traveled extensively before we *bought* our summer home.

2. **(1)** We *had traveled* in Europe and Asia before we went to South America.

3. **(2)** For the past year, however, we *have been* inclined to stay home.

4. **(1)** Family travel *has become* so expensive over the past few years that we can no longer afford it.

5. **(5)** No error. The helping words *will have* show that the decision to travel occurred in the past, before the children were grown.

6. **(3)** As soon as they become independent of us, we *will become* independent of them.

7. **(4)** During the past several years, the children's increasing activities *have hampered* our independence.

8. **(2)** Before we started a family, we *had not traveled* as much as we should have.

Chapter 10

PRONOUNS

I had only just arrived at the club when I bumped into Roger. After we had exchanged a few pleasantries, he lowered his voice and asked, "What do you think of Martha and I as a potential twosome?"

"That," I replied, "would be a mistake. Martha and me is more like it."

"You're interested in Martha?"

"I'm interested in clear communication."

"Fair enough," he agreed. "May the best man win." Then he sighed. "Here I thought we had a clear path to becoming a very unique couple."

"You couldn't be a very unique couple, Roger."

"Oh? And why is that?"

"Martha couldn't be a little pregnant, could she?"

"Say what? You think that Martha and me. . . ."

"Martha and I."

"Oh." Roger blushed and set down his drink. "Gee, I didn't know."

"Of course you didn't," I assured him. "Most people don't."

"I feel very badly about this."

"You shouldn't say that: I feel bad. . . ."

"Please, don't," Roger said. "If anyone's at fault here, it's me!"

By Lawrence Bush
The New York Times Op-Ed, 4/5/94.

A Word With You . . .

Poor Roger. If he had only read this chapter, he would have understood that his friend had no interest in Martha. The author had a strong desire to use (and have others use) pronouns correctly. The loser here, of course, is Martha. She will never understand why Roger stops calling her. Review all the pronoun clues—your future could depend on it.

Rules Concerning Pronoun Usage

Pronouns are used as performers/subjects or as words that receive action. *For example:*

performer

Lloyd ran home.

performer pronoun

He ran home.

subject

Lloyd is pleasant.

subject pronoun

He is pleasant.

performer

receives action

Elana gave a bright smile to Tom.

performer

pronoun that receives action

Elana gave a bright smile to him.

performer   receives action

Maria gave Tom an icy stare.

performer   pronoun that receives action

Maria gave him an icy stare.

Perfomer/Subject Pronouns	Pronouns That Receive Action
I	me
you	you
he	him
she	her
it	it
we	us
they	them
who	whom

Practice I

Directions: Complete each sentence using a pronoun from the above list. More than one choice may be correct.

1. _____ won the election.
2. _____ campaigned all week.
3. The National Organization for Women gave the citation to _____.
4. The student hitchhiker got a lift from _____.
5. _____ was responsible for legislation providing consumer protection?
6. For _____ did the witness testify?

Pronoun Clue 1:

Don't be confused by *who* and *whom*. As you can see in the preceding list, *who* is a subject/performer and *whom* is a pronoun that receives action.

IF: *He* painted the house.
THEN: *Who* painted the house?
IF: The phone call is for *him*.
THEN: For *whom* is the phone call?
IF: Jane hired Crisala (her).
THEN: Crisala is the woman *whom* Jane hired.

Practice II

Directions: Underline the pronoun that correctly completes each sentence.

EXAMPLE:

(*Who*—Whom) rang the doorbell?
Clue: *He* rang the doorbell.

1. (Who—Whom) did you call?
2. (Who—Whom) answered your letter?
3. (Who—Whom) will help with this project?
4. *Consumer Reports* cites manufacturers from (who—whom) we can expect quality products.
5. Mariah Carey is the singer (who—whom) Tony likes best.

Pronoun Clue 2:

Don't be confused by more than one subject.

IF: He won the election.
THEN: Macon and *he* won the election.

Because it is incorrect to say:

Him won the election.

It is also incorrect to say:

Macon and *him* won the election.

Practice III

Directions: Underline the pronoun that correctly completes each sentence.

1. Zoey and (he, him) ran the fair.
2. (They, Them) and their father went fishing.

3. My friend and (I, me) are planning a camping trip.
4. (She, her) and (he, him) were delegates to the convention.
5. The Walters and (we, us) go to the shore each summer.
6. (Who, whom), along with Susan, will work on this committee?

Pronoun Clue 3:

Don't be confused by more than one word receiving the action.

IF: I gave the present to *her*.
THEN: I gave the present to Tom and *her*.

Because it is incorrect to say:

I gave the present to *she*.

It is also incorrect to say:

I gave the present to Tom and *she*.

IF: Sam bought her lunch.
THEN: Sam bought Robert and *her* lunch.

Because it is incorrect to say:

Sam bought *she* lunch.

It is also incorrect to say:

Sam bought Robert and *she* lunch.

Practice IV

Directions: Underline the pronoun that correctly completes each sentence.

1. When the plans for the new community center are completed, call Mr. Faldez and (I, me).
2. The supermarket manager gave discount coupons to Olga and (she, her).
3. When they question you about the accident, tell Paul and (they, them) the truth.
4. Will you be speaking to Hiroko and (he, him)?
5. The MacDonalds sent regards to Joanna and (we, us).

Pronoun Clue 4:

Don't be confused by a condensed thought.

IF: Elmer runs more quickly *than I do*.
THEN: Elmer runs more quickly *than I*.

Because it is incorrect to say:

> Elmer runs more quickly *than me do*.

It is also incorrect to say:

> Elmer runs more quickly *than me*.

Practice V

Directions: Underline the pronoun that correctly completes each sentence.

1. Mary is a better cook than (I, me).
2. I sew better than (she, her).
3. You don't feel as sorry as (he, him).
4. The Ortegas are better swimmers than (we, us).
5. Their neighbors don't argue as often as (they, them).

Pronoun Clue 5:

A sentence in which a linking verb is connecting the subject to a word that means the same thing as the subject, is reversible.

If:	Carl is the mayor.
Then:	The mayor is Carl.
If:	He is the mayor.
Then:	The mayor is he.

Because it is incorrect to say:

> *Him* is the mayor.

It is also incorrect to say:

> The mayor is *him*.

Practice VI

Directions: Underline the pronoun that correctly completes each sentence.

1. My secretary is (she, her).
2. The winner of the contest was (he, him).
3. (Who, whom) seems most likely to get the promotion?
4. The culprits were (they, them).
5. The person who called you was (I, me).
6. If there is a couple who enjoys dancing, it is (we, us).

Pronoun Clue 6:

Certain pronouns—*my, your, his, her, its, our, their*—may be used as descriptive words.

EXAMPLE:

I like the *red* hat.
I like *his* hat.

Descriptive pronouns are never a problem in the above context. However, errors tend to be made in sentences such as the following:

INCORRECT: I do not like *him* smoking.
CORRECT: I do not like *his* smoking.
INCORRECT: Of course I approve of *you* jogging.
CORRECT: Of course I approve of *your* jogging.

Practice VII

Directions: Underline the pronoun that correctly completes each sentence.

1. Tom is very proud of (him, his) karate.
2. I don't like (you, your) calling me at the office.
3. The professor was glad to hear about (me, my) writing a story.
4. We wondered (who's, whose) contribution to medicine was greatest.
5. I don't like (them, their) refusing to take BHA and BHT out of foods.

Pronoun Clue 7:

Words such as *to, from, between, except, among* are followed by pronouns that receive action. Here are some examples.

1. Between you and *me*, I don't enjoy cooking.
2. The package is for *her*.
3. Please divide the workload among *them*.
4. Everyone, except *us*, is attending the meeting.

Practice VIII

Directions: Underline the pronoun that correctly completes each sentence.

1. From (who, whom) did you learn that myth about not eating before swimming?
2. Many secrets have passed between you and (he, him).
3. The personnel director gave notices to John and (they, them).
4. Everyone, except (she, her), plans to take the test.
5. The host and his friends divided the four bottles of beer among (they, them).

Pronoun Clue 8:

A pronoun must agree in number with the word to which it refers. Here are some examples.

1. One of the men in the back of the room could not project *his* voice.
   His refers to one. Both words are singular.
2. All of those women left *their* coats after the rally.
   Their refers to *all*. Both words are plural.

Practice IX

Directions: Select the word that correctly completes each sentence.

1. Everyone must decide for (himself, themselves).
2. Each of the painters worked (his, their) best.
3. They each performed to the best of (his, their) ability.
4. All of the members brought (his, their) spouses.

Review Exercises

Practice X

Directions: Blacken the circle that corresponds to the number of the incorrect word in each sentence. If there is no error, blacken number 5.

1. <u>He</u> and <u>his</u> brother strenuously object to <u>me</u> <u>smoking</u>.   ① ② ③ ④ ⑤
     1   2   3   4
   <u>No error</u>
     5

2. Although <u>she</u> is interesting and <u>she's</u> witty, I don't think that   ① ② ③ ④ ⑤
              1   2
   <u>she</u> is the right girl for <u>my</u> friend. <u>No error</u>
    3   4   5

3. Sam finds <u>my</u> singing offensive, but <u>he</u> enjoys <u>me</u> playing <u>the</u>   ① ② ③ ④ ⑤
            1   2   3   4
   piano. <u>No error</u>
         5

4. The man <u>who</u> you called is out and <u>his</u> assistant insists <u>that</u>   ① ② ③ ④ ⑤
           1   2   3
   <u>he</u> will not return again today. <u>No error</u>
    4   5

5. If you are wondering <u>who</u> it was <u>who</u> called <u>you</u> earlier in the   ① ② ③ ④ ⑤
                      1   2   3
   week, it was <u>him</u>. <u>No error</u>
          4   5

6. Although _he_ plays tennis better than _I_ do, _I_ bowl better than
        1   2   3
   him. _No error_
    4   5
① ② ③ ④ ⑤

7. Would _you_ please buy tickets for the football game _for him_
        1   2   3
   and _I_? _No error_
     4   5
① ② ③ ④ ⑤

8. _He_ invited Jim and _she_ to join _his_ car pool _that_ day. _No error_
   1   2   3   4   5
① ② ③ ④ ⑤

9. Don wanted _us_, John and _I_, to help _him_ build _his_ new
              1   2   3   4
   garage. _No error_
         5
① ② ③ ④ ⑤

10. Jane and _me_ invited _our_ husbands and _them_ to join _our_ yoga
          1   2   3   4
   class. _No error_
       5
① ② ③ ④ ⑤

Practice XI

Directions: Blacken the circle that corresponds to the number of the incorrect sentence in each group. If there is no error, blacken number 5.

1. (1) Them and us play gin rummy each Wednesday.
   (2) Please write to the folks and me while you're away.
   (3) The friendliest person on the street is he.
   (4) I did not give the information about the adverse effects of food additives to him.
   (5) No error
① ② ③ ④ ⑤

2. (1) Who told you that oil drilling equipment does not cause pollution?
   (2) Rita is a more knowledgeable gardener than me.
   (3) For whom did you buy that impractical gift?
   (4) The person responsible for creating the Equal Rights Amendment is she.
   (5) No error
① ② ③ ④ ⑤

3. (1) In the bright light, Theresa and I could see their faces clearly.
   (2) Either she or I am working late.
   (3) A package just arrived, and it is marked for either him or her.
   (4) The person who gave the lecture did not speak well.
   (5) No error
① ② ③ ④ ⑤

4. (1) Since they went for marriage counseling, Simon fights more fairly than she.
    (2) In 1998, Nina and me saw Mark McGwire hit his 70th home run of the season.
    (3) Arthur and he claim to have seen several UFO's.
    (4) At whose request do I send this letter?
    (5) No error
    ① ② ③ ④ ⑤

5. (1) Who's going to pay for education if all funding legislation is defeated?
    (2) Please call Jake and I as soon as you get into town.
    (3) Do you really approve of his playing football?
    (4) Arlene will always be younger than I.
    (5) No error
    ① ② ③ ④ ⑤

6. (1) Who called?
    (2) After you've repaired the sink, give the tools to John and him.
    (3) Mike and me will carry the steel beam.
    (4) In case you didn't know, the new supervisor is he.
    (5) No error
    ① ② ③ ④ ⑤

7. (1) We hope the new police commissioner will be as friendly as him.
    (2) The Jensens and they organize a block party each year to raise money for the Fresh Air Fund.
    (3) Who do you think will run his campaign?
    (4) Give responsible jobs to Kate and her because they have had the most experience.
    (5) No error
    ① ② ③ ④ ⑤

8. (1) Dominic and I are meeting them for dinner.
    (2) I have always worked harder than he.
    (3) If you don't do the job, who will?
    (4) He really shouldn't have objected to me leaving since my work had been finished.
    (5) No error
    ① ② ③ ④ ⑤

9. (1) I was very pleased with them for thinking of me when they decided to expand their company.
    (2) If it is his turn, then allow him to take it.
    (3) Davis has always been more punctual than us.
    (4) The Boss is one of those musicians who are full of surprises.
    (5) No error
    ① ② ③ ④ ⑤

10. (1) Give me your word that you and he will comply with our terms.
    (2) Jean and I completed the forms and left them at the front desk.
    (3) If I can find you and her, I will give you his instructions.
    (4) According to *Time Magazine*, Rudy Giuliani was the Person of the Year in 2001.
    (5) No error
    ① ② ③ ④ ⑤

Chapter 10 Pronouns

Practice I *Page 89.*

Answers will vary.

   Sample answers:

1. I, You, He, She, We, They
2. I, You, He, She, We, They
3. him, her, you, them
4. him, me, you, her, us, them
5. Who
6. whom

Practice II *Page 90.*

For explanations of these answers, see *Pronoun Clue 1.*

1. *Whom* did you call?
2. *Who* answered?
3. *Who* will help?
4. from *whom*
5. *whom* Tony likes

Practice III *Page 90.*

For explanations of these answers, see *Pronoun Clue 2.*

1. *he* ran
2. *They* went
3. My friend and *I* are
4. *She, he* were
5. *we* go
6. *Who* will work

Practice IV *Page 91.*

For explanations of these answers, see *Pronoun Clue 3.*

1. call *me*
2. gave to *her*
3. Tell *them*
4. speaking to *him*
5. sent to *us*

Practice V *Page 92.*

For explanations of these answers, see *Pronoun Clue 4.*

1. than *I* (am)
2. than *she* (sews)
3. as *he* (feels)
4. than *we* (are)
5. as *they* (argue)

Practice VI *Page 92.*

For explanations of these answers, see *Pronoun Clue 5.*

1. *she* (is my secretary)
2. *he* (was the winner)
3. *who* (seems)
4. *they* (were the culprits)
5. *I* (was the person)
6. *we* (are it)

Practice VII *Page 93.*

For explanations of these answers, see *Pronoun Clue 6.*

1. *his* karate
2. *your* calling
3. *my* writing
4. *whose* contribution
5. *their* refusing

Practice VIII *Page 93.*

For explanations of these answers, see *Pronoun Clue 7.*

1. from *whom*
2. between you and *him*
3. to John and *them*
4. except *her*
5. among *them*

Practice IX *Page 94.*
For explanations of these answers, see *Pronoun Clue 8.*

1. *himself* refers to everyone (singular).
2. *his* refers to each (singular).
3. *their* refers to they (plural).
4. *their* refers to all (plural).

Practice X *Page 94.*

1. **(3)** *my* smoking
   See Pronoun Clue 6.
2. **(5)** No error
3. **(3)** *my* playing
   See Pronoun Clue 6.
4. **(1)** *whom*
   See Pronoun Clues 3 and 7.
5. **(4)** *he* was it
   See Pronoun Clue 5.
6. **(4)** he (bowls)
   See Pronoun Clue 8.
7. **(4)** for *me*
   See Pronoun Clues 3 and 7.
8. **(2)** he invited *her*
   See Pronoun Clue 3.
9. **(2)** Don wanted *me*
   See Pronoun Clue 3.
10. **(1)** *I* invited
    See Pronoun Clue 2.

Practice XI *Page 95.*

1. **(1)** *They* and *we* play gin rummy each Wednesday.
2. **(2)** Rita is a more knowledgeable gardener than *I* (am).
3. **(5)** No error
4. **(2)** In 1988, Nina and *I* saw Mark McGwire hit his 70th home run of the season.
5. **(2)** Please call Jake and *me* as soon as you get into town.
6. **(3)** Mike and *I* will carry the steel beam.
7. **(1)** We hope the new police commissioner will be as friendly as *he* (is).
8. **(4)** He really shouldn't have objected to *my* leaving since my work had been finished.
9. **(3)** Davis has always been more punctual than *we* (have been).
10. **(5)** No error

Chapter 11

CUMULATIVE REVIEW

This review covers:

- Agreement in Time and Number
- Correct Use of Descriptive Words and Phrases
- Recognizing Complete and Incomplete Thoughts
- Special Problems in Agreement
- Special Problems in Time
- Correct Use of Pronouns

After completing the Cumulative Review exercises, evaluate your ability using the SUMMARY OF RESULTS chart on page 105. Acceptable scores for each practice are given.

To learn your areas for skill improvement, find the question numbers you answered incorrectly on the SKILLS ANALYSIS table. The table will show which of your skills need improvement and the necessary chapters to review.

Practice Exercises

Practice I

Directions: Blacken the circle that corresponds to the number of the incorrect word in each sentence. If there is no error, blacken number 5.

1. The *angry* man *ran* *hurriedly* into the crowded room and   ① ② ③ ④ ⑤
      1   2   3
shouted *loud* at the guest. *No error*
        4   5

2. Airman Donald G. Farrell *grimaced* as *he* *squeezed* into the   ① ② ③ ④ ⑤
                       1   2   3
simulated space cabin *that was* to be his home for seven days.
                       4

No error
  5

3. *What is* the *social* implications of the *small* car? *No error*   ① ② ③ ④ ⑤
    1   2   3   4   5

4. Although Jan *worked* all day, she *did* not *feel good*. *No error*   ① ② ③ ④ ⑤
              1   2   3 4   5

5. There again, I must *insist* that I *do* not like *you* smoking in   ① ② ③ ④ ⑤
                  1   2   3

   my home. *No error*
    4   5

6. Just between *we* two, I *believe* Jim did not *write* the contract   ① ② ③ ④ ⑤
            1   2   3

   properly. *No error*
     4   5

7. Without *fail*, Carlo and *she attend monthly* board of education   ① ② ③ ④ ⑤
        1   2   3   4

   meetings. *No error*
         5

8. Neither the congressman *nor* the people *whom* he *represents*   ① ② ③ ④ ⑤
                      1   2   3

   approves of this bill. *No error*
    4   5

9. *Somehow* a misunderstanding about *this* situation   ① ② ③ ④ ⑤
    1   2

   has developed between you and *me*. *No error*
     3   4   5

Practice II

Directions: Blacken the circle that corresponds to the number of the incorrect sentence in each group. If there is no error, blacken number 5.

1. (1) Mark and Eloise gave gifts to Bill and her.   ① ② ③ ④ ⑤
   (2) A waiting room crowded with impatient patients were common at Dr. Rizzo's.
   (3) George Sampson is one man whom I trust.
   (4) Every one of those boxes represents a large investment.
   (5) No error

2. (1) Is this the man who you gave the information to?   ① ② ③ ④ ⑤
   (2) Mrs. Stover is one of those teachers who relish new ideas.
   (3) If anyone can be unfailingly stubborn, it is she.
   (4) The L.A. Dodgers and their manager are in the dugout.
   (5) No error

3. (1) All of our energy should be directed toward maintaining a clean environment. ① ② ③ ④ ⑤
   (2) Please remind all of the members of your organization to vote for Alex and him.
   (3) There was several short stories in the magazine, but the last was by far the best one.
   (4) Whoever calls the radio station within three minutes with the name of the third vice president of the United States will win the contest.
   (5) No error

4. (1) There goes Chester Kallow and his wife, Olga, to their weekly bowling game. ① ② ③ ④ ⑤
   (2) Mrs. Jana, along with her teacher's aide, initiates a new science project each week.
   (3) There are no correct or incorrect answers when speaking of the interpretations of dreams.
   (4) If the inflation continues and the political scandal goes on, we are headed for hard times.
   (5) No error

5. (1) When you can't find the solution to a problem and help is not forthcoming and you don't know where to turn. ① ② ③ ④ ⑤
   (2) Of all the recipes for quiche, this is the quickest.
   (3) The musician who lives in the downstairs apartment plays ragtime piano loudly.
   (4) The cold, icy wind cut through the cabin walls and made sleeping uncomfortable.
   (5) No error

6. (1) The young boy and his companion spent the afternoon pretending that the pond was a lake and that they were explorers. ① ② ③ ④ ⑤
   (2) Neither the merchants nor their customers approve of the town ordinance to close at 6 P.M.
   (3) Kicking and splashing, the dog finished his bath.
   (4) Before signing the order, on the telephone the salesman finished his conversation.
   (5) No error

7. (1) Of all the women in the race, Amelia runs quickest. ① ② ③ ④ ⑤
   (2) Everyone in our group believes that the organization must collect dues in order to sustain itself.
   (3) Please hire whomever you think is best suited for this exacting job.
   (4) Do you agree that whoever speaks last will make the most lasting impression upon the audience?
   (5) No error

8. (1) The rising price of food, coupled with a recession, would make it impossible for an average family to obtain even the slightest luxury. ① ② ③ ④ ⑤
   (2) Although she enjoys fishing, Theresa becoming dizzy because of the motion of the sea and increasingly nauseated by the smell of the fish.
   (3) Any of the three dresses is suitable for this occasion.
   (4) Here is the file that you requested.
   (5) No error

Practice III

Directions: Blacken the circle that corresponds to the correct rewriting of the underlined portion of the sentence. Choice 1 is always the same as the underlined portion and is sometimes the right answer.

1. The shy young woman <u>stood hesitantly</u> in the doorway before she entered the crowded bar. ① ② ③ ④ ⑤
   (1) stood hesitantly
   (2) standed hesitantly
   (3) has stood hesitantly
   (4) had stood hesitantly
   (5) stands hesitantly

2. <u>Either the grass or the shrubs need</u> cutting weekly. ① ② ③ ④ ⑤
   (1) Either the grass or the shrubs need
   (2) Either the grass or the shrubs needs
   (3) Either the shrubs or the grass need
   (4) Either the grass or the shrubs needing
   (5) Either the shrubs or the grass needing

3. <u>Here's</u> my mother and father. ① ② ③ ④ ⑤
   (1) Here's
   (2) Here is
   (3) Here are
   (4) Here was
   (5) Here were

4. Last week I <u>went to the boringest party</u>. ① ② ③ ④ ⑤
   (1) went to the boringest party.
   (2) went to the most boringest party.
   (3) went to the more boring party.
   (4) had gone to the most boring party.
   (5) went to the most boring party.

5. David performed the difficult experiment <u>more precisely than any student</u> in the class. ① ② ③ ④ ⑤
   (1) more precisely than any student
   (2) most precisely than any student
   (3) more precise than any student
   (4) more precisely than any other student
   (5) more precise than any other student

Practice IV

Directions: Blacken the circle that corresponds to the number of the incorrect sentence in each group. If all sentences are correct, blacken number 5.

1. (1) Neither Mrs. Jones nor any of her children were at the school play.
   (2) Each of the three entries in the 4-H contest has merit.
   (3) Any one of those sandwich meats is an excellent choice for lunch.
   (4) That painting hangs in my mother's hallway of which I am proud.
   (5) No error

   ① ② ③ ④ ⑤

2. (1) That lecturer, about whom I've told you, has agreed to speak at our meeting.
   (2) Any of the four volunteers would serve well.
   (3) Neither the child nor his father want to take the responsibility for walking the dog.
   (4) The cheese in the refrigerator is no longer fresh.
   (5) No error

   ① ② ③ ④ ⑤

3. (1) This excellent thesis surpasses all others and presented the facts most coherently.
   (2) He is a terrible golfer, but the most tenacious would-be sportsman I know.
   (3) If you are wondering who left the book in your mailbox, it was I.
   (4) When you visit Yosemite Park, please take a deep breath for Marty and me.
   (5) No error

   ① ② ③ ④ ⑤

4. (1) Isaac Asimov, Frank Herbert, and Robert Heinlein wrote good science fiction.
   (2) All of the twelve contestants are talented.
   (3) The tall, handsome man, wearing a plaid jacket and striped pants, stepping snappily off the curb.
   (4) An English garden, filled with a variety of colors and strains, is an enchanting sight.
   (5) No error

   ① ② ③ ④ ⑤

5. (1) Tom and she frequently read the same books.
   (2) If you don't see us, leave.
   (3) In addition to being rude, he is the most stubborn man I know.
   (4) How can you expect everyone to do his best when you place them under constant pressure?
   (5) No error

   ① ② ③ ④ ⑤

6. (1) This is the worst project I've ever been involved in.   ① ② ③ ④ ⑤
   (2) According to a spokesman for the members, they each gave
       their own opinions at the meeting.
   (3) The stapler belongs to that woman on the table.
   (4) Of the two methods of bidding, I like this one better.
   (5) No error

7. (1) None of our group is ready for the meet.   ① ② ③ ④ ⑤
   (2) There's several avenues of approach open to us.
   (3) The gymnast performed the difficult exercise so well that he
       received a near-perfect score.
   (4) I do not.
   (5) No error

8. (1) Of the two airplanes, the DC 10 ascends quicker.   ① ② ③ ④ ⑤
   (2) No one understands the situation better than he.
   (3) Maria and I climbed a street that wound around like a spiral
       staircase.
   (4) Neither Sheila nor I was particularly pleased with the color
       of the paint.
   (5) No error

9. (1) I, myself, completed the difficult job.   ① ② ③ ④ ⑤
   (2) Before they completed the building, the contractors
       discovered that the heating system was insufficient.
   (3) The Jacksons and the Walters take day trips together each
       summer and visit each other frequently in the winter.
   (4) This is the liveliest color combination of all.
   (5) No error

10. (1) Henry and Will have been living in their parents' house for   ① ② ③ ④ ⑤
        eight years.
    (2) When I was a child, my family went to the beach every
        summer.
    (3) Please check the calendar to see if you are available on the
        20th.
    (4) If you arrive at the theater earlier than me, please buy my
        ticket.
    (5) No error

After reviewing the Answer Key on page 106, chart your scores below for each practice exercise.

SUMMARY OF RESULTS

Practice Number	Number Correct	Number Incorrect (Including Omissions)	Acceptable Score
I			7 Correct
II			6 Correct
III			4 Correct
IV			8 Correct

To identify your areas for skill improvement, locate the questions you answered incorrectly and circle the numbers on this Skills Analysis chart. Wherever you have circled errors, review the chapters listed in the last column.

SKILLS ANALYSIS

Skill	Question Number	Review Chapter
Practice I		
Correct Use of Descriptive Words	1, 4	3
Agreement of Subject and Action or Linking Word in Number	2, 7	2 and 7
Correct Use of Pronouns	5, 6	10
Agreement: Special Problems	3, 8	8
Practice II		
Agreement: Special Problems	3, 4	8
Correct Use of Pronouns	2	10
Complete and Incomplete Thoughts	5, 8	1
Agreement of Subject and Linking Word	1	7
Correct Use of Descriptive Phrases	6	5
Correct Use of Descriptive Words	7	3
Practice III		
Time: Special Problems	1	9
Agreement: Special Problems	2, 3	8
Correct Use of Descriptive Words	4, 5	4
Practice IV		
Correct Use of Descriptive Phrases	1, 6	5
Agreement: Special Problems	2, 7	8
Action Words: Agreement in Time	3	2
Complete and Incomplete Thoughts	4	1
Correct Use of Descriptive Words	8	4
Time: Special Problems	9	9
Correct Use of Pronouns	5, 10	10

Chapter 11   Cumulative Review

Practice I *Page 99.*

1. **(1)** *Loudly* describes shouted.
2. **(5)** No error
3. **(2)** *Are* agrees with the plural subject, *implications*.
4. **(4)** *Well* describes a state of health.
5. **(3)** *Your* describes smoking.
6. **(1)** Use *us* after between.
7. **(5)** No error
8. **(4)** *Approve* agrees with the plural performer, *people*.
9. **(5)** No error

Practice II *Page 100.*

1. **(2)** A waiting room (crowded with impatient patients) *was*. *Was* agrees with the singular subject, *room*.
2. **(1)** *whom* you gave the information to (to whom). Use whom after *to*.
3. **(3)** Several short stories *were* there. *Were* agrees with the plural performer, *stories*.
4. **(1)** Chester Kallow and his wife, Olga, *go*. *Go* agrees with the plural performer, *Chester Kallow and his wife*.
5. **(1)** Incomplete thought. Possible thought completion: When you can't find the solution to a problem, and help is not forthcoming, and you don't know where to turn, *call me*.
6. **(4)** Before signing the order, the salesman finished his conversation on the telephone. *On the telephone* describes conversation and should be placed after it.

7. **(1)** runs most *quickly*. Descriptive words ending in *-ly* describe actions; therefore, the correct form is *most quickly*.
8. **(2)** Incomplete thought. Possible thought completion: Although she enjoys fishing, Theresa, becoming dizzy because of the motion of the sea and the smell of the fish, *asked to return to shore*.

Practice III *Page 102.*

1. **(4)** *Stood* occurred *before* entered, so you must use the helping word *had* with *stood*.
2. **(1)** *Need* agrees with the closest performer, *shrubs*, which is plural.
3. **(3)** *Are* agrees with the plural subject, mother and father.
4. **(5)** *Most boring*. Do not add *-er* or *-est* to a descriptive word ending in *-ing*; use *more* or *most*.
5. **(4)** *Any other* (He did not perform more precisely than himself.)

Practice IV *Page 103.*

1. **(4)** That painting, of which I am proud, hangs in my mother's hallway. *Of which I am proud* describes painting, not hallway.
2. **(3)** Neither the child nor his father *wants* to take the responsibility for walking the dog. In an either/or neither/nor construction, the action or linking verb agrees in number with the closest performer or subject.

3. **(1)** This excellent thesis surpasses all others and *presents* the facts most coherently. *Presents* should have the same form as *surpasses*.

4. **(3)** Incomplete thought. Possible thought completion: The tall, handsome man, wearing a plaid jacket and striped pants, and stepping snappily off the curb, *tripped*.

5. **(4)** How can you expect everyone to do his best when you place *him* under constant pressure? Because *everyone* is singular and *his* is singular, use *him* rather than *them* to balance the sentence.

6. **(3)** The stapler on the table belongs to that woman. *On the table* describes stapler and should be next to it.

7. **(2)** There are several avenues of approach open to us. *Are* must agree with the plural subject, *avenues*.

8. **(1)** Of the two airplanes, the DC 10 ascends *more quickly*. Descriptive words ending in -*ly* describe actions; therefore the correct form is *more quickly*.

9. **(2)** Before they *completed* the building, the contractors *had discovered* that the heating system was insufficient. *Discovered* occurred *before completed*, so you must use the helping word *had* with *discovered*.

10. **(4)** If you arrive at the theater earlier than *I* (do), please buy my ticket. Since you would not say, If you arrive earlier than *me do*, you do not say, If you arrive earlier than *me*.

Chapter 12

BALANCED SENTENCES

One of the things that used to irritate me in my junior high English classes was the corrections some teachers made in the margins of my compositions. I didn't mind when they wrote "sp." and circled the misspelled word on the line, or "cap." to indicate that I had written "french" with a small "f."

What got me all riled up, however, were the mysterious jottings such as "awk." and "frag." And one term I had a former C.I.A. agent as a teacher, and he used secret codes, it seemed to me. His favorite was a couple of parallel lines in the margin—and his cryptic explanation to my query was "lack of parallelism." I never got to know what he meant, and, at the time, couldn't see that anything was wrong with "I like swimming, hunting, and to fish."

—Paul Allen
Trouble Deaf Heaven

A Word With You . . .

Paul Allen's teacher did a good job in spotting the error in "I like swimming, hunting, and to fish" but he failed to show his students why it was incorrect. The parallel slash marks in the margins were no substitute for a lesson explaining the need for balance in sentence structure.

You will find that the mystery is removed from that topic in the following pages and why in Paul Allen's published work we can find a sentence such as, "*Listening* to Beverly Sills, *looking* at a Rembrandt, and *sipping* Chivas Regal all give me goose pimples."

Understanding Correct Sentence Structure

Correctly and effectively written sentences are balanced sentences. *A balanced sentence is one in which related actions, descriptions, or ideas are presented in the same form.* The following sentences are not balanced. Why not?

1. He liked swimming and *to dive.*
2. Mei is pleasant and *has intelligence.*
3. Tennis is both stimulating and *makes me exhausted.*
4. Gary is not only a good carpenter *but a fine electrician also.*

In sentence 1 the related actions are not expressed in the same form. One action word ends with *ing*; the other action takes an entirely different form, using *to.* Now, you must choose the form you prefer. Either one would be correct, but the same form must be used for both action words.

He liked swimming and diving.

or

He liked to swim and to dive.

In sentence 2, what are the two terms that describe Mrs. Thompson?_____ and _____. You've probably chosen *pleasant* and *has intelligence.* The sentence would be balanced if *has intelligence* were replaced by one word. *Pleasant* is a descriptive word, describing Mei. What descriptive word means *has intelligence?* In other words, how do you change the form of *has intelligence* to balance with *pleasant?*

EXAMPLE:

Mei is pleasant and *intelligent.*

In sentence 3, what are the two terms that describe tennis? _____ and _____. You've probably chosen *stimulating* and *makes me exhausted.* The sentence would be balanced if *makes me exhausted* were replaced by one word. *Stimulating* is a descriptive word, describing tennis. What descriptive word means *makes me exhausted?* In other words, how do you change the form of *makes me exhausted* to balance with *stimulating?*

EXAMPLE:

Tennis is both stimulating and *exhausting.*

In sentence 4, Gary is two things. He is a *good carpenter* and a *fine electrician.* What two phrases relate carpenter to electrician? _____ and _____. You've probably chosen *not only* and *but.* The relationship is shown, however, by *not only* and *but also.* Just as *not only* comes immediately before *a good carpenter,* so must *but also* come immediately before *a fine electrician.*

EXAMPLE:

Gary is not only a good carpenter *but also a fine electrician.*

Look at a few more examples:

INCORRECT: I like to walk in the rain, to sing in the shower, and stamping in puddles.
CORRECT: I like to walk in the rain, to sing in the shower, and to stamp in puddles.
INCORRECT: The eagle has majesty, strength, and is graceful.
CORRECT: The eagle has majesty, strength, and grace.

Practice I

Directions: Blacken the circle that corresponds to the number of the word or phrase that correctly completes each sentence.

1. The long-time servant was faithful and   ① ② ③ ④
   (1) honestly.
   (2) with honesty.
   (3) honest.
   (4) honesty.
2. Please write your evaluation carefully, truthfully, and   ① ② ③ ④
   (1) concise.
   (2) concisely.
   (3) with concision.
   (4) be concise.
3. The advertisement said that at the "Y" Camps our children would   ① ② ③ ④
   learn to swim, play tennis, row boats, and
   (1) how to get along with others.
   (2) getting along with others.
   (3) friendship.
   (4) get along with others.
4. Henry is not only a good doctor   ① ② ③ ④
   (1) but also an excellent friend.
   (2) but he is also an excellent friend.
   (3) but he is an excellent friend also.
   (4) but is also an excellent friend.
5. If you want this job,   ① ② ③ ④
   (1) you must be prompt.
   (2) one must be prompt.
   (3) they must be prompt.
   (4) you must have been prompt.
6. This book is a monument to its author and   ① ② ③ ④
   (1) it pays tribute to its subject.
   (2) a tribute to its subject.
   (3) it tributes its subject.
   (4) pays tribute to its subject.

7. This summer Arthur will clean the garage, mow the lawn, and ① ② ③ ④
   (1) paints the house.
   (2) he plans to paint the house.
   (3) paint the house.
   (4) will be painting the house.
8. The teenage boy's mother insisted that he hang up his clothes and ① ② ③ ④
   (1) make his bed.
   (2) he should make his bed.
   (3) why doesn't he make his bed.
   (4) to make his bed.
9. The tennis game was invigorating and ① ② ③ ④
   (1) excitement.
   (2) had excitement.
   (3) excited.
   (4) exciting.

Practice II

Directions: Blacken the circle that corresponds to the number of the incorrect word or group of words in each paragraph. If there is no error, blacken number 5.

1. Soft drinks _satisfy_ the appetite, _offer_ absolutely nothing   ① ② ③ ④ ⑤
                1   2

   toward building health, _taking_ up valuable space, and
                              3

   particularly _crowd_ out valuable nutrients. _No error_
               4   5

2. Personal health educators would be people who know the   ① ② ③ ④ ⑤

   basic facts of _nutrition_, _food buying_, _cooking_, physical fitness,
                  1   2   3

   how to motivate people, and interviewing. _No error_
            4   5

3. _Doctors are doing_ very little health education. They _are not_   ① ② ③ ④ ⑤
       1   2

   oriented or trained to be health educators, _cannot make money_
                                   3

   dispensing health education, and _there is no interest_ in being
                             4

   health educators. _No error_
        5

Practice III

Directions: Balance each of the following sentences by rewriting them in the spaces provided.

1. The winner's attitude toward the loser was conciliatory yet not with condescension.

   _____

   _____

2. Mrs. Santos is conservative not only in business but also politically.

   _____

   _____

3. The judge asked the defendant to swear to tell the truth and if he would cite the evidence.

   _____

   _____

4. I cannot abide congested subways or elevators with crowds in them.

   _____

   _____

5. This project is to be a benefit to the neighborhood and it will credit the sponsors.

   _____

   _____

6. Math, reading, and to write are my favorite subjects.

   _____

   _____

7. The professor lectured on anthropology, and he was outlining the child-rearing habits of the Polynesians.

   _____

   _____

8. I splashed cold water on my face and looking into the mirror.

   _____

   _____

9. The rain splashes onto the walk and soaked into the ground.

   _____

   _____

10. Outside the wind rustled the leaves in the trees, while inside the children sleep quietly.

   _____

   _____

Practice IV

Directions: In each of the following groups of sentences, one sentence contains an error in either agreement, placement of a descriptive phrase, or balance. Blacken the circle that corresponds to the number of the incorrect sentence in each group.

1. (1) After taking the jewelry, the thief out of the window jumped.   ① ② ③
   (2) Harry S. Truman enjoyed reading not only fiction but also nonfiction.
   (3) The labor negotiations were deadlocked.

2. (1) Many people believe in stronger consumer protection and better   ① ② ③
       consumer information.
   (2) Walking quickly down the street, I lost my balance.
   (3) I enjoy knitting and to crochet.

3. (1) Don't automation deprive many of jobs?   ① ② ③
   (2) Neither the supervisor nor the assemblymen report directly to
       the president.
   (3) While reading a dull book, I was interrupted.

4. (1) A true guru must have discipline and concentration.   ① ② ③
   (2) The attainment of full benefits and achieving a four-day work
       week were their goals.
   (3) None of the representatives is lying.

5. (1) Although the system has defects, it still functions well.   ① ② ③
   (2) I not only support his decision but also encourage it.
   (3) The mayor divided among his largest contributors the best municipal
       positions.

6. (1) The reasons for shortening the work day is logical.   ① ② ③
   (2) Dashing home from work, the busy woman prepared a menu in her
       mind.
   (3) Clouds hang heavily in the sky, signaling rain.

7. (1) While talking on the telephone, the painting on the kitchen wall   ① ② ③
       caught my eye.
   (2) In the summer, the rosebushes climb along the side of the house.
   (3) My feelings were hurt, so I cried a little.

8. (1) Spring is enjoyable, pretty, and fragrant.   ① ② ③
   (2) A duck swam across the lake and dived under the water.
   (3) Many people in the wealthiest nation in the world are destitute,
       malnourished, and don't have jobs.

9. (1) Before ending their dispute, the doorbell interrupted the two women.   ① ② ③
   (2) They each pass the dish to their right.
   (3) Several women in the book club play softball.

10. (1) Bacon and eggs is my favorite breakfast.   ① ② ③
    (2) Each of the topics on the agenda sound interesting.
    (3) Chicken soup is a common cure-all.

Chapter 12   Balanced Sentences

Practice I *Page 110.*

1. **(3)** *honest* agrees with faithful.
2. **(2)** *concisely* agrees with carefully and truthfully.
3. **(4)** *get (along with others)* agrees with swim, play, and row.
4. **(1)** Henry is two things: *a good doctor, an excellent friend. Not only* precedes *a good doctor,* and *but also* precedes *an excellent friend.*
5. **(1)** *you* agrees with you.
6. **(2)** *a tribute* agrees with a monument.
7. **(3)** *paint* agrees with clean and mow.
8. **(1)** *make* agrees with hang.
9. **(4)** *exciting* agrees with *invigorating.*

Practice II *Page 111.*

1. **(3)** *take* agrees with satisfy, offer, and crowd.
2. **(4)** *motivation* agrees with nutrition, buying, cooking, and interviewing.
3. **(4)** *are not interested* agrees with are doing, are not oriented or trained, and cannot make.

Practice III *Page 112.*

(Note: Although there is more than one way of rewriting these sentences to make them balanced, the following answers indicate and explain one possible way.)

1. The winner's attitude toward the loser was conciliatory yet not condescending. *Yet not condescending* agrees with conciliatory.
2. Mrs. Santos is conservative not only in business but also in politics. *In politics* agrees with in business.

3. The judge asked the defendant to swear to tell the truth and to cite the evidence. *To cite the evidence* agrees with to swear to tell the truth.
4. I cannot abide congested subways or crowded elevators. *Crowded elevators* agrees with congested subways.
5. This project is to be a benefit to the neighborhood and a credit to the sponsors. *A credit to the sponsors* agrees with a benefit to the neighborhood.
6. Math, reading, and writing are my favorite subjects. *Writing* agrees with math and reading.
7. The professor lectured on anthropology, and he outlined the child-rearing habits of the Polynesians. *Outlined* agrees with lectured.
8. I splashed cold water on my face and looked into the mirror. *Looked* agrees with splashed.
9. The rain splashes onto the walk and soaks into the ground. *Soaks* agrees with splashes.
10. Outside, the wind rustled the leaves in the trees, while inside the children slept quietly. *Slept* agrees with rustled.

Practice IV *Page 113.*

1. **(1)** After taking the jewelry, the thief *jumped out of the window.*
2. **(3)** I enjoy *knitting* and *crocheting.*
3. **(1)** *Doesn't automation* deprive many of jobs?
4. **(2)** The attainment of full benefits and *achievement* of a four-day work week were their goals.

5. **(3)** The mayor divided the *best munici-pal positions among his largest contributors.*

6. **(1)** The *reasons* for shortening the work day *are* logical.

7. **(1)** While talking on the telephone, *I noticed* the painting on the kitchen wall.

8. **(3)** Many people in the wealthiest nation in the world are destitute, malnour-ished, and *jobless.*

9. **(1)** Before ending their dispute, *the two women were interrupted* by the doorbell.

10. **(2)** *Each* of the topics on the agenda *sounds* interesting.

Chapter 13

PUNCTUATION

To punctuate or not to punctuate that is the question
is it better in the long run to omit the periods and
question marks of English sentences or to include them
against a large number of misunderstandings by using
them we end all misinterpretation all the problems and
confusion that the reader faces this is a result to be
greatly valued

> Adaptation of a monologue in
> William Shakespeare's
> *Hamlet*, Act III, Scene 1

A Word With You . . .

Hamlet pondered the question, "To be or not to be." To punctuate or not to punctuate is not open to question. In order to write clearly and meaningfully, we must punctuate. Standard rules of punctuation help all of us gain the same meaning from written material. In this chapter, we review with you some of the more common rules of punctuation.

End Marks

Punctuation is simply a way of keeping ideas straight. The most commonly used forms of punctuation are end marks, which are used at the ends of sentences. These include the period (.), the question mark (?), and the exclamation mark (!). Read the following paragraph to see the confusion that results from not using end marks.

Paragraph 1:

Preheat oven to 375° in a medium saucepan, melt 3 tablespoons butter stir in flour, salt, and pepper add milk and cook, stirring constantly, until thickened add mushrooms and parsley cook noodles as package directs.

Now place end marks where necessary in order to clarify the recipe.

Consider the following paragraph and place the proper end marks.

Paragraph 2:

We have always considered heartbeat and breathing the basic signs of life Legally and medically, their absence indicates death But heartbeat and breathing are controlled by the brain Is a patient still alive when these functions occur only through the use of a machine A clinical decision to turn off the machines is either a recognition that life is over or a form of murder Many will agree with the former, but an equal number will cry, "Murder"

Turn to the answer key on page 124 to see if you've punctuated correctly.

Commas

The comma is the most difficult form of punctuation because of its varied uses. After studying the Comma Style Sheet and Common Errors, do Practice I to determine where your comma strengths and areas for improvement lie.

COMMA STYLE SHEET

1. Commas are used to separate items in a series to ensure clarity.

   EXAMPLE:

   Check the tires, the oil, and the battery.

2. Commas separate more than one descriptive word describing the same word.

   EXAMPLE:

   Racing car drivers like long, low, streamlined cars.

3. Commas separate words or groups of words that interrupt the flow of the sentence.

   EXAMPLES:

   Jimmy Doolittle, Air Force squadron leader during WW II, was admired by those who flew with him.
   The letter, if you must know, is from my brother.

4. The words *therefore, however, nevertheless, inasmuch as,* are set off by commas when they interrupt a complete thought.

   EXAMPLES:

   Unfortunately for Herbert Hoover, however, he became president a year before the crash of 1929.
   Can we, therefore, call environmentalists overcautious?

5. A comma separates an introductory word or group of words from the complete thought.

   EXAMPLES:

   Before the New Deal, laissez-faire economics was practiced.
   Before Roosevelt introduced the New Deal, laissez-faire economics was practiced.

COMMA STYLE SHEET

6. Commas separate two complete thoughts that are joined by a connecting word such as *and*, *or*, *but*, or *for*.

   EXAMPLE:

   The office building will be torn down, and a parking lot will replace it.

7. A comma always separates the day from the year, and a comma separates the year from the rest of the sentence.

   EXAMPLE:

   His son graduated on June 14, 1999, from New York University.

8. Separate a direct quotation from the rest of the sentence by using commas.

   EXAMPLES:

   "I cannot attend," he said.
   The master of ceremonies shouted, "Attention, ladies and gentlemen!"
   "I can understand how you feel," he said, "but please try to see it my way."

9. A comma separates the name of a city from the name of a state or country.

   EXAMPLES:

   Madeline Manning Jackson is from Cleveland, Ohio.
   Paul Martin will be stationed in Paris, France.

10. A comma follows the salutation in a friendly letter.
    A comma follows the closing in a friendly letter, as well as in a business letter.

    EXAMPLES:

    Dear Tom,

    Sincerely,
    Harvey

Common Comma Errors

Frequently, commas are included where they should not be. Following are two common examples.

1. A comma is *not* used to separate two actions if the sentence has one performer.

   INCORRECT: *I returned* to the library, and *left* the unread book.
   CORRECT: *I returned* to the library_and *left* the unread book.

2. When a sentence begins with a complete thought followed by an incomplete thought, a comma is not used.

   INCORRECT: The party became lively, when John arrived.
   CORRECT: The party became lively_when John arrived.

Practice I

Directions: Insert the missing commas in the sentences below. Use the Comma Style Sheet.

1. The "Day in the City" tour included visits to the Metropolitan Museum the Museum of Natural History the Planetarium and Central Park Zoo.
2. The local theater group presented *Death of a Salesman* on June 14 2002.
3. The company transferred my brother from Cleveland Ohio to New York City.
4. After escaping from his pursuers the innocent victim ran breathlessly into the room and he collapsed into a chair.
5. Dear Joe
    We arrived in Phoenix Arizona on July 10 and we were fortunate to find pleasant accommodations. We will see you in January.
    Love
        Mom
6. Michael Jordan the basketball player left baseball.
7. After reading the newspaper Terence Morgan decided to write to his congressperson.
8. Will stood up when Mrs. Sullivan the mayor's wife entered the room.
9. "Please bring your camera to the game" said Juan.
10. "I would like to" Mitchell replied "but I can't afford the film."

Practice II

Directions: Blacken the circle that corresponds to the number of the incorrectly punctuated sentence in each group. If there is no error, blacken number 5.

1. (1) Before eating breakfast, Tom ran two miles.   ① ② ③ ④ ⑤
   (2) Tom ran two miles before eating breakfast.
   (3) Tom's brother jogs, before eating breakfast.
   (4) Before any physical activity, John eats breakfast.
   (5) No error
2. (1) Because he was late John missed most of the lecture.   ① ② ③ ④ ⑤
   (2) Professor Simmons always begins on time.
   (3) John often misses the opening remarks because he is late.
   (4) Whenever he is late, he copies my notes.
   (5) No error
3. (1) Hubert Humphrey, as well as Adlai Stevenson accepted the   ① ② ③ ④ ⑤
       Democratic nomination but lost the election.
   (2) Jimmy Carter ran for a second term as president of the U. S.
       in 1980 but did not win.
   (3) When I attend the lectures, I bring a notebook, a pencil, my
       eyeglasses, and a *People* magazine.
   (4) Each morning the sun rises, and each evening it sets.
   (5) No error

4. (1) Teddy, along with his friends, enjoys stripping cars.   ① ② ③ ④ ⑤
   (2) The local Memorial Day Committee plans many exciting events for this summer and the Committee will continue to function each summer.
   (3) I cannot drive when the roads are icy.
   (4) Ricky was elated because he won the car.
   (5) No error

5. (1) Because she had overslept, Rosa was late for work.   ① ② ③ ④ ⑤
   (2) *Fit or Fat* by Covert Bailey helps people lose weight and put new vitality in their lives.
   (3) The thief stole a bracelet, a diamond ring, a wallet containing $100 and a fur coat.
   (4) I cannot smile when I am angry.
   (5) No error

Practice III

Directions: Blacken the circle or circles that correspond to the number of each error in the passage below.

Many consumer groups and individuals are worried about the   ① ② ③ ④

genetic engineering of food. For example, www.safefood.org is one of
                                        1
many sites to publish information, references, and links, regarding
                        2   3   4
the dangers.

One of the many health concerns is the difficulty of tracing certain   ⑤ ⑥ ⑦ ⑧
                        1
allergic reactions. One cited article _ on the subject of allergies,
                                5   6
appeared in the *New England Journal of Medicine*, on March 14,
                                                        7   8
1996.

The article refers to a soya bean, that was genetically crossed with   ⑨ ⑩ ⑪ ⑫
                                9
the genes from a brazil nut. As a result, people allergic to brazil nuts
                                        10
showed allergic responses, to the altered soybean_in seven out of
                        11   12
nine cases.

Semicolons

The semicolon is a strong mark of punctuation. It signals the end of a thought. Two short, complete, related thoughts may be separated by a semicolon instead of a period. Either is correct, but using semicolons adds variety and interest to your writing. The other way to separate complete thoughts is with a comma and a small connecting word.

The following are the three ways to separate complete, related thoughts.

1. Use a period.

EXAMPLES:

No one will forget the Great Houdini's feats of escape. He earned the world's praise. Magicians used to keep their secrets. Now many give them away as part of the show.

2. Use a comma and a word such as *and, but, or, nor, for,* or *so.*

EXAMPLES:

No one will forget the Great Houdini's feats of escape, and he earned the world's praise.
Magicians used to keep their secrets, but now many give them away as part of the show.

EXAMPLES:

No one will forget the Great Houdini's feats of escape; he earned the world's praise.
Magicians used to keep their secrets; now many give them away as part of the show.

ADDITIONAL EXAMPLES:

Penn and Teller use bugs, guns, and fake blood in their acts; they are known as the bad boys of magic.
The magician made my wife disappear; I thought I was off the hook, but then he brought her back.

Practice IV

Directions: Each of the following sentences is missing either a comma or a semicolon. If the sentence is missing a comma, blacken circle 1. If there is a missing semicolon, blacken circle 2.

1. In 1871, Kate O'Leary's cow kicked over a lamp_the City of Chicago ① ②
   burned to the ground.
2. We accepted the invitation_but we canceled because of illness. ① ②
3. Our backs were weak_but our spirit was strong.
4. The Louisiana Purchase enlarged America by about 140 percent in ① ②
   area_fifteen states were later carved from it.

5. Lemmings travel toward the sea_and they eat everything that is available on the way.   ① ②

6. Dr. Toselli, our physician, was delayed at the hospital_my husband left.   ① ②

7. An ancient temple in Mexico was cut out of a mountain_and water was the natural stonecutting tool used by its builders.   ① ②

8. Please walk in_don't run.   ① ②

9. Julius Caesar knew that it would be dangerous to transport an army across rough waters_but it was the only way he could learn more about Britain.   ① ②

10. I am working late tonight_don't expect me for dinner.   ① ②

Occasionally, one or both of two complete and related thoughts will contain commas.

EXAMPLE:

John, my older brother, is not a very good pool player; but even though he never wins, he enjoys the game.

Notice that in this type of sentence, in order to avoid the confusion that too many commas can cause, a semicolon is used to separate the two complete thoughts even though a connecting word is present. Study these examples:

Although Jane is five years old, she has never been swimming; and, personally, I think that is a shame.

When you are ready, please call me; and I, although occupied, will meet you at once.

The following large connecting words are always preceded by a semicolon and followed by a comma when connecting two complete thoughts:

therefore
nevertheless
however
inasmuch as
For example:

I don't like the terms of the contract; therefore, I will not sign it.

Practice V

Directions: Blacken the circle that corresponds to the number of the incorrect sentence in each group. If there is no error, blacken number 5.

1. (1) We, therefore, cannot accept your terms.   ① ② ③ ④ ⑤
   (2) The first universities began as scholastic guilds, and arose gradually and with great difficulty.
   (3) The contract is unfair; therefore, we cannot sign it.
   (4) The day was very hot; we cooled ourselves in the park.
   (5) No error

2. (1) I had wanted to attend, nevertheless, other commitments prevented my doing so. ① ② ③ ④ ⑤
   (2) You look, however, as though you like this bargain.
   (3) The aristocratic Watusi are towering African men with fine features, and they are also remarkable athletes.
   (4) My friend, Jane Smith, whom you met last week, arrived today; and, in spite of her long trip, she was eager to see the town.
   (5) No error

3. (1) I went home after work; John went to the game. ① ② ③ ④ ⑤
   (2) The town plans to demolish the old buildings, and to replace them with new structures.
   (3) The painters plan to remove all of the old paint, and they are going to repaint the entire house.
   (4) Our neighbors, the Wilsons, went on their first camping trip; they loved it.
   (5) No error

4. (1) The ancient people adapted their construction methods to the quality of their stone, and they used the forces of nature that were available. ① ② ③ ④ ⑤
   (2) Clem is a chef, and his speciality is vegetarian dishes.
   (3) I worked on the project all day; however, I was not successful.
   (4) My checkbook balance, however, will not support that purchase.
   (5) No error

5. (1) Joe was late; therefore, he missed the essence of the lecture. ① ② ③ ④ ⑤
   (2) I cannot smile when I'm angry, and I'm not smiling today.
   (3) James Beckwourth was the son of an African-American soldier, nevertheless, James was known to the Crow Indians as the brave Medicine Calf.
   (4) When the science demonstration began, the children looked bored; when the lava started flowing, their eyes widened with excitement.
   (5) No error

Chapter 13 Punctuation

END MARKS

Introductory Paragraph 1 *Page 116.*
Preheat oven to 375°. In a medium saucepan, melt 3 tablespoons butter. Stir in flour, salt, and pepper. Add milk and cook, stirring constantly, until thickened. Add mushrooms and parsley. Cook noodles as package directs.

Introductory Paragraph 2 *Page 116.*
We have always considered heartbeat and breathing the basic signs of life. Legally and medically, their absence indicates death. But heartbeat and breathing are controlled by the brain. Is a patient still alive when these functions occur only through the use of a machine? A clinical decision to turn off the machines is either a recognition that life is over or a form of murder. Many will agree with the former, but an equal number will cry, "Murder!"

COMMAS

Practice I *Page 119.*

1. The "Day in the City" tour included visits to the Metropolitan Museum, the Museum of Natural History, the Planetarium, and the Central Park Zoo.
2. The local theater group presented *Death of A Salesman* on June 14, 2002.
3. The company transferred my brother from Cleveland, Ohio to New York City.
4. After escaping from his pursuers, the innocent victim ran breathlessly into the room, and he collapsed into a chair.
5. Dear Joe,

   We arrived in Phoenix, Arizona on July 10, and we were fortunate to find pleasant accommodations. We will see you in January.

   Love,

   Mom

6. Michael Jordan, the basketball player, left baseball.
7. After reading the newspaper, Terence Morgan decided to write to his congressman.
8. Will stood up when Mrs. Sullivan, the mayor's wife, entered the room.
9. "Please bring your camera to the game," said Juan.
10. "I would like to," Mitchell replied, "but I can't afford the film."

Practice II *Page 119.*

1. **(3)** Tom's brother jogs before eating breakfast.

   When a sentence begins with a complete thought followed by an incomplete thought, a comma is not used.
2. **(1)** Because he was late, John missed most of the lecture.

   An introductory word or group of words is separated from the complete thought by a comma.
3. **(1)** Hubert Humphrey, as well as Adlai Stevenson, accepted the Democratic nomination but lost the election.

   As well as Adlai Stevenson interrupts the flow of the sentence. Hubert Humphrey accepted the Democratic nomination but lost the election is the main idea of the sentence; therefore, *as well as Adlai Stevenson* must be set off by commas.
4. **(2)** The local Memorial Day Committee plans many exciting events for this summer, and the Committee will continue to function each summer.

   When two complete thoughts are connected by *and*, *and* must be preceded by a comma.

5. **(3)** The thief stole a bracelet, a diamond ring, a wallet containing $100, and a fur coat.

A comma precedes the *and* in a list of three or more items to ensure clarity.

Practice III *Page 120*.

(4) Many consumer groups and individuals are worried about the genetic engineering of food. For example, www.safefood.org is one of many sites to publish information, references, and links_regarding the
4
dangers.

(6, 7) One of the many health concerns is the difficulty of tracing certain allergic reactions. One cited article on the subject of allergies _appeared in the *New England*
6
*Journal of Medicine*_on March
7
14, 1996.

(9, 11) The article refers to a soya bean_that was genetically
9
crossed with the genes from a Brazil nut. As a result, people allergic to Brazil nuts showed allergic responses_to the altered
11
soybean in seven out of nine cases.

COMMAS AND SEMICOLONS

Practice IV *Page 121*.

1. **(2)** Use a semicolon to connect two complete, related thoughts when there is no connecting word such as *and*, *but*, *or.*

2. **(1)** Use a comma when connecting two complete thoughts joined by *and*, *but*, *or.*

3. **(1)** See answer 2 above.
4. **(2)** See answer 1 above.
5. **(1)** See answer 2 above.
6. **(2)** See answer 1 above.
7. **(1)** See answer 2 above.
8. **(2)** See answer 1 above.
9. **(1)** See answer 2 above.
10. **(2)** See answer 1 above.

Practice V *Page 122*.

1. **(2)** *guilds and* No comma; *and arose gradually and with great difficulty* is not a complete thought.

2. **(1)** *attend; nevertheless,* When connecting two complete thoughts by *nevertheless, however*, etc., precede the connecting word with a semicolon and follow it with a comma.

3. **(2)** *buildings and* See answer 1 above.

4. **(5)** No error

5. **(3)** *soldier; nevertheless,* See answer 2 above.

Chapter 14

CUMULATIVE REVIEW

This review covers:

- Balanced Sentences
- Correct Sentence Structure
- Punctuation That Affects Sentence Structure

After completing the Cumulative Review exercises, evaluate your ability using the SUMMARY OF RESULTS chart on page 133. Acceptable scores for each practice are given.

To learn your areas for skill improvement, find the question numbers you answered incorrectly on the SKILLS ANALYSIS table. The table will show which of your skills need improvement and the necessary chapters to review.

Practice Exercises

Practice I

Directions: Blacken the circle that corresponds to the correct rewriting of the underlined portion of the sentence. Choice 1 is always the same as the underlined portion and is sometimes the right answer.

1. In the autumn of 3001 we prepared for the colonization of Venus. ① ② ③ ④ ⑤
   We encountered *difficulties although* our technology was advanced.
   (1) difficulties although
   (2) difficulties, although
   (3) difficulties! Although
   (4) difficulties. Although
   (5) difficulties; although
2. My Aunt Bell, the woman in the *green dress speaks five languages.* ① ② ③ ④ ⑤
   (1) green dress speaks five languages.
   (2) green dress, speaks five languages.
   (3) green dress; speaks five languages.
   (4) green dress. speaks five languages.
   (5) green dress? She speaks five languages.

3. _After the baseball game we_ bought lettuce, tomatoes, onions, luncheon meats, and Italian bread and made hero sandwiches. ① ② ③ ④ ⑤
   - (1) After the baseball game we
   - (2) After the baseball game. We
   - (3) After the baseball game, we
   - (4) After the baseball game ended we
   - (5) After the baseball game; we

4. She was an attractive woman, an excellent _speaker and a charming hostess; but_ she dressed outlandishly. ① ② ③ ④ ⑤
   - (1) speaker and a charming hostess; but
   - (2) speaker and a charming hostess, but
   - (3) speaker, and a charming hostess; but
   - (4) speaker, and a charming hostess, but
   - (5) speaker, and a charming hostess but

Practice II*

Directions: Blacken the circle that corresponds to the correct rewriting of the underlined portion of the sentence. Choice 1 is always the same as the underlined portion and is sometimes the right answer.

1. The bicycle is a fairly pleasant machine for limited use by a few _people, but claims_ that it can substitute for the automobile as a device for moving people around town are grossly overstated. ① ② ③ ④ ⑤
   - (1) people, but claims
   - (2) people, But claims
   - (3) people but claims
   - (4) people; but claims
   - (5) people, but, claims

2. Most old people will not be happy aboard _it, and mothers who must take along small children during a shopping trip to the supermarket won't be either._ ① ② ③ ④ ⑤
   - (1) it, and mothers who must take along small children during a shopping trip to the supermarket won't be either.
   - (2) it, and mothers who must take along small children during a shopping trip to the supermarket won't be.
   - (3) it, nor will mothers who must take along small children during a shopping trip to the supermarket.
   - (4) it, or will mothers who must take along small children during a shopping trip to the supermarket.
   - (5) it, for mothers who take along small children during a shopping trip to the supermarket.

---

* Practice II is adapted from Russell Baker's "Backwards Wheels the Mind," _The New York Times_, July 1, 1973. © 1973 by The New York Times Company. Reprinted by permission.

3. It is an exhausting and brutal machine in cities built on _hills,_   ① ② ③ ④ ⑤
    and being the most unattractive way to travel wherever and
    whenever the temperature is over 90° and under 30°.
    (1) hills, and being
    (2) hills, and is said to be
    (3) hills, and it is
    (4) hills, and has been
    (5) hills, but being

4. If parked, even chained, out of eyesight for more than 10   ① ② ③ ④ ⑤
    minutes; it is a cinch to be stolen.
    (1) minutes; it is
    (2) minutes it, is
    (3) minutes it is
    (4) minutes, it is
    (5) minutes. It is

5. And _then, of course,_ there is the awkward question of courage.   ① ② ③ ④ ⑤
    (1) then, of course,
    (2) then, of course
    (3) then of course,
    (4) then; of course
    (5) then; of course;

Practice III

Directions: Blacken the circle that corresponds to the correct rewriting of the underlined
portion of the sentence. Choice 1 is always the same as the underlined portion and is
sometimes the right answer.

1. Because he did not enjoy last week's _lecture, Tom_ decided   ① ② ③ ④ ⑤
    to skip this week's.
    (1) lecture, Tom
    (2) lecture! Tom
    (3) lecture Tom
    (4) lecture; Tom
    (5) lecture. Tom

2. The carnival was exciting, the games were _fun but_ the children   ① ② ③ ④ ⑤
    became very tired.
    (1) fun but
    (2) fun; but
    (3) fun, but
    (4) fun. But
    (5) fun, the

3. We decided to play tennis, have lunch_, and then we played bridge._   ① ② ③ ④ ⑤
    (1) , and then we played bridge.
    (2) , and played bridge.
    (3) ; and then we played bridge.
    (4) , and play bridge.
    (5) ; we played bridge

4. Their living room lights were _shining we_ decided to stop to say   ① ② ③ ④ ⑤
   hello.
   (1) shining we
   (2) shining, we
   (3) shining. And we
   (4) shining; and we
   (5) shining; we

5. We should first measure the room, then order the carpeting,   ① ② ③ ④ ⑤
   and, finally, _we will paint the walls._
   (1) we will paint the walls.
   (2) we would paint the walls.
   (3) paint the walls.
   (4) we will be painting the walls.
   (5) to paint the walls.

6. Among all the causes of sedition and basic changes of _the state;_   ① ② ③ ④ ⑤
   none is more important than excessive wealth of the few and
   extreme poverty of the many.
   (1) the state; none
   (2) the state none
   (3) the state? None
   (4) the state, none
   (5) the state, so none

7. From a thousand feet, flapping his wings as hard as he could,   ① ② ③ ④ ⑤
   he pushed over into a blazing steep dive toward the _waves, and_
   learned why seagulls don't make blazing steep power-dives.*
   (1) waves, and
   (2) waves and
   (3) waves; and
   (4) waves. And
   (5) waves and,

8. The beach was extremely _crowded, nevertheless,_ we found Joan.   ① ② ③ ④ ⑤
   (1) crowded, nevertheless,
   (2) crowded; nevertheless,
   (3) crowded; nevertheless
   (4) crowded nevertheless
   (5) crowded, nevertheless

9. Because the landlord has refused _to testify our attorney_ will have   ① ② ③ ④ ⑤
   to subpoena him.
   (1) to testify our attorney
   (2) to testify. Our attorney
   (3) to testify; our attorney
   (4) to testify our attorney,
   (5) to testify, our attorney

---

* Quote from Richard Bach's _Jonathan Livingston Seagull._ © 1975, Macmillan Publishing Co., Inc. Reprinted by
permission.

10. Della Mason is a competent accountant _and she cooks well._   ① ② ③ ④ ⑤
    (1) and she cooks well.
    (2) , and she cooks well.
    (3) and a good cook.
    (4) and she cooks competently.
    (5) ; and she cooks well.

Practice IV

Directions: Blacken the circle that corresponds to the number of the incorrect sentence in each group. If there is no error, blacken number 5.

1. (1) Increasing unemployment, in my opinion, is a major problem   ① ② ③ ④ ⑤
      of the decade.
   (2) Our baby-sitter never cleans the kitchen and leaves the den
      in a mess.
   (3) I, however, spoke to John and alerted him to expect the
      shipment.
   (4) I like the painting, but not enough to buy it.
   (5) No error

2. (1) The aphids have eaten the roses, the mealworms have destroyed   ① ② ③ ④ ⑤
      the cucumbers, and the cinchbugs have ruined the lawn.
   (2) After we had paid the painter, we called the mason for an
      estimate on rebuilding the front stairs.
   (3) When the carpenter ants invade your kitchen, and the ter-
      mites swarm under your porch, you know that spring is here.
   (4) Owning a home is a pleasurable experience; however, there is
      a great deal of work involved.
   (5) No error

3. (1) Having considered the backgrounds of the prospective   ① ② ③ ④ ⑤
      candidates, the members of the Republican National Committee
      began to consider its options.
   (2) Although history records the names of many famous women,
      many important women remain anonymous.
   (3) According to great coaches, confidence, self-discipline, and
      experience are prerequisites for a successful pitcher.
   (4) After a massive stroke, President Woodrow Wilson was par-
      tially paralyzed; nevertheless, the White House functioned
      under the leadership of Edith Bolling Wilson, the president's
      wife.
   (5) No error

4. (1) The best web sites instruct, inform, and entertain.   ① ② ③ ④ ⑤
   (2) Arthur rushed out of the barber shop, his face buried in
      lather; however, the meter maid already had written out his
      parking ticket.
   (3) Although the software was expensive, it was well worth it.
   (4) Coughing, sneezing, and wheezing, the speaker descended
      from the stage.
   (5) No error

5. (1) I enjoy sad movies, but I dislike books that depress me. ① ② ③ ④ ⑤
   (2) The young author had a compulsion to do the research, assemble his notes, and write the paper in one evening.
   (3) If you believe that I am correct, then why won't you support me publicly?
   (4) The community pool is not only crowded, but also shadeless.
   (5) No error
6. (1) If you don't like the heat, get out of the kitchen. ① ② ③ ④ ⑤
   (2) Don't jump!
   (3) During our trip to London, we visited Westminster Abbey, we also viewed the Crown Jewels in the Tower of London and saw the Changing of the Guard.
   (4) Because they were planning a picnic lunch, the children asked for pretzels, potato chips, cookies, and marshmallows.
   (5) No error
7. (1) Although, in recent years, many efforts have been made; we can never compensate for the injustice inflicted upon the American Indian. ① ② ③ ④ ⑤
   (2) I could wait no longer because I had promised to begin the meeting promptly at eight o'clock.
   (3) Once one attains freedom of purpose, any task is possible.
   (4) The current hearings are interesting, but last year's scandal bored me.
   (5) No error

Practice V

Directions: Blacken the circle that corresponds to the number of the incorrect word in each group. If there is no error, blacken number 5.

1.* Men are bent intently over *chessboards. They* are men of all ① ② ③ ④ ⑤
            1

   ages, but most are closer to life's twilight than its *dawn. They*
       2   3

   are in battle with one *another, the* chessboard is their
                              4

   battlefield. *No error*
       5

---

* Practice V is from Leo Rosen's "Even Bobby Fischer Would Have His Hands Full," *The New York Times,* July 25, 1972.

2.   The sun is _hot. Never_ mind. Sometimes a drizzle _begins. Never_   ① ② ③ ④ ⑤
                    1   2

mind. This is not some silly pastime to idle time _away, this_ is
                                                        3

chess! This outdoor chess congregation is the only one of its
        4

kind in the borough. _No error_
                        5

3.   _Yet, it_ boasts not a single authentic chess master. Is this   ① ② ③ ④ ⑤
        1

sad? No, it's irrelevant. _For, if_ a man is seeking out excellence
        2   3

in _chess he_ would do well to stay away from St. James Park.
        4

No error
        5

4.   What he would find here is _grimness, determination, anguish,_   ① ② ③ ④ ⑤
                                    1   2

wisdom after the fact, bitterness under the breath, and
                3

there are a number of accidental brilliances. No error
                        4   5

5.   Good chess is not being played in St. James _Park, but_ life is   ① ② ③ ④ ⑤
                                                    1

being played. Here sits _Liebowitz,_ he has escaped again from
                                2

his wife. She will be along about 7 o'clock to remind him loudly
that he is a married man with children. "Your supper is cold again,
Liebowitz!" She has never called him Liebowitz anywhere in the
world but in St. James Park. It is the circumstances, the men there,
        3

the _lateness_ of the hour. _No error_
            4   5

After reviewing the Answer Key on page 134, chart your scores below for each practice exercise.

SUMMARY OF RESULTS

Practice Number	Number Correct	Number Incorrect (Including Omissions)	Acceptable Score
I			3 Correct
II			4 Correct
III			7 Correct
IV			5 Correct
V			4 Correct

To identify your areas for skill improvement, locate the questions you answered incorrectly and circle the numbers on this Skills Analysis chart. Wherever you have circled errors, review the chapters listed in the last column.

SKILLS ANALYSIS

Skill	Question Number	Review Chapter
Practice I		
Balanced Sentences	3, 4	12
Punctuation That Affects Sentence Structure	2	13
Practice II		
Punctuation That Affects Sentence Structure	1, 4, 5	13
Balanced Sentences	2, 3	12
Practice III		
Punctuation That Affects Sentence Structure	1, 4, 6, 7, 8, 9	13
Balanced Sentences	2, 3, 5, 10	13
Practice IV		
Balanced Sentences	1, 5, 7	12
Punctuation That Affects Sentence Structure	6	13
Practice V		
Balanced Sentences	4	12
Punctuation That Affects Sentence Structure	1, 2, 3, 5	13

Chapter 14 Cumulative Review

Practice I *Page 126.*

1. **(1)** No error
2. **(2)** My Aunt Bell, the woman in the green dress, speaks five languages.
3. **(3)** After the baseball game, we bought lettuce, tomatoes, onions, luncheon meats, and Italian bread and made hero sandwiches.
4. **(3)** She was an attractive woman, an excellent speaker, and a charming hostess; but she dressed outlandishly.

Practice II *Page 127.*

1. **(1)** The bicycle is a fairly pleasant machine for limited uses by a few *people, but claims* that it can substitute for the automobile as a device for moving people around town are grossly overstated.

   Use a comma between two complete thoughts connected by *and, but, or.*

2. **(3)** Most old people will not be very happy aboard *it, nor will mothers who must take along small children during a shopping trip to the supermarket.*

   This choice states the idea most clearly.

3. **(3)** It is an exhausting and brutal machine in cities built on *hills, and it is* a most unattractive way to travel wherever and whenever the temperature is over 90° or under 30°.

   And it is agrees with *It is* at the beginning of the sentence.

4. **(4)** If parked, even chained, out of eyesight for more than 10 *minutes, it is* a cinch to be stolen.

   When a sentence begins with an incomplete thought followed by a complete thought, the two are separated by a comma.

5. **(1)** And *then, of course,* there is the awkward question of courage.

   Set off an interrupting group of words with commas.

Practice III *Page 128.*

1. **(1)** Because he did not enjoy last week's *lecture, Tom* decided to skip this week's.
2. **(3)** The carnival was exciting, the games were *fun, but* the children became very tired.
3. **(4)** We decided to play tennis, have lunch, *and play bridge.*
4. **(5)** Their living room lights were *shining; we* decided to stop to say hello.
5. **(3)** We should first measure the room, then order the carpeting, and, finally, *paint the walls.*
6. **(4)** Among all the causes of sedition and basic changes of *the state, none* is more important than excessive wealth of the few and extreme poverty of the many.

7. **(2)** From a thousand feet, flapping wings as hard as he could, he pushed over into a blazing steep dive toward the _waves and_ learned why seagulls don't make blazing steep power-dives.

8. **(2)** The beach was extremely _crowded; nevertheless,_ we found Joan.

9. **(5)** Because the landlord has refused _to testify, our attorney_ will have to subpoena him.

10. **(3)** Della Mason is a competent accountant _and a good cook._

Practice IV _Page 130._

1. **(2)** Our baby-sitter never cleans the kitchen or the den.

2. **(5)** No error

3. **(5)** No error

4. **(5)** No error

5. **(1)** I enjoy sad movies, but I dislike depressing books.

6. **(3)** During our trip to London, we visited Westminster Abbey; we also viewed the Crown Jewels in the Tower of London, and saw the Changing of the Guard.

7. **(4)** The current hearings are interesting, but last year's scandal was boring.

Practice V _Page 131._

1. **(4)** another_;_ the _or_ another_, and_ the _or_ another_. T_he

2. **(3)** away_; this or_ away_. T_his

3. **(4)** chess_, h_e

4. **(4)** _a number of accidental brilliances_

5. **(2)** Liebowitz_; h_e _or_ Liebowitz_. H_e

Chapter 15

EFFECTIVE EXPRESSION

A Word With You . . .

The common errors pointed out by the poet are all treated in Chapter 15. She "paid her dues" by learning how to avoid such repetitive expressions and how to write in a clear, concise, uncluttered fashion.

Care to pay your dues?

Style and Clarity

Many sentences that seem correctly written are, in fact, incorrect because of:

- the misuse of words or phrases.
- the addition of unnecessary words or phrases.

See if you can locate the errors in style and clarity in the following paragraphs. Mark your corrections directly in the paragraph.

Paragraph A

My reason for sending the children to Happy Days Camp was that I thought they might learn to swim. Much of the time, the weather was cloudy, but they didn't go swimming. At the end of the season, the campers gave a party for their parents, but they didn't enjoy it. Since our expectations were not fulfilled, we signed the children up for the next year.

Did you find these errors?

1. INCORRECT: My reason for sending the children to Happy Days Camp was that I thought they might learn to swim.

   PROBLEM: The incorrect sentence uses too many words to make the point. "My reason . . . was that" can be condensed simply to "I sent the children to Happy Days Camp because . . ."

   CORRECT: I sent the children to Happy Days Camp *because* I thought they might learn to swim.

2. INCORRECT: Much of the time, the weather was cloudy, but they didn't go swimming.

   PROBLEM: The sentence states that they didn't go swimming *in spite of* the cloudy weather. In fact, they didn't go swimming *because of* the cloudy weather.

   CORRECT: a. Much of the time, the weather was cloudy, so they didn't go swimming.

   b. Much of the time, the weather was cloudy; therefore, they didn't go swimming.

   c. Much of the time, they didn't go swimming because the weather was cloudy.

3. INCORRECT: At the end of the season, the campers gave a party for their parents, but they didn't enjoy it.

   PROBLEM: It is unclear whether *they* refers to the campers or their parents. The sentence must be changed in order to convey the true meaning.

   CORRECT: a. At the end of the season, the campers gave a party for their parents, but the campers didn't enjoy it.

   b. At the end of the season, the campers gave a party for their parents, but their parents didn't enjoy it.

   c. Although they didn't enjoy it, at the end of the season, the campers gave a party for their parents.

   d. At the end of the season, the campers gave a party for their parents, who didn't enjoy it.

4. INCORRECT: Since our expectations were not fulfilled, we signed the children up for next year.

   PROBLEM: The sentence states that we enrolled the children for next year *since* our expectations were not fulfilled. In fact, we enrolled the children for next year *although* our expectations were not fulfilled.

   CORRECT: Although our expectations were not fulfilled, we enrolled the children for next year.

The corrected paragraph would look like this:

I sent the children to Happy Days Camp because I thought they might learn to swim. Much of the time, the weather was cloudy, so they didn't go swimming. At the end of the season, the campers gave a party for their parents, but the campers didn't enjoy it. Although our expectations were not fulfilled, we enrolled the children for next year.

Paragraph B

The bus tour of Philadelphia on the bus was interesting. I don't never remember a livelier group. The highlight of the trip was when we saw the Liberty Bell. The reason I enjoyed that sight was because I love history. The bus driver, he gave an informative speech.

Did you find these errors?

1. INCORRECT: The bus tour of Philadelphia on the bus was interesting.
   PROBLEM: The phrase *on the bus* is a repetition. Bus *tour* means that the tour was on the bus.
   CORRECT: The bus tour of Philadelphia was interesting.
2. INCORRECT: I don't never remember a livelier group.
   PROBLEM: The incorrect sentence uses a double negative, *don't never*. These two negative words, in effect, cancel each other. Other negative words that should not be used in combination are: hardly, scarcely, neither, only, never, no one, nobody, no, none, nothing, not.
   CORRECT: I don't ever remember a livelier group.
3. INCORRECT: The highlight of the trip was when we saw the Liberty Bell.
   PROBLEM: The use of *was when* is poor style. A more concise form of expression should be chosen.
   CORRECT: The highlight of the trip was seeing the Liberty Bell.
4. INCORRECT: The reason I enjoyed that sight was because I love history.
   PROBLEM: *The reason . . . was because* creates an awkward sentence. Simplify the sentence by stating *A* because *B* without the unnecessary words.
   CORRECT: I enjoyed that sight because I love history.
5. INCORRECT: The bus driver, he gave an informative speech.
   PROBLEM: Wordiness results from the repetition in the phrase *the bus driver, he*. Use one or the other, but not both terms. In this sentence you need to use *bus driver*, since there has been no prior reference to him.
   CORRECT: The bus driver gave an informative speech.

The corrected paragraph would look like this:

The bus tour of Philadelphia was interesting. I don't ever remember a livelier group. The highlight of the trip was seeing the Liberty Bell. I enjoyed that sight because I love history. The bus driver gave an informative speech.

Practice I

Directions: Blacken the circle that corresponds to the number of the incorrect sentence in each group. If there is no error, blacken number 5.

1. (1) He hardly never writes home.   ① ② ③ ④ ⑤
   (2) Charlie accepted the job because the pay was good.
   (3) I hardly ever visit my childhood friend, Eddie.
   (4) Manuel doesn't like fishing.
   (5) No error

2. (1) My reasons for leaving the firm are personal.   ① ② ③ ④ ⑤
   (2) Leonardo da Vinci, he painted *The Last Supper*.
   (3) I had scarcely opened the book when I fell asleep.
   (4) Albert Einstein was one man whom many people admired.
   (5) No error

3. (1) Money was very tight during the early 1980s, so major   ① ② ③ ④ ⑤
       automobile manufacturers offered customer rebates.
   (2) Britons and Americans have never spoken the same
       language.
   (3) Since I enjoy music, I never attend concerts.
   (4) Although the hour was late, Congress voted to remain in
       session.
   (5) No error

4. (1) Since the weather has been unusually dry, forests are in   ① ② ③ ④ ⑤
       danger of burning.
   (2) Dolores visited her former employer, Martha Cummins, and
       she gave her a lovely gift.
   (3) Although I like to play chess online, I cannot play now.
   (4) I have never known anyone else who has so consistently
       disregarded the rules.
   (5) No error

5. (1) There isn't no easy way of solving the problem.   ① ② ③ ④ ⑤
   (2) Since Martin Luther King had been an advocate of non-
       violence, his violent death was particularly shocking.
   (3) An impasse occurs when either party refuses to listen.
   (4) If you regulate your sleeping habits, you will feel better.
   (5) No error

6. (1) Good sense told the ambassador not to continue in that area   ① ② ③ ④ ⑤
       of conversation.
   (2) When my young neighbor asked for permission to use my car,
       I denied it.
   (3) My brother, he refused to admit that he'd broken the stereo.
   (4) After he had signed the bill, the president gave the Boy Scout
       leader the pen.
   (5) No error

7. (1) The librarian had given no one permission to use the   ① ② ③ ④ ⑤
       reference books.
   (2) Susan B. Anthony was a pioneer for women's suffrage during
       a period in history when it was hardly popular for a woman
       to be an activist.
   (3) The babysitter gave the child her lunch and she continued to
       play.
   (4) Since the crew had heard the twelve o'clock whistle, they
       knew it was lunchtime.
   (5) No error

8. (1) If the play is not a success, the reason is because the actors never learned their lines well.   ① ② ③ ④ ⑤
   (2) A green-eyed, black cat darted in front of us.
   (3) A high school graduate is neither too young nor too inexperienced for that job.
   (4) As the bus rounded the corner, the tourists could see the traffic jam.
   (5) No error

9. (1) Rupert cannot understand your unclear notes.   ① ② ③ ④ ⑤
   (2) Maria washed her car this morning, so she is tired.
   (3) Don't say that you haven't been warned.
   (4) The reason I called this meeting is because there have been some misunderstandings.
   (5) No error

10. (1) Didn't Mattie say that she would complete the job?   ① ② ③ ④ ⑤
   (2) Why don't you ask her if she would?
   (3) The ancient, old castle stood on the hill.
   (4) We visited an old, well-kept inn.
   (5) No error

Practice II

Directions: Blacken the circle that corresponds to the correct rewriting of the underlined portion of the sentence. Choice 1 is always the same as the underlined portion and is sometimes the right answer. These sentences are presenting a story.

1. Our *family, we* went to the craft show.   ① ② ③ ④ ⑤
   (1) family, we
   (2) we
   (3) whole family, we
   (4) family
   (5) family, when we

2. The *craft show* included displays of pottery, needlepoint, jewelry,   ① ② ③ ④ ⑤
   leaded-glass, and other crafts.
   (1) craft show
   (2) crafts show
   (3) show of crafts
   (4) show
   (5) craft's show

3. My favorite part of the afternoon *was when I tried* the potter's wheel.   ① ② ③ ④ ⑤
   (1) was when I tried
   (2) was trying
   (3) was the time I tried
   (4) was when trying
   (5) is when I tried

4. I *didn't never do anything* that creative before.   ① ② ③ ④ ⑤
   (1) didn't never do anything
   (2) never did nothing
   (3) didn't ever do nothing
   (4) never did anything
   (5) did not never do anything

5. I had difficulty trying the spinning wheel, *and* I had never   ① ② ③ ④ ⑤
   done it before.
   (1) and
   (2) therefore
   (3) but
   (4) however
   (5) since

6. The artists permitted the children to try their media,   ① ② ③ ④ ⑤
   and they enjoyed sharing this creative experience.
   (1) and they enjoyed
   (2) and the artists enjoyed
   (3) and then they enjoyed
   (4) and they also enjoyed
   (5) and, despite this, they enjoyed

7. When I was a child, *nobody never* took me to such an exciting event.   ① ② ③ ④ ⑤
   (1) nobody never
   (2) anybody never
   (3) anybody ever
   (4) no one never
   (5) nobody ever

Practice III

Directions: Blacken the circle that corresponds to the correct rewriting of the underlined portion of the sentence. Choice 1 is always the same as the underlined portion and is sometimes the correct answer.

1. The graduates and their teachers gathered in the auditorium   ① ② ③ ④ ⑤
   where they received diplomas.
   (1) where they received diplomas.
   (2) in which they received diplomas.
   (3) where the graduates received their diplomas.
   (4) to receive diplomas.
   (5) where diplomas were received.

2. The mailman *he comes promptly* at noon.   ① ② ③ ④ ⑤
   (1) he comes promptly
   (2) who comes promptly
   (3) comes promptly
   (4) coming promptly
   (5) he come promptly

3. *The reason I bought the outfit was because it was on sale.*   ① ② ③ ④ ⑤
    (1) The reason I bought the outfit was because it was on sale.
    (2) The reason I bought the outfit was it was on sale.
    (3) I bought the outfit for the reason that it was on sale.
    (4) I bought the outfit because it was on sale.
    (5) The reason it was on sale was because I bought the outfit.

4. The polite time to comment *was when he finished his entire speech.*   ① ② ③ ④ ⑤
    (1) was when he finished his entire speech.
    (2) was when he had finished his entire speech.
    (3) was when he was finishing his speech.
    (4) was while he was finishing his speech.
    (5) came after he had finished his speech.

5. *Don't you never* have to work on weekends?   ① ② ③ ④ ⑤
    (1) Don't you never
    (2) Don't you ever
    (3) Didn't you never
    (4) Haven't you never
    (5) Do you not never

6. All of the graduates *who graduated in the class of '94* met at   ① ② ③ ④ ⑤
    the school for a party.
    (1) who graduated in the class of '94
    (2) whom graduated in the class of '94
    (3) graduated in the class of '94
    (4) who graduate in the class of '94
    (5) of the class of '94

7. *Since I had cooked dinner, we did not go out to eat.*   ① ② ③ ④ ⑤
    (1) Since I had cooked dinner, we did not go out to eat.
    (2) Since I had cooked dinner, we went out to eat.
    (3) We went out to eat since I had cooked dinner.
    (4) We went out to eat because I cooked dinner.
    (5) Since I cooked dinner, we did not go out to eat.

Practice IV

Directions: Blacken the circle that corresponds to the number of the proper completion for each sentence below.

1. Paula entered the room laughing,   ① ② ③ ④
    (1) because she tripped at the doorway.
    (2) when she saw that her father was angry.
    (3) but stopped when she saw that her father was angry.
    (4) but stopped when she saw her father who was not laughing
        because he was angry.

2. Lyndon Johnson chose not to run for reelection in 1968   ① ② ③ ④
   (1) since the growing antiwar sentiment did not influence him.
   (2) because the growing antiwar sentiment did not influence him.
   (3) because the growing antiwar sentiment influenced him.
   (4) because his reason was that the growing antiwar sentiment influenced him.

3. The roads were flooded   ① ② ③ ④
   (1) , so we went for a drive.
   (2) since we went for a drive.
   (3) although we turned back.
   (4) , so we turned back.

4. Because the building was old and irreparable,   ① ② ③ ④
   (1) the city planners decided to use it for student housing.
   (2) the city planners decided that the thing to do was that they should tear it down.
   (3) the city planners decided to tear it down.
   (4) the city planners asked the students if they would tear it down.

5. After climbing thirty flights of stairs,   ① ② ③ ④
   (1) the package was still in the delivery boy's hands.
   (2) the feet of the delivery boy were sore he said.
   (3) the delivery boy he refused to walk home.
   (4) the delivery boy's feet were sore.

6. The combined meeting of the bus drivers and taxi drivers   ① ② ③ ④
   (1) resulted from the passenger boycott.
   (2) was for the men who drove buses and taxis.
   (3) was because of the passenger boycott.
   (4) met for the bus drivers and taxi drivers.

7. I'm very sorry for leaving early,   ① ② ③ ④
   (1) but I couldn't never understand the speaker.
   (2) so I couldn't understand the speaker.
   (3) but I couldn't hardly understand the speaker.
   (4) but I couldn't understand the speaker.

8. Although we celebrated the occasion,   ① ② ③ ④
   (1) we were very happy about it.
   (2) was because we were happy about it.
   (3) we were not very happy about it.
   (4) was that we were happy about it.

9. Thomas Jefferson, the President of the United States,   ① ② ③ ④
   (1) he was a creative thinker.
   (2) who was a creative thinker.
   (3) who thought creatively.
   (4) was a creative thinker.

10. If you did not enjoy that movie,   ① ② ③ ④
    (1) the reason is because you have no sense of humor.
    (2) the reason is because that you have no sense of humor.
    (3) you have no sense of humor.
    (4) it could also be the reason is because you have no sense of humor.

Problems With Logic*

When you use a descriptive word or phrase in a sentence, be sure your sentence also includes the word being described. Look at what happens to logic when the word being described is left out of the sentence.

1. INCORRECT: Tired from the long climb, a rest seemed in order.
   PROBLEM: As it is written, the sentence means that a *rest was tired*. The people being described as *tired* are missing from the sentence.
   CORRECT: Tired from the long climb, *we* thought a rest seemed in order.
   ANOTHER SOLUTION: Move the person or thing being described to the beginning of the sentence.
   CORRECT: Because *we* were *tired* from the long climb, a rest seemed in order.
2. INCORRECT: After taking the picture, the camera was given to the Elsie.
   PROBLEM: As it is written, the sentence means that the camera—with no help from a person—took the picture. The person who used the camera to take the picture is missing from the sentence.
   CORRECT: After taking the picture, Shayna gave the camera to Elsie.
   ANOTHER SOLUTION: After Shayna took the picture, she gave the camera to Elsie.

Practice V

Directions: The following items are based on a paragraph containing numbered sentences. Some of the sentences may contain errors in logic. Other sentences are correct as they appear in the paragraph. Read the paragraph and then answer the questions based on it. Choose the one best answer for each item.

(1) Hot air balloons are based on the scientific law, or principle, that warmer air rises in cooler air. (2) Using a device called a burner, the hot air lifts the balloon. (3) Stored, the pilot has gas in the balloon basket. (4) A sheep, a duck, and a chicken were the first passengers on a balloon craft test flight in 1783. (5) This early model flew by straw and manure.

1. Sentence 1: Hot air balloons are based on the scientific law, or ① ② ③ ④ ⑤ principle, that warmer air rises in cooler air.
   What correction should be made to this sentence?
   (1) Insert *it* after hot air balloon.
   (2) Change *are* to *is*.
   (3) Remove the comma after *law*.
   (4) Remove the comma after *principle*.
   (5) No correction is necessary.

---

* Adapted from P. Dutwin and H. Diamond's *Grammar In Plain English.* © 1989, Barron's Educational Series, Inc.

2. Sentence 2: Using a device called a burner, the hot air lifts ① ② ③ ④ ⑤
   the balloon.
   What would be a more accurate way to rewrite the sentence?
   Start with: <u>Using a device called a burner,</u>
   (1) the basket holds the passengers.
   (2) the heat lifts the balloon.
   (3) the pilot blows hot air.
   (4) the pilot sends hot air into the balloon to make it rise.
   (5) No correction is necessary.
3. Sentence 3: Stored, the pilot has gas in the balloon basket. ① ② ③ ④ ⑤
   What would be a more accurate way to rewrite the sentence?
   (1) The pilot stores gas in the basket.
   (2) Stored, the gas is in the basket.
   (3) The basket is stored with gas.
   (4) The basket has gas.
   (5) No correction is necessary.
4. Sentence 4: A sheep, a duck, and a chicken were the first ① ② ③ ④ ⑤
   passengers on a balloon craft test flight in 1783.
   What correction should be made to this sentence?
   (1) Put a comma after *chicken*.
   (2) Add *in the year of* before 1783.
   (3) Replace *in 1783* with *on 1783*.
   (4) Change *passengers* to *animals*.
   (5) No correction is necessary.
5. Sentence 5: This early model flew by straw and manure. ① ② ③ ④ ⑤
   What correction should be made to this sentence?
   (1) This early model flew with straw and manure.
   (2) This early model flew on straw and manure.
   (3) This early model gave gas with straw and manure.
   (4) This early model was fueled by straw and manure.
   (5) No correction is necessary.

Reminder: In Chapter 5 you learned to place descriptive phrases close to the words they describe. Follow that rule to ensure that your sentences are clear and logical.

1. INCORRECT:	Problems are solved by computer scientists that are very complicated.	
PROBLEM:	Written this way, the sentence states that scientists are very complicated. The descriptive words, *that are very complicated* are placed incorrectly.	
CORRECT:	Problems that are very complicated are solved by computer scientists.	
ANOTHER SOLUTION:	Computer scientists solve problems that are very complicated.	
2. INCORRECT:	The scientists types questions and the computer answers on the keyboard.	
PROBLEM:	According to this sentence, answers appear on the keyboard. The descriptive words *on the keyboard* are placed incorrectly.	
CORRECT:	The scientist types questions on the keyboard and the computer answers.	

Practice VI

Directions: The sentences that follow are illogical because they contain incorrectly placed descriptive phrases. Correct the errors using the spaces provided.

1. We noticed a small dog in the back of the kennel that was a perfect choice for us.

   _____

2. We had seen a dog also in the window of a local store that we liked. (CAUTION: Find *two* placement errors here.)

   _____

3. The cafeteria serves lunch to everyone from noon to two o'clock in my office.

   _____

4. Students blocked the hall who were strolling to the final class of the day.

   _____

5. He said he had seen a man in the cab wearing a cowboy hat.

   _____

Chapter 15 Effective Expression

Practice I *Page 138.*

1. **(1)** Do not use a negative word such as never with *hardly* or *scarcely*. The sentence should read: He hardly *ever* writes home.

2. **(2)** *He* is repetitious. The sentence should read: *Leonardo da Vinci painted The Last Supper.*

3. **(3)** The second part of the sentence is contradictory to the first. The sentence should read: Since I enjoy music, *I frequently attend* concerts.

4. **(2)** The use of *she* and *her* makes the sentence unclear. Who gave the gift to whom? The sentence should read: Dolores *visited* her former employer, Martha Cummins, and *gave her* a lovely gift.

5. **(1)** Don't use *not* and *no* together. The sentence should read: There *is no* easy way of solving the problem. or There *isn't any* easy way of solving the problem.

6. **(3)** *He* is repetitious. The sentence should read: *My brother refused* to admit that he'd broken the stereo.

7. **(3)** The use of *her* and *she* make the sentence unclear. The sentence should read: The baby-sitter gave the child lunch, *and the child* continued to play.

8. **(1)** *The reason is because* makes the sentence unwieldy. The sentence should read: If the play is not a success, *it is because* the actors never learned their lines well.

9. **(4)** See #8. The sentence should read: *I called this meeting because* there have been some misunderstandings.

10. **(3)** *Old* is repetitious. The sentence should read: The *ancient castle* stood on a hill.

Practice II *Page 140.*

1. **(4)** *We* is repetitious. The sentence should read: Our <u>family</u> went to the craft show.

2. **(4)** *Craft* is repetitious. The sentence should read: The <u>show</u> included displays of pottery, needlepoint, jewelry, beaded glass objects, and other crafts.

3. **(2)** *Was when* is an awkward construction. The sentence should read: My favorite part of the afternoon <u>was trying</u> the potter's wheel.

4. **(4)** Don't use *didn't* and *never* together. The sentence should read: I <u>never did anything</u> that creative before.

5. **(5)** *Since* coordinates the two thoughts; *and* does not. The sentence should read: I had difficulty trying the spinning wheel, <u>since</u> I had never done it before.

6. **(2)** The word to which *they* refers is unclear. The sentence should read: The artists permitted the children to try their media, <u>and the artists</u> enjoyed sharing this creative experience.

7. **(5)** Don't use *nobody* and *never* together. The sentence should read: When I was a child, <u>nobody ever</u> took me to such an exciting event.

Practice III *Page 141.*

1. **(3)** The graduates and their teachers gathered in the auditorium *where the graduates received their diplomas.*

2. **(3)** The mailman *comes promptly* at noon.

3. **(4)** *I bought the outfit because it was on sale.*

4. **(5)** The polite time to comment *came after he had finished his speech.*

5. **(2)** *Don't you ever* have to work on weekends?

6. **(5)** All of the graduates *of the class of '94* met at the school for a party.

7. **(1)** *Since I had cooked dinner, we did not go out to eat.*

Practice IV *Page 142.*

1. **(3)** Paula entered the room laughing, but stopped when she saw that her father was angry.

2. **(3)** Lyndon Johnson chose not to run for reelection in 1968 because the growing antiwar sentiment influenced him.

3. **(4)** The roads were flooded, so we turned back.

4. **(3)** Because the building was old and irreparable, the city planners decided to tear it down.

5. **(4)** After climbing thirty flights of stairs, the delivery boy's feet were sore.

6. **(1)** The combined meeting of the bus drivers and taxi drivers resulted from the passenger boycott.

7. **(4)** I'm very sorry for leaving early, but I couldn't understand the speaker.

8. **(3)** Although we celebrated the occasion, we were not very happy about it.

9. **(4)** Thomas Jefferson, the president of the United States, was a creative thinker.

10. **(3)** If you did not enjoy that movie, you have no sense of humor.

Practice V *Page 144.*

1. **(5)** No correction is necessary.

2. **(4)** The pilot sends hot air into the balloon to make it rise.

3. **(1)** The pilot stores gas in the basket.

4. **(5)** No correction is necessary.

5. **(4)** This early model was fueled by straw and manure.

Practice VI *Page 146.*

1. We noticed a small dog *that was a perfect choice for us* in the back of the kennel.

2. We *also* had seen a dog *that we liked* in the window of a local store.

3. The cafeteria serves lunch to everyone *in my office* from noon to two o'clock.

4. Students *who were strolling to the final class of the day* blocked the hall.

5. He said he had seen a man *wearing a cowboy hat* in the cab.

Chapter 16

MORE PUNCTUATION

A Word With You . . .

Charlie Brown knows that strong writers don't just "sprinkle in the little curvy marks" or any other mark of punctuation. Punctuation, used correctly, guides your reader through your writing. This chapter introduces marks of punctuation that many people avoid. Learn to use them correctly, and your writing will stand out.

Quotation Marks

Quotation marks are used to set off the *exact* words said by somebody or taken from a source.

DIRECT QUOTATION: The young mother remarked, "Thank goodness for my company's new on-site day care center."

INDIRECT QUOTATION: The young mother remarked that she was grateful for her company's new on-site day care center.

In the first sentence, the woman's exact words are quoted. In the second sentence, the word *that* signals the fact that the sentence is a report of what was said, not a direct quotation.

QUOTATION MARK STYLE SHEET

1. Use quotation marks to set off the exact words of a speaker. Note the comma between the speaker and the words spoken in each example. Note the period *inside* the quotation marks at the end of the first sentence.

    EXAMPLES:

    The teacher instructed, "Complete the vocabulary list at home."
    "Review the vocabulary list for our last class," the teacher instructed.

2. Use quotation marks to set off both parts of a broken quotation. Do not capitalize the first word of the second part of the quotation unless it is the beginning of a new sentence.

    EXAMPLES:

    "Well," exclaimed Anita, "what did you expect?"
    "Stop complaining, Billy," said his brother. "It won't help."

3. Place a semicolon after the closing quotation marks.

    EXAMPLE:

    You said, "Wait until you see me"; so I waited.

4. Never use two forms of punctuation at the end of a quotation. When the entire sentence is a question but the quoted portion is not, place a question mark *after* the closing quotation marks.

    When the quoted portion is a question, place the question mark *inside* the quotes.

    EXAMPLES:

    Did Jane say, "Meet at our house"?
    The interviewer shook my hand and asked, "When can you start?"

5. Never use two forms of punctuation at the end of a quotation. When the entire sentence is an exclamation but the quoted portion is not, place the exclamation point *after* the closing quotation marks.

    When the quoted portion is an exclamation, place the exclamation mark *inside* the quotes.

    EXAMPLES:

    I could scream each time you call and say, "I'll be late for dinner tonight, dear"!
    The guard shouted, "Stop him! Stop him!"

QUOTATION MARK STYLE SHEET

6. Use single quotation marks for a quotation within a quotation.

EXAMPLE:

The history student asked, "Is it true that Patrick Henry said, 'Give me liberty or give me death' when America's freedom was in question?"

7. Use quotation marks to enclose titles of poems, articles, chapters, or any part of a book or magazine. If the quoted title is followed by a comma, the comma should be placed inside the quotation marks.

EXAMPLE:

The third chapter of *Our World,* entitled, "Views of the Middle East," is the most interesting.

Common Errors With Quotation Marks

Quotations require marks of punctuation in addition to quotation marks. The most common errors in quotations involve the omission or misuse of commas, periods, and capital letters. Following are common examples.

1. Place a comma between what is quoted and the person quoted.

INCORRECT: "When you finish packing the last box, start loading all of them onto the truck" the shipping manager instructed.

CORRECT: "When you finish packing the last box, start loading all of them onto the truck," the shipping manager instructed.

2. In a broken quotation, do not capitalize the first word of the second part of the quotation unless it is the beginning of a new sentence.

INCORRECT: "When you finish packing the last box," the shipping manager instructed. "Start loading all of them onto the truck."

CORRECT: "When you finish packing the last box," the shipping manager instructed, "start loading all of them onto the truck."

CORRECT: "You have finished packing the last box," the foreman said. "Start loading all of them onto the truck."

3. Place the period inside the quotation marks at the end of a sentence.

INCORRECT: Dr. D'Amato said, "Before you leave the office, please give your Medicare number to the nurse".

CORRECT: Dr. D'Amato said, "Before you leave the office, please give your Medicare number to the nurse."

4. Place a question mark *after* the closing quotation marks when the entire sentence is a question, but the quoted portion is not.

   INCORRECT: Did Dr. D'Amato say, "Please leave your Medicare number with the nurse?"
   CORRECT: Did Dr. D'Amato say, "Please leave your Medicare number with the nurse"?

5. Place a question mark *inside* the closing quotation marks when the quoted portion is a question, but the entire sentence is not.

   INCORRECT: Dr. D'Amato asked, "Is this your correct Medicare number"?
   CORRECT: Dr. D'Amato asked, "Is this your correct Medicare number?"

Practice I

Directions: Punctuate the following sentences.

1. The manager said three men must work overtime
2. The manager said that three men must work overtime
3. Three men said the manager must work overtime
4. The manager asked who will work overtime
5. Why didn't the manager say everyone must work
6. Imagine if the manager had said everyone must work overtime
7. Imagine if the manager had said that everyone must work overtime
8. The manager shouted everyone must work overtime

Practice II

Directions: Blacken the circle that corresponds to the number of the error in each sentence. If there is no error, blacken number 5.

1. Mrs. Romano exclaimed, Frankie, the parakeet has   ① ② ③ ④ ⑤
                1   2   3
   disappeared!" *No error*
       4   5

2. Frankie answered, "Mom, I don't know why; it was there   ① ② ③ ④ ⑤
                 1   2   3
   when I tried to clean it with the vacuum cleaner. *No error*
                                     4   5

3. "You will never catch me!" shouted Batman. The pursuers   ① ② ③ ④ ⑤
    1   2   3
   vowed to catch him. *No error*
        4   5

4. The student sai_d t_hat he now understands the theory behind
         1

   these problems_. He said_, "_S_uddenly, everything falls into
            2   3

   place_." _No error_
       4   5
   ① ② ③ ④ ⑤

5. The author said_, "_You can learn to write only through
            1

   writing_." He said that one can never learn to write by
            2

   reading _how-to_ book_s. No error_
            3   4   5
   ① ② ③ ④ ⑤

6. Alice told Marion sh_e w_as to stay at home and be a
                       1

   babysitte_r. Marion exclaimed_, "_w_hat a sham_e!" No error_
             2   3   4   5
   ① ② ③ ④ ⑤

7. "_C_lean your room_; take the laundry to the basement_; and
    1   2   3

   wash the car_," instructed Mother. _No error_
              4   5
   ① ② ③ ④ ⑤

8. _A_fter you turn over the eart_h, a_dd some plant food and water.
    1   2

   Then you'll be ready to plant the flower_," c_oncluded the
                                           3

   gardene_r. No error_
          4   5
   ① ② ③ ④ ⑤

9. _W_as it Elsa who said_, "_O_ur sales meeting begins at 9:30 A.M.
    1   2 3

   sharp_?" No error_
        4   5
   ① ② ③ ④ ⑤

10. "_W_hen will you ever_," asked the foreman, "_A_rrive at work on
     1   2   3

    time_?" No error_
        4   5
   ① ② ③ ④ ⑤

11. "_I_ know when I will arrive on tim_e," answered Marie. "_i_t will
     1   2   3

    be when my alarm clock is finished being repaired_." No error_
                                                      4   5
   ① ② ③ ④ ⑤

12. The show is called "Day After Day;" it starts at 2:30 P.M.   ① ② ③ ④ ⑤
                  1   2   3 4

    No error
     5

13. He replied encouragingly, "Remember that Ted said, "Let   ① ② ③ ④ ⑤
                         1   2 3

    Irene wait. I'll interview her as soon as I return.'" No error
                                              4   5

14. After having read the third chapter, entitled "Spring-time   ① ② ③ ④ ⑤
                                       1   2

    Planting", I felt that I was ready to tackle the gardening
             3

    job. No error
     4   5

15. After the vicious dog had attacked the trespasser, the dog's   ① ② ③ ④ ⑤
    owner said, "Didn't you see the sign that reads 'Beware of
             1   2

    Dog' before you entered my property?" No error
     3   4   5

Other Marks of Punctuation: Colon, Hyphen, Apostrophe, Dash, Parentheses, Brackets

You have already studied the major punctuation marks. There are several marks of punctuation that we encounter less frequently. These are the colon, the hyphen, the apostrophe, the dash, parentheses, and brackets.

OTHER MARKS OF PUNCTUATION STYLE SHEET

1. **Colon** Use a colon to introduce a list. Don't use a colon when the list is preceded by an action or linking verb.

EXAMPLE:

Bring the following equipment: a tent, a cot or sleeping bag, basic cooking utensils, and matches. Necessary equipment for such a trip includes a tent, a cot or sleeping bag, basic cooking utensils, and matches.

OTHER MARKS OF PUNCTUATION STYLE SHEET

2. Use a colon after the salutation in a business letter.

EXAMPLES:

Dear Mr. Williams:
Dear Sir:

3. Use a colon between numbers to show time.

EXAMPLE:

4:15 P.M.

4. **Hyphen** Use a hyphen to divide a word at the end of a line. Divide between syllables with a hyphen.

EXAMPLE:

The new skyscraper downtown is enormous and imposing, yet mostly un-ornamented.

5. Use a hyphen to divide compound numbers from twenty-one to ninety-nine.

EXAMPLE:

twenty-two, eighty-seven

6. Hyphenate descriptive words that are brought together to form a new word.

EXAMPLE:

well-to-do, fly-by-night, half-yearly, self-supporting

7. Hyphenate certain prefixes and the words to which they are added. For example, ex-husband.

EXAMPLE:

My favorite art form is pre-Columbian sculpture.

8. **Apostrophe** Use an apostrophe to show the omission of a letter from a word.

EXAMPLE:

We aren't (are not) responsible for breakage.

OTHER MARKS OF PUNCTUATION STYLE SHEET

9. Use an apostrophe to show possession. Note that apostrophes are placed differently according to whether the word is singular or plural and according to the way the word forms its plural. Exceptions: *Its* is the possessive form of *it*. *It's* means *it is*. *His* and *hers* are the possessive forms of *he* and *she*.

EXAMPLE:

the dog's collar, the dogs' kennels, the man's tie, the men's department, the lady's hat, ladies' hats

10. Use an apostrophe to show the plural of letters when necessary to avoid confusion. Use the apostrophe with all lower case letters and with those upper case/lower case combinations that create words.

EXAMPLES:

A's, B's, I's, r's, v's, U's, T's

11. **Dash** Use dashes to emphasize an interruption within a sentence.

EXAMPLE:

Be home on time—no later than midnight—or I shall be very worried.

12. **Parentheses** Use parentheses for words not strictly related to the main thought of the sentence. Do not use a capital letter or final punctuation (except the question mark) within the parentheses.

EXAMPLES:

I managed (somehow or other) to drag three heavy suitcases to the terminal.
I called you last night (or was it Friday?) to give you the message.

13. **Brackets** Use brackets within parentheses and within a quotation.

EXAMPLES:

They tried some French wines (Bordeaux [Medoc], Burgundy, and Chablis).
We were asked to read a poem and Tom said, "The one I've chosen [by Wilde] is called 'The Ballad of Reading Gaol.'"

Practice III

Directions: Blacken the circle that corresponds to the number of the error in each sentence. If there is no error, blacken number 5.

1. The presiden*t's* desk was covered with all sorts of business

         1

paper*s;* invoices, receipts, minutes of his last meetin*g,* and

    2   3

projected plans for the new buildin*g* *No error*

                                    4   5
                           ①②③④⑤

2. We expect to arrive at Kennedy Airport at *8 15* P.M. on

                                        1

Thursda*y,* June *8, 199*6*. No error*

    2   3   4   5
                           ①②③④⑤

3. Although we had met only once*,* he recognized me

                            1

immediately and began to regale me with the followin*g:* he

                                           2

had just arrived in tow*n;* he had bought a hous*e;* and he had

                     3   4

just been promoted within his company. *No error*

                                      5
                           ①②③④⑤

4. Do you really *believe* that you were a different person at

               1

twenty nine from the one you are at *thirty* *?* *No error*

    2   3   4   5
                           ①②③④⑤

5. If you are planning to send a present to Lauri*e,* go to the

                                          1

half-yearly sale in the children*s'* departmen*t. No error*

    2   3   4   5
                           ①②③④⑤

6. *Dont* forget to write two *r's* in *"d*eferre*d." No error*

   1   2   3   4   5
                           ①②③④⑤

7. When I arrived (*after a four-hour drive*), I found that my

                        1

cousin's *weren't* at hom*e. No error*

    2   3   4   5
                           ①②③④⑤

8. The *ex Senator* hoped that his *protege's* bill would pass the

           1   2

two-thirds mar*k. No error*

   3   4   5
                           ①②③④⑤

9. Although Septembe<u>r,</u> Jun<u>e,</u> and April have thirty day<u>s.</u>   ① ② ③ ④ ⑤
              1   2   3

    December and January have *thirty-one* days. *No error*
                                4   5

10. At <u>11:45</u> A.M. the <u>*commuter's*</u> <u>*train*</u> pulled them into the   ① ② ③ ④ ⑤
      1   2   3

    <u>*jam-packed*</u> station. *No error*
        4   5

Practice IV

Directions: Blacken the circle that corresponds to the number of the incorrect sentence in each group. If there is no error, blacken number 5.

1. (1) Let's talk about Mozart's music first.   ① ② ③ ④ ⑤
   (2) If you leave after I do, do this: put the cat out, close the windows, and lock the front door.
   (3) Henrys new car seems to be a poor sample of this year's cars.
   (4) Mr. Jones is a good example of a self-satisfied person.
   (5) No error

2. (1) In November, 2002, unusually high temperatures reached the 70s and even the 80s.   ① ② ③ ④ ⑤
   (2) Dot your i's and cross your t's.
   (3) Who's going to Ellen's party?
   (4) It's wheel is no longer round.
   (5) No error

3. (1) Many experts skills have been brought to bear upon our energy needs.   ① ② ③ ④ ⑤
   (2) Mr. Evans hadn't stepped out of the room before the whispering began.
   (3) After her work's finished, she'll be home.
   (4) My mother-in-law's house was the scene of our recent reunion.
   (5) No error

4. (1) The United Nations' subcommittees meet regularly.   ① ② ③ ④ ⑤
   (2) Have you ever bought tickets to the Firemens' Ball?
   (3) My friends' letters demand that I be a good correspondent.
   (4) The children's club meets at 3:45 P.M. on Tuesdays.
   (5) No error

5. (1) Yesterday I had lunch with Mr. Templeton.   ① ② ③ ④ ⑤
   (2) Learn the meanings of the following words—"petition," "council," and "electorate."
   (3) The children—in the midst of our frantic activity—asked for chocolate ice cream sundaes.
   (4) Take the bicycle (John's), and don't forget my fishing rod.
   (5) No error

6. (1) If you consult James Beard's newest cookbook, you will find some excellent shellfish recipes.   ① ② ③ ④ ⑤
   (2) I'd rather you didn't do that.
   (3) When I heard (last night) that you were ill, I drove all night to get here.
   (4) Is that pen his or her's?
   (5) No error

7. (1) Take my shirts to the laundry tomorrow!   ① ② ③ ④ ⑤
   (2) We listed the stolen items a ring, a bracelet, and a TV set.
   (3) All of this pre-Christmas rush has ruined Terry's disposition.
   (4) Jan's sister-in-law agreed to join us for bridge.
   (5) No error

8. (1) When it is 10:30 A.M. in New York, what time is it in Chicago?   ① ② ③ ④ ⑤
   (2) A famous critic (Lionel Trilling) said that a nation's literature reflects its deepest philosophies.
   (3) Listening to everyone's ideas sometimes confuses me.
   (4) I've decided to take a year's subscription to *Your Health.*
   (5) No error

9. (1) We've discovered that students' absences have decreased this month.   ① ② ③ ④ ⑤
   (2) The seashore is only an hour's ride from here.
   (3) Have you read *The Record*'s lead article?
   (4) This book's theme is the development of the Puritan ethic.
   (5) No error

10. (1) A person's health depends somewhat upon his mental attitude.   ① ② ③ ④ ⑤
    (2) Don't call him un American because he disagrees with your opinions.
    (3) While you're at the store, buy wire, nails, and a hammer.
    (4) Almost three-fourths of our organization voted against the admission of new members.
    (5) No error

Chapter 16   More Punctuation

QUOTATION MARKS

Practice I *Page 152*

1. The manager said, "Three men must work overtime."

2. The manager said that three men must work overtime.

3. "Three men," said the manager, "must work overtime."

4. The manager asked, "Who will work overtime?"

5. Why didn't the manager say, "Everyone must work"?

6. Imagine if the manager had said, "Everyone must work overtime"!

7. Imagine if the manager had said that everyone must work overtime!

8. The manager shouted, "Everyone must work overtime!"

Practice II *Page 152.*
For explanations of answers, refer to the style sheet beginning on page 150.

1. **(2)** Mrs. Romano exclaimed, "*F*rankie, the parakeet has disappeared!"
See Rule 1.

2. **(4)** Frankie answered, "Mom, I don't know why; it was there when I tried to clean it with the vacuum cleaner*."*
See Rule 1.

3. **(5)** No error

4. **(5)** No error

5. **(5)** No error

6. **(3)** Alice told Marion she was to stay at home and be a babysitter. Marion exclaimed*, "W*hat a shame!"

See Rule 1.

7. **(5)** No error

8. **(1)** "*After* you turn over the earth, add some plant food and water. Then you'll be ready to plant the flower," concluded the gardener.
See Rule 1.

9. **(4)** Was it Elsa who said, "Our sales meeting begins at 9:30 A.M. shar*p"?*
See Rule 4.

10. **(3)** "When will you ever," asked the foreman, "*arrive* at work on time?"
See Rule 2.

11. **(3)** "I know when I will arrive on time," answered Marie. "*It* will be when my alarm clock is finished being repaired."
See Rule 2.

12. **(2)** The show is called "Day After Da*y":*
it starts at 2:30 P.M.
See Rule 3.

13. **(3)** He replied encouragingly, "Remember that Ted said, '*L*et Irene wait. I'll interview her as soon as I return.'"
See Rule 6.

14. **(3)** After having read the third chapter, entitled "Spring-time Planting*," I* felt that I was ready to tackle the gardening job.
See Rule 7.

15. **(4)** After the vicious dog had attacked the trespasser, the dog's owner said, "Didn't you see the sign that reads 'Beware of Dog' before you entered my propert*y?"*
See Rule 4.

OTHER MARKS OF PUNCTUATION

Practice III *Page 157.*

For explanations of answers, refer to the style sheet beginning on page 154.

1. **(2)** The president's desk was covered with all sorts of business pape*rs: in*-voices, receipts, minutes of his last meeting, and projected plans for the new building.
   See Rule 1.

2. **(1)** We expect to arrive at Kennedy Airport at *8:15* on Thursday, June 8, 1983.
   See Rule 3.

3. **(1)** Although we had met only once, he recognized me immediately.
   See Rule 4.

4. **(2)** Do you really believe that you were a different person at *twenty-nine* from the one you are at thirty?
   See Rule 5.

5. **(3)** If you are planning to send a present to Laurie, go to the half-yearly sale in the *children's* department.
   See Rule 8.

6. **(1)** *Don't* forget to write two r's in "deferred."
   See Rule 8.

7. **(2)** When I arrived (after a four-hour drive), I found that my *cousins* weren't at home.
   See Rule 8.

8. **(1)** The *ex-Senator* hoped that his protege's bill would pass the two-thirds mark.

   See Rule 7.

9. **(5)** No error

10. **(2)** At 11:45 A.M., the *commuters'* train pulled them into the jam-packed station.
    See Rule 9.

Practice IV *Page 158.*

For explanations of answers, refer to the style sheet beginning on page 154.

1. **(3)** *Henry's* new car seems to be a poor sample of this year's cars.
   See Rule 9.

2. **(4)** *Its* wheel is no longer round.
   See Rule 9.

3. **(1)** Many *experts'* skills have been brought to bear upon our energy needs.
   See Rule 8.

4. **(2)** Have you ever bought tickets to the *Firemen's Ball?*
   See Rule 9.

5. **(2)** Learn the meanings of the following *words:* petition, council, and electorate.
   See Rule 1.

6. **(4)** Is that pin his or *hers?*
   See Rule 9.

7. **(2)** We listed the stolen *items:* a ring, a bracelet, and a TV set.
   See Rule 1.

8. **(5)** No error

9. **(4)** This book's theme is the *development* of the Puritan ethic.
   See Rule 4.

10. **(2)** Don't call him *un-American* because he disagrees with your opinions.
    See Rule 7.

Chapter 17

CAPITALIZATION

When I was a young writer, submitting poems and thought pieces to arty little magazines, I refused to capitalize anything—not my own name, not kentucky, not broadway, not belgium, not even e. e. cummings or don marquis' cockroach, archy.

It was a period I was going through when I explained to my courtiers that only God was deserving of capitalization. You can't imagine how that nonsensical pose won approbation with my admirers, but, come to think of it, it never made much of an impression on the editors of *Partisan Review.* When they sent me my usual rejection slip, they always used CAPITAL LETTERS.

—Tim Wolfe
The Child That's Got His Own

A Word With You . . .

Some writers, for purposes best known to themselves, use lowercase letters at all times, refusing to capitalize anything. Instead of "Dear Sir" in the salutation of a letter, they prefer "dear sir," that is, when they take the trouble to write a formal letter.

When one is a professional writer with a philosophical point of view about capitalization, one can afford to use lowercase letters. The rest of us had better learn where and when to capitalize. Chapter 17 will help.

Capitalization, like punctuation, is applied according to rules. Study the style sheet and then take the survey test that follows.

CAPITALIZATION STYLE SHEET

1. Capitalize the first letter of the first word in a sentence, unless it is a sentence within parentheses.

   EXAMPLE:

   Language changes continually (note all the once-slang words in your current dictionary) but slowly.

CAPITALIZATION STYLE SHEET

2. Capitalize the first word of a direct quotation.

   EXAMPLE:

   He cautioned, "If you buy a ticket beforehand, you will secure a seat for the performance."

3. Capitalize the word *I*.

   EXAMPLE:

   In case you are late, *I* will cover for you.

4. Capitalize the deity, place names, street names, persons' names, organization names, languages, and specific course names.

   EXAMPLES:

   God and His universe, Blue Ridge Mountains, Delaware River, Forty-second Street, John Masters, Knights of Columbus, Spanish, History II, Algebra (Algebra and history are capitalized only because they are being used as course titles. When used in a sentence (not as a title), algebra and history are not capitalized.)

5. Capitalize names of important historical events, documents, and ages.

   EXAMPLES:

   World War I, Magna Carta, Declaration of Independence, Victorian Era

6. Capitalize days of the week, months, and special holidays.

   EXAMPLES:

   Monday, January, Memorial Day

7. Capitalize east, west, north, and south only when they are used as sections of the country, not as directions.

   EXAMPLES:

   Rod Lewis lived in the East for three years, then moved to the Midwest.
   Turn east at the next corner.

8. In a title (of a movie, play, book, poem, magazine, etc.) capitalize the first word and each important word.

   EXAMPLES:

   Pulp Fiction, Death of a Salesman, The Odyssey, The Wasteland, Newsweek

---
CAPITALIZATION STYLE SHEET
---

9. Capitalize the initials of a person's name.

   EXAMPLE:

   T. J. Phillips

10. Capitalize a title when it is used as a form of address. *Do not* capitalize a title when it is not used as a form of address.

    EXAMPLES:

    Captain T. J. Phillips
    T. J. Phillips, captain of *Star Lady*, . . .
    The captain of *Star Lady*, T. J. Phillips. . . .

Survey Test

Directions: Place capital letters where they are needed in the following sentences.

1. after considering all the facts, i have chosen an appropriate action.
2. don't you think that fred might enjoy owning a french-english dictionary?
3. he said, "leave new jersey at noon, and you will reach new york city by 1 p.m. at the latest."
4. john is planning to take german, geography, history, and economics this year at city college.
5. we're expecting guests for dinner on friday night. i hope you can join us.
6. mary stark bought a chevrolet last tuesday, although she hadn't planned on buying a car this year.
7. in history II we will study the industrial revolution, world war I, world war II, and the atomic age.
8. this course will be offered to adults on mondays, wednesdays, and fridays in the spring only.
9. his original home, in california, was his favorite; and he plans on returning to the west in november.
10. captain and mrs. ryan made reservations at island beach motel on the cape's north shore for labor day.

Before beginning Practice 1, check your answers on the Survey Test and review the rules pertaining to the errors you made.

Practice I

Directions: Blacken the circle that corresponds to the number of the capitalization error in each group. If there is no error, blacken number 5.

1. *Our History* course this semester highlights *civilizations* of
      1   2   3
   the *East. No error*
       4   5
   ① ② ③ ④ ⑤

2. *My* family plans to move to *Cypress street* in *Millville, Ohio.*
     1   2   3   4
   No error
    5
   ① ② ③ ④ ⑤

3. *"If* you plan see the entire *art* exhibit," *Joan said,* *"Be* sure
    1   2   3   4
   to arrive at 10 A.M." *No error*
                5
   ① ② ③ ④ ⑤

4. The *Thompkins'* plans for *Labor day* include a *visit* to the
        1   2   3
   beach. No error
     4   5
   ① ② ③ ④ ⑤

5. *Proceed* two blocks *north* to the traffic light, and turn right
     1   2
   onto *Rumson Lane. No error*
        3   4   5
   ① ② ③ ④ ⑤

6. I asked *father* to lend me the *Chevrolet* so that we can drive
         1   2
   to the *Rosemont Club,* which is on the *east* side of town.
         3   4
   No error
    5
   ① ② ③ ④ ⑤

7. Speaking to the *town's Community Action Council,*
                   1   2
   Dr. j. l. Raio suggested revamping mental health *services.*
     3   4
   No error
    5
   ① ② ③ ④ ⑤

8. This *September,* both of my children, Bob and Ronny, will be
         1
   attending *Cedar High school. No error*
          2   3   4   5
   ① ② ③ ④ ⑤

9. Waiting for the *Twenty-second Street* bus, we had time to
                 1
   admire the *arrow shirts* displayed in *Stone's Haberdashery.*
            2   3   4
   No error
    5
   ① ② ③ ④ ⑤

10. *"Why* don't you read the *Winston Item,"* said *Mother, "and*
     1   2   3   4
    check for sales on air conditioners?" *No error*
                       5
    ① ② ③ ④ ⑤

11. *Uncle* John and my *father* are going to *Crystal Lake* on
    1   2   3
    saturday to try out their new fishing gear. *No error*
    4   5
① ② ③ ④ ⑤

12. I've already crossed the *Atlantic ocean* by air; but this
                         1   2
    summer, in *July.* I hope to make the crossing on an *Italian*
               3   4
    freighter. *No error*
            5
① ② ③ ④ ⑤

13. *More* and more elementary *schools* are teaching in *spanish*
    1   2   3
    in order to meet the needs of the *community. No error*
                                    4   5
① ② ③ ④ ⑤

14. You recall *Reverend Hempstead* saying that he will study
              1   2
    religious philosophies of the *east. No error*
    3   4   5
① ② ③ ④ ⑤

15. The Ridgedale *Garden club* developed a hybrid *rose* and
               1   2   3
    named it *Everlasting Beauty. No error*
              4   5
① ② ③ ④ ⑤

16. Including *caucasians, African-Americans,* and *Asians,* the
          1   2   3
    population of *Winfield,* Pennsylvania has grown to one and a
                    4
    half million. *No error*
              5
① ② ③ ④ ⑤

Practice II

Directions: Blacken the circle that corresponds to the number of the incorrect sentence in each group. If there is no error, blacken number 5.

1. (1) Each year our community celebrates the Fourth Of July with races, entertainment, and fireworks.
    (2) Because of its beauty and natural resources, the state of Colorado now boasts many new residents.
    (3) John works for the Ford Motor Company in Cleveland.
    (4) I asked Gerry, "Do you think we'll get to the game in time for the first quarter?"
    (5) No error
① ② ③ ④ ⑤

2. (1) Last year we celebrated that Holiday on a Monday.
    (2) This year the holiday falls in the third week of September.
    (3) Shall we cross the bridge or take the tunnel?
① ② ③ ④ ⑤

    (4) Archaeologists found evidence that the pagan gods were worshipped on that spot.

    (5) No error

3. (1) Dean Jones just became an administrator this September.   ① ② ③ ④ ⑤

    (2) Andy joined the travel-American Club and enjoyed a six week tour with the group.

    (3) We have a subscription to the *Reader's Digest.*

    (4) *The Bridges of Madison County* was a very popular book.

    (5) No error

4. (1) "Don't forget your umbrella," Aunt Jean said, "for you know   ① ② ③ ④ ⑤ the forecast indicates rain for today."

    (2) At Ohio State university, students take courses year-round.

    (3) Our curriculum needs to stress reading skills in the areas of science, social studies, and American literature.

    (4) Evan Greene, who lives in Syracuse, New York, joined the Professional Photographers Club.

    (5) No error

5. (1) The train trip was most scenic since the route wound through   ① ② ③ ④ ⑤ the White Mountains and ended at Pleasant Lake.

    (2) when did you say that Bud had called me?

    (3) Last summer, in July, we camped in Colorado.

    (4) That company, Ferro Metals, has increased its volume of business through advanced advertising and promotion techniques.

    (5) No error

6. (1) In the West, we plan to visit the Grand Canyon as well as the   ① ② ③ ④ ⑤ southern half of California.

    (2) The course, interestingly enough, was entitled, "God and His Relationship to Man."

    (3) Let's make a date to meet on Sunday, June 2nd.

    (4) *Who wants to Be a Millionaire?* averaged 29 million viewers per night the first season it aired in the United States.

    (5) No error

7. (1) We're leaving Kennedy International Airport at 8 P.M., and we   ① ② ③ ④ ⑤ arrive in Lisbon seven hours later.

    (2) My friend, Fred, was elected President of the Rescue Squad.

    (3) "This new wing contains our intensive care unit," explained the director.

    (4) France and Belgium are both French-speaking countries.

    (5) No error

8. (1) The group turned its attention to a tall, drawling Texan in its   ① ② ③ ④ ⑤ midst.

    (2) A well-known senator was accused of un-American activities.

    (3) "Don't do that!" said Jack. "you'll ruin the machine!"

    (4) Each time I see the Tappan Zee Bridge, I am impressed by its size and beauty.

    (5) No error

9. (1) A river in Wisconsin is called the Fox River.   ① ② ③ ④ ⑤
   (2) The Indian language is composed of many dialects.
   (3) The Empire State Building is still an impressive sight although it is no longer the tallest building in the world.
   (4) While you are in London, be sure to shop at Simpson's, Ltd.
   (5) No error

10. (1) It was two years ago that judge Billings was appointed to the bench.   ① ② ③ ④ ⑤
    (2) I remember seeing Uncle John at the family gathering; but, as I recall, my aunt was not there.
    (3) Our study group discussed a few books of the Bible.
    (4) An essay question regarding the French Revolution might involve the major causes leading up to the disquiet of the times.
    (5) No error

Chapter 17 Capitalization

Survey Test *Page 164.*

1. After considering all the facts, I have chosen an appropriate action.
2. Don't you think that Fred might enjoy owning a French-English dictionary?
3. He said, "Leave New Jersey at noon, and you will reach New York City by 1 P.M. at the latest."
4. John is planning to take German, geography, history, and economics this year at City College.
5. We're expecting guests for dinner on Friday night. I hope you can join us.
6. Mary Stark bought a Chevrolet last Tuesday, although she hadn't planned on buying a car this year.
7. In History II we will study the Industrial Revolution, World War I, World War II, and the Atomic Age.
8. This course will be offered to adults on Mondays, Wednesdays, and Fridays in the spring only.
9. His original home, in California, was his favorite; and he plans on returning to the West in November.
10. Captain and Mrs. Ryan made reservations at Island Beach Motel on the Cape's north shore for Labor Day.

Practice I *Page 164.*

1. **(2)** Our *history* course this semester highlights civilizations of the East.
   Capitalize only *specific* course names, ie., History IA.
2. **(2)** My family plans to move to *Cypress Street* in Millville, Ohio.
   Capitalize entire street names.

3. **(4)** "If you plan to see the entire art exhibit," Joan said, *"be* sure to arrive at 10 A.M."
   Do not capitalize the first word in a broken quotation unless it is the beginning of a complete thought.
4. **(2)** The Thompkins' plans for *Labor Day* include a visit to the beach.
   Capitalize the name of a holiday.
5. **(5)** No error
6. **(1)** I asked *Father* to lend me the Chevrolet so that we can drive to the Rosemont Club, which is on the east side of town.
   Capitalize Father or Mother when they are used as names.
7. **(3)** Speaking to the town's Community Action Council, Dr. *J. L.* Raio suggested revamping mental health services.
   Capitalize initials in a name.
8. **(4)** This September both of my children, Bob and Ronny, will be attending Cedar High *School.*
   Capitalize the entire name of a school.
9. **(2)** Waiting for the Twenty-second Street bus, we had time to admire the *Arrow* shirts displayed in Stone's Haberdashery.
   Capitalize the name of a company.
10. **(5)** No error
11. **(4)** Uncle John and my father are going to Crystal Lake on *Saturday* to try out their new fishing gear.
   Capitalize the names of the days of the week.

12. **(2)** I've already crossed the Atlantic *Ocean* by air; but this summer, in July, I hope to make the crossing on an Italian freighter.

Capitalize the entire name of an ocean.

13. **(3)** More and more elementary schools are teaching in *Spanish* in order to meet the needs of the community.

Capitalize the name of a language.

14. **(4)** You recall Reverend Hempstead saying that he will study religious philosophies of the *East*.

Capitalize North, South, East, and West when they designate an area.

15. **(2)** The Ridgedale Garden *Club* developed a hybrid rose and named it Everlasting Beauty.

Capitalize the entire name of a club.

16. **(1)** Including *Caucasians,* African-Americans and Asians, the population of Winfield, Pennsylvania, has grown to one and a half million.

Capitalize the name of a race.

Practice II *Page 166.*

1. **(1)** Each year our community celebrates the Fourth *of* July with races, entertainment, and fireworks.

2. **(1)** Last year we celebrated that *holiday* on a Monday.

3. **(2)** Andy joined the *Travel-American Club* and enjoyed a six-week tour with the group.

4. **(2)** At Ohio State *University,* students take courses year-round.

5. **(2)** *When* did you say that Bud had called me?

6. **(4)** *Who Wants to Be a Millionaire?* averaged 29 million viewers per night the first season it aired in the United States.

7. **(2)** My friend, Fred, was elected *president* of the Rescue Squad.

8. **(3)** "Don't do that!" said Jack. *"You'll* ruin the machine!"

9. **(5)** No error

10. **(1)** It was two years ago that *Judge* Billings was appointed to the bench.

Chapter 18

SPELLING

"The other people that was involved in the Lincoln assination later exequded or killed themselves. Mary Tood Lincoln locked herself up in a closet and went crazy. She was declared mentally insane and put in a insane silome.
One day a long time later a man walked into Lincoln's office and found his son, Robert Tood, burning some of his daddy's old pappers. The man asked him why he was burning the pappers and Robert Tood said, 'Maybe they will criminate one of the members of the goverment,' which his daddy was in."

—Bill Lawrence, Editor
Then Some Other Stuff Happened

A Word With You ...

It isn't easy to become a good speller; in fact, many people never master the art. The high school student whose work is quoted above proves our point.

One famous English writer, George Bernard Shaw, was critical of our many spelling rules and the strange appearance of many of our words. He invested a goodly sum of money in a campaign to reform certain spelling practices. Shaw, however, was an excellent speller, regardless of his complaints.

There is no magic formula for learning how to spell. The ability to spell correctly results from persistent study. Here are some useful suggestions for studying spelling:

1. Use a small notebook exclusively for recording your personal spelling problem words.
2. Each time that you discover a problem word, enter it in your notebook. Check a dictionary for the correct syllabification and pronunciation.
3. Look at the word and say it in syllables.
4. Try to apply a rule that will help you to understand *why* the word is spelled as it is.
5. Close your eyes and picture the way the word looks.
6. Write the word. Check it. Rewrite it if necessary.
7. Review words you have already studied until you are absolutely sure that you know how to spell them.

Some words are correctly spelled in more than one way. For example, the word *catalogue* appears in one dictionary in the following way:

cat-a-logue, n. Also **catalog** ...

In another dictionary, the entry says:

catalogue or **catalog**, n. ...

In the examples above, the use of the words *also* and *or* is important. For example, while *or* means that both spellings are equally common, *also* means that the first spelling is more common. How do you know for sure what policy a dictionary follows? Look at the front of the dictionary where all the rules and standards for that dictionary are explained. When in doubt, choose the first spelling unless the dictionary entry explains that there is a special reason for choosing the second.

There are many commonly misspelled words. Careful study of the list beginning on page 189 of this chapter will improve your spelling. There are also a number of hints and rules that are helpful in learning to spell.

Building Blocks of Words: Consonants, Vowels, Syllables

Of the twenty-six letters in the alphabet, twenty-one letters are consonants: b, c, d, f, g, h, j, k, l, m, n, p, q, r, s, t, v, w, x, y, z. The other five letters of the alphabet are vowels: a, e, i, o, u. Sometimes the consonant y is used as a vowel.

A syllable is a single, uninterrupted sound. A syllable is either a single vowel or a combination of one or more vowels or consonants. One syllable can be a word or just a part of a word.

EXAMPLES:

<u>one syllable</u>
ki
un
ing

<u>one-syllable words</u>
oh
let
pound

Learning to spell a long word is a much easier task if you divide the word into syllables.

EXAMPLE:

complacency = com • pla • cen • cy

You can learn to spell each syllable and, finally, put the word together.

Adding to Words

Many words are formed by adding to the root (basic part) of the word. Prefixes are added to the beginning of a word, whereas suffixes are added to the end of a word.

prefix	root	suffix
*dis*quiet	quiet	quiet*ly*

Rules Concerning Spelling

Rule 1:

In most cases, a prefix can be added to a word without changing the spelling of that word.

Prefix	(Meaning)	Word Combination
il	(not)	literate = illiterate
ir	(not)	regular = irregular

Practice I

Directions: Add the correct prefix from the list below to each of the following words.

ac-	il-	in-	mis-	over-	mal-
dis-	ir-	un-	re-	im-	co-

1. _____ instate
2. _____ illusion
3. _____ necessary
4. _____ operate
5. _____ mortal
6. _____ spell
7. _____ reverent
8. _____ legal
9. _____ climate
10. _____ rate
11. _____ content
12. _____ accurate

Rule 2:

When adding a suffix that begins with a consonant, the spelling of most words does not change.

	Word	Suffix
	careless	ness = carelessness
	active	ly = actively
Exceptions:	true	ly = truly
	due	ly = duly

Rule 3:

Suffixes do change the spelling of words that end in *y*.

Word	Suffix
happy	ness = happiness
hearty	ly = heartily

Rule 4:

When adding a suffix that begins with a vowel to a word that ends in *e*, drop the final *e*.

Word	Suffix
fame	ous = famous
continue	ous = continuous

Exceptions: Words that end in *-ge* or *-ce* must retain the final *e* to maintain the soft sound of the *g* or *c*.

Word	Suffix
courage	ous = courageous
notice	able = noticeable

Another exception is the word *dye*.

Word	Suffix
dye	ing = dyeing

Practice II

Directions: Opposite each word below is a suffix that, when combined with the word, forms a new word. In the space provided, write the new word, making sure to spell it correctly.

	Word	Suffix
1.	announce	ment = _____
2.	dye	ing = _____
3.	snappy	ness = _____
4.	associate	ion = _____
5.	dispense	able = _____
6.	definite	ly = _____
7.	economic	al = _____
8.	courage	ous = _____
9.	move	able = _____
10.	necessary	ly = _____
11.	practical	ly = _____
12.	port	able = _____
13.	rude	ness = _____
14.	guide	ance = _____
15.	true	ly = _____

Practice III

Directions: Blacken the circle that corresponds to the number of the incorrectly spelled word in each group. If there is no error, blacken number 5.

1. (1) unimportant
   (2) revelation
   (3) cumulative
   (4) irational
   (5) no error
   ① ② ③ ④ ⑤

2. (1) brighter
   (2) happyness
   (3) unaccustomed
   (4) berate
   (5) no error
   ① ② ③ ④ ⑤

3. (1) impossible
   (2) cooperation
   (3) inactive
   (4) mispell
   (5) no error
   ① ② ③ ④ ⑤

4. (1) commencment
   (2) coverage
   (3) practically
   (4) extraction
   (5) no error
   ① ② ③ ④ ⑤

5. (1) safty
   (2) forgiveness
   (3) shining
   (4) amusement
   (5) no error
   ① ② ③ ④ ⑤

6. (1) becoming
   (2) truly
   (3) plainness
   (4) actually
   (5) no error
   ① ② ③ ④ ⑤

7. (1) adorable
   (2) contagious
   (3) acumulate
   (4) supervise
   (5) no error
   ① ② ③ ④ ⑤

8. (1) loneliness
   (2) personal
   (3) barely
   (4) noticable
   (5) no error
   ① ② ③ ④ ⑤

9. (1) continuation
   (2) arguement
   (3) ridiculous
   (4) usage
   (5) no error
   ① ② ③ ④ ⑤

10. (1) surprised
    (2) acquisitiveness
    (3) carefully
    (4) virtuous
    (5) no error
    ① ② ③ ④ ⑤

The Role of Accent Marks

A word that contains more than one syllable has an accent on one of those syllables. Say this word in syllables: punc • tu • ate. Which syllable is stressed? Yes, the first syllable is stressed or accented, and its accent is marked in this way:

punc´ • tu • ate

Practice IV

Directions: The following words have been divided into syllables. In each word, place an accent mark to show which syllable is stressed. The first word is done for you.

1. paint´ • er
2. pri • vate
3. of • fice
4. e • con • o • my
5. ad • vise
6. bal • ance
7. dis • sat • is • fy
8. de • vel • op • ment

9. in • di • vid • u • al
10. pre • fer
11. pref • er • ence
12. psy • chol • o • gy
13. vac • il • late
14. u • nan • i • mous
15. wretch • ed

Rule 5:

When changing the form of a one-syllable action word that ends in a consonant preceded by a vowel, double the final consonant.

plan   planned
sun   sunning
run   runner

Rule 6:

Double the final consonant when changing the form of a two-syllable word that ends in a consonant preceded by a vowel *and* that is accented on the second syllable.

refer   referred
occur   occurred
occur   occurrence

Rule 7:

In a two- or three-syllable word, if the accent changes from the final syllable to a preceding one when a suffix is added (prefer, preference), do not double the final consonant.

refer   reference
confer   conference

Practice V

Directions: Blacken the circle that corresponds to the number of the incorrectly spelled word in each group. If there is no error, blacken number 5.

1. (1) referred
   (2) preferrence
   (3) stunning

   (4) winding
   (5) no error

   ① ② ③ ④ ⑤

2. (1) thinner   (4) detered   ① ② ③ ④ ⑤
   (2) conferred
   (3) reference   (5) no error

3. (1) binder   (4) reared   ① ② ③ ④ ⑤
   (2) funnier
   (3) pictured   (5) no error

4. (1) cunning   (4) banning   ① ② ③ ④ ⑤
   (2) preferable
   (3) deterent   (5) no error

5. (1) preferred   (4) occurence   ① ② ③ ④ ⑤
   (2) canning
   (3) fanned   (5) no error

Rule 8:

Use *i* before *e* except after *c*. *Examples:* relief, receipt. *Exception:* Use *e* before *i* in words that sound like ā. *Examples:* neighbor, weigh.

Other exceptions: weird, seize, either, leisure, neither.

Practice VI

Directions: Complete the following words with *ei* or *ie*.

1. n_____ce   6. rec_____ve
2. dec_____ve   7. conc_____ve
3. th_____f   8. bel_____f
4. rel_____ve   9. n_____ther
5. n_____gh   10. s_____ze

Rule 9:

There are rules for forming the plurals of words. Following are the rules and a few examples of each.

A. Most words form plurals by adding *s*.

radio	radios
towel	towels
chair	chairs
tray	trays

B. Words ending in *y* preceded by a consonant form plurals by changing *y* to *i* and adding *es*.

sky	skies
story	stories

C. Words ending in *o* preceded by a consonant form plurals by adding *es*.

tomato	tomatoes
hero	heroes

Exception: words ending in *o*, preceded by a consonant, but referring to music, form their plurals by adding only *s*.

alto	altos
piano	pianos

D. Words ending in *s*, *sh*, *ch*, and *x* form plurals by adding *es*.

bunch	bunches
sex	sexes
boss	bosses
crush	crushes

E. A compound word forms its plural by adding *s* to the principal word.

fathers-in-law
baby*sitters*

F. Words ending in *-ful* form their plurals by adding *s*.

mouthfuls
cupfuls

G. Some words have one spelling for singular and plural.

deer
trout
Chinese
sheep

H. Some words form their plurals by irregular changes.

thief	thieves
knife	knives
leaf	leaves
woman	women
child	children
tooth	teeth
louse	lice
crisis	crises
alumnus	alumni
datum	data
appendix	appendices

Practice VII

Directions: Blacken the circle that corresponds to the number of the incorrectly spelled word in each group. If there is no error, blacken number 5.

1. (1) geese (4) firemen ① ② ③ ④ ⑤
    (2) mouthsful
    (3) commanders-in-chief
    (5) no error
2. (1) Chinese's (4) 10's ① ② ③ ④ ⑤
    (2) bases
    (3) workmen
    (5) no error
3. (1) bacilli (4) handkerchiefs ① ② ③ ④ ⑤
    (2) son-in-laws
    (3) series
    (5) no error
4. (1) women (4) mice ① ② ③ ④ ⑤
    (2) alumni
    (3) passersby
    (5) no error
5. (1) 8s (4) men-of-war ① ② ③ ④ ⑤
    (2) Frenchmen
    (3) alumni
    (5) no error

Rule 10:

Following are rules regarding *sede*, *ceed*, and *cede*.

A. Only one word is spelled with a *sede* ending:

supersede

B. Only three words are spelled with a *ceed* ending:

succeed   exceed   proceed

C. All other words of this type are spelled with a *cede* ending:

precede   recede   concede

Spelling Review

Practice VIII

Directions: Blacken the circle that corresponds to the number of the incorrectly spelled word in each group. If there is no error, blacken number 5.

1. (1) acknowledge (4) commodity ① ② ③ ④ ⑤
    (2) fireman
    (3) conclusivly
    (5) no error
2. (1) incurred (4) herald ① ② ③ ④ ⑤
    (2) coranation
    (3) voluntary
    (5) no error
3. (1) simular (4) quizzes ① ② ③ ④ ⑤
    (2) bulletin
    (3) bored
    (5) no error
4. (1) duchess (4) fertile ① ② ③ ④ ⑤
    (2) achevement
    (3) monarchial

5. (1) distribute   (4) tonnage   ① ② ③ ④ ⑤
   (2) sieze   (5) no error
   (3) premises

6. (1) monthly   (4) dupped   ① ② ③ ④ ⑤
   (2) primarily   (5) no error
   (3) condemned

7. (1) cancellation   (4) utilize   ① ② ③ ④ ⑤
   (2) derrick   (5) no error
   (3) pertinant

8. (1) nowadays   (4) guardian   ① ② ③ ④ ⑤
   (2) courtesies   (5) no error
   (3) negotiate

9. (1) loot   (4) axle   ① ② ③ ④ ⑤
   (2) faculties   (5) no error
   (3) loveable

10. (1) fragrance   (4) athletic   ① ② ③ ④ ⑤
   (2) accompanied   (5) no error
   (3) preference

Practice IX

Directions: Blacken the circle that corresponds to the number of the incorrectly spelled word in each group. If there is no error, blacken number 5.

1. (1) liquify   (4) dissolve   ① ② ③ ④ ⑤
   (2) disappear   (5) no error
   (3) swirling

2. (1) inexorable   (4) arboreal   ① ② ③ ④ ⑤
   (2) mercyful   (5) no error
   (3) potable

3. (1) disolution   (4) diseases   ① ② ③ ④ ⑤
   (2) agreeable   (5) no error
   (3) planned

4. (1) minimize   (4) candidacy   ① ② ③ ④ ⑤
   (2) sophomore   (5) no error
   (3) attorneys

5. (1) unnecessary   (4) judgment   ① ② ③ ④ ⑤
   (2) carnage   (5) no error
   (3) wierd

6. (1) roses   (4) churches   ① ② ③ ④ ⑤
   (2) goverment   (5) no error
   (3) absence

7. (1) emergency   (4) citizen   ① ② ③ ④ ⑤
   (2) eager   (5) no error
   (3) cordialy

8. (1) benefit   (4) peice   ① ② ③ ④ ⑤
   (2) boxes   (5) no error
   (3) consequence

9. (1) journey   (4) relief   ① ② ③ ④ ⑤
   (2) majority
   (3) necessarily
10. (1) yacht   (4) principle   ① ② ③ ④ ⑤
    (2) traveler   (5) no error
    (3) profession

Practice X

Directions: Blacken the circle that corresponds to the number of the incorrectly spelled word in each group. If there is no error, blacken number 5.

1. (1) overrate   (4) greenness   ① ② ③ ④ ⑤
   (2) misapprehend   (5) no error
   (3) habitualy
2. (1) deferred   (4) defference   ① ② ③ ④ ⑤
   (2) hoping   (5) no error
   (3) approval
3. (1) candys   (4) files   ① ② ③ ④ ⑤
   (2) valleys   (5) no error
   (3) torches
4. (1) immaterial   (4) unabated   ① ② ③ ④ ⑤
   (2) dissapoint   (5) no error
   (3) practically
5. (1) potatos   (4) sopranos   ① ② ③ ④ ⑤
   (2) teeth   (5) no error
   (3) radios
6. (1) preparing   (4) controlled   ① ② ③ ④ ⑤
   (2) writing   (5) no error
   (3) propeling
7. (1) crises   (4) trucksful   ① ② ③ ④ ⑤
   (2) geese   (5) no error
   (3) concertos
8. (1) truely   (4) famous   ① ② ③ ④ ⑤
   (2) moving   (5) no error
   (3) running
9. (1) shelves   (4) churches   ① ② ③ ④ ⑤
   (2) benches   (5) no error
   (3) knives
10. (1) salarys   (4) nameless   ① ② ③ ④ ⑤
    (2) basketfuls   (5) no error
    (3) reddest
11. (1) disagree   (4) casually   ① ② ③ ④ ⑤
    (2) benefited   (5) no error
    (3) gases
12. (1) oxen   (4) solves   ① ② ③ ④ ⑤
    (2) desirable   (5) no error
    (3) data

Practice XI

Directions: Blacken the circle that corresponds to the number of the incorrectly spelled word in each group. If there is no error, blacken number 5.

1. (1) belief   (4) weigh   ① ② ③ ④ ⑤
    (2) achieve   (5) no error
    (3) neice
2. (1) yield   (4) releif   ① ② ③ ④ ⑤
    (2) neighbor   (5) no error
    (3) deceive
3. (1) benefited   (4) equipped   ① ② ③ ④ ⑤
    (2) appealed   (5) no error
    (3) refered
4. (1) preference   (4) colonel   ① ② ③ ④ ⑤
    (2) reference   (5) no error
    (3) asessment
5. (1) stationery   (4) similar   ① ② ③ ④ ⑤
    (2) stationary   (5) no error
    (3) sophomore
6. (1) primarily   (4) receit   ① ② ③ ④ ⑤
    (2) principal   (5) no error
    (3) principle
7. (1) aquired   (4) height   ① ② ③ ④ ⑤
    (2) brief   (5) no error
    (3) contemptible
8. (1) erred   (4) lieutenent   ① ② ③ ④ ⑤
    (2) millionaire   (5) no error
    (3) misanthrope
9. (1) adjournament   (4) digestible   ① ② ③ ④ ⑤
    (2) caucus   (5) no error
    (3) contagious
10. (1) cheff   (4) preceding   ① ② ③ ④ ⑤
    (2) calendar   (5) no error
    (3) macaroni

Practice XII

Directions: Blacken the circle that corresponds to the number of the incorrectly spelled word in each group. If there is no error, blacken number 5.

1. (1) changeable   (4) fortissimo   ① ② ③ ④ ⑤
    (2) atheletic   (5) no error
    (3) grammar
2. (1) filial   (4) treachery   ① ② ③ ④ ⑤
    (2) leisure   (5) no error
    (3) temperture

3. (1) bulletin (4) kindergarten ① ② ③ ④ ⑤
 (2) amendment (5) no error
 (3) incessent
4. (1) legitiment (4) courtesies ① ② ③ ④ ⑤
 (2) vivisection (5) no error
 (3) pervade
5. (1) prefer (4) patrolled ① ② ③ ④ ⑤
 (2) preferred (5) no error
 (3) preference
6. (1) ninth (4) hideous ① ② ③ ④ ⑤
 (2) correspondent (5) no error
 (3) canon
7. (1) apparently (4) forfeit ① ② ③ ④ ⑤
 (2) foreign (5) no error
 (3) carriage
8. (1) aggregate (4) tetnus ① ② ③ ④ ⑤
 (2) massacre (5) no error
 (3) omissions
9. (1) exceed (4) procedure ① ② ③ ④ ⑤
 (2) intercede (5) no error
 (3) proceed
10. (1) fundimental (4) penitentiary ① ② ③ ④ ⑤
 (2) misspell (5) no error
 (3) odyssey

Practice XIII

Directions: Blacken the circle that corresponds to the number of the incorrectly spelled word in each group. If there is no error, blacken number 5.

1. (1) torches (4) shelves ① ② ③ ④ ⑤
 (2) salaries (5) no error
 (3) valleys
2. (1) absense (4) citizen ① ② ③ ④ ⑤
 (2) gases (5) no error
 (3) accident
3. (1) executive (4) eager ① ② ③ ④ ⑤
 (2) divide (5) no error
 (3) discusion
4. (1) contrary (4) banquet ① ② ③ ④ ⑤
 (2) athaletic (5) no error
 (3) critical
5. (1) association (4) decide ① ② ③ ④ ⑤
 (2) character (5) no error
 (3) earliest
6. (1) Wenesday (4) executive ① ② ③ ④ ⑤
 (2) knives (5) no error
 (3) concerning

7. (1) appreciate (4) numerous ① ② ③ ④ ⑤
  (2) except (5) no error
  (3) scene

8. (1) national (4) volume ① ② ③ ④ ⑤
  (2) posession (5) no error
  (3) industrious

9. (1) patient (4) probably ① ② ③ ④ ⑤
  (2) quantity (5) no error
  (3) boundary

10. (1) warrant (4) libary ① ② ③ ④ ⑤
  (2) laboratory (5) no error
  (3) interesting

Practice XIV

Directions: Blacken the circle that corresponds to the number of the incorrectly spelled word in each group. If there is no error, blacken number 5.

1. (1) biased (4) vacuum ① ② ③ ④ ⑤
  (2) aberation (5) no error
  (3) wholly

2. (1) capitol (4) essential ① ② ③ ④ ⑤
  (2) ecstasy (5) no error
  (3) embarrass

3. (1) asertain (4) diocese ① ② ③ ④ ⑤
  (2) correlation (5) no error
  (3) abeyance

4. (1) ninth (4) official ① ② ③ ④ ⑤
  (2) resileince (5) no error
  (3) nickel

5. (1) salable (4) policy ① ② ③ ④ ⑤
  (2) ordinance (5) no error
  (3) illegitimate

6. (1) subversive (4) prairie ① ② ③ ④ ⑤
  (2) predatory (5) no error
  (3) lucritive

7. (1) pacifist (4) surfiet ① ② ③ ④ ⑤
  (2) senior (5) no error
  (3) source

8. (1) weild (4) transaction ① ② ③ ④ ⑤
  (2) vacillate (5) no error
  (3) vengeance

9. (1) queue (4) marital ① ② ③ ④ ⑤
  (2) masquerade (5) no error
  (3) loose

10. (1) psicology (4) impeccable ① ② ③ ④ ⑤
  (2) possession (5) no error
  (3) imminent

Practice XV

Directions: Blacken the circle that corresponds to the number of the incorrectly spelled word in each group. If there is no error, blacken number 5.

1. (1) derogatory   (4) yacht   ① ② ③ ④ ⑤
   (2) neglagible   (5) no error
   (3) rehearsal
2. (1) queue   (4) gelatin   ① ② ③ ④ ⑤
   (2) jeopardy   (5) no error
   (3) forfiet
3. (1) bureau   (4) harass   ① ② ③ ④ ⑤
   (2) blamable   (5) no error
   (3) desecration
4. (1) falibility   (4) remnant   ① ② ③ ④ ⑤
   (2) heinous   (5) no error
   (3) myriad
5. (1) hygienic   (4) prommisory   ① ② ③ ④ ⑤
   (2) medallion   (5) no error
   (3) midget
6. (1) complacency   (4) realize   ① ② ③ ④ ⑤
   (2) efemeral   (5) no error
   (3) exaggerate
7. (1) lacquer   (4) emolument   ① ② ③ ④ ⑤
   (2) currency   (5) no error
   (3) exortation
8. (1) apologetic   (4) exzema   ① ② ③ ④ ⑤
   (2) coroner   (5) no error
   (3) clique
9. (1) disatisfied   (4) surgeon   ① ② ③ ④ ⑤
   (2) moribund   (5) no error
   (3) warrant
10. (1) defered   (4) intercede   ① ② ③ ④ ⑤
    (2) extraordinary   (5) no error
    (3) journal

Practice XVI

Directions: Blacken the circle that corresponds to the number of the incorrectly spelled word in each group. If there is no error, blacken number 5.

1. (1) responsibility   (4) rhetoric   ① ② ③ ④ ⑤
   (2) resonence   (5) no error
   (3) rheostat
2. (1) salient   (4) parliament   ① ② ③ ④ ⑤
   (2) patronize   (5) no error
   (3) pateint

3. (1) secretery (4) innocuous ① ② ③ ④ ⑤
   (2) piquancy (5) no error
   (3) integrity

4. (1) diphtheria (4) cemetery ① ② ③ ④ ⑤
   (2) distinguised (5) no error
   (3) category

5. (1) abscess (4) ingenuous ① ② ③ ④ ⑤
   (2) chamois (5) no error
   (3) effects

6. (1) accessible (4) inimitable ① ② ③ ④ ⑤
   (2) chauffur (5) no error
   (3) elaborate

7. (1) impromptu (4) precede ① ② ③ ④ ⑤
   (2) incongruity (5) no error
   (3) permissable

8. (1) tremendous (4) tariff ① ② ③ ④ ⑤
   (2) punctilious (5) no error
   (3) recognizible

9. (1) reasonable (4) repetitious ① ② ③ ④ ⑤
   (2) mischivous (5) no error
   (3) picnicking

10. (1) sobriquet (4) stretch ① ② ③ ④ ⑤
    (2) soveriegn (5) no error
    (3) staunch

Practice XVII

Directions: Blacken the circle that corresponds to the number of the incorrectly spelled word in each group. If there is no error, blacken number 5.

1. (1) addressee (4) murmuring ① ② ③ ④ ⑤
   (2) carburator (5) no error
   (3) intercede

2. (1) biscut (4) preceding ① ② ③ ④ ⑤
   (2) financier (5) no error
   (3) previous

3. (1) hearth (4) heritage ① ② ③ ④ ⑤
   (2) bounteous (5) no error
   (3) judgment

4. (1) aversion (4) bookkeeping ① ② ③ ④ ⑤
   (2) aquatic (5) no error
   (3) facilitation

5. (1) dilapidated (4) regrettable ① ② ③ ④ ⑤
   (2) function (5) no error
   (3) relevent

6. (1) dearth (4) wethar ① ② ③ ④ ⑤
   (2) deceive (5) no error
   (3) proceed

7. (1) excede (4) vacuum   ① ② ③ ④ ⑤
   (2) feudal   (5) no error
   (3) grandeur

8. (1) realize (4) matinee   ① ② ③ ④ ⑤
   (2) foriegn (5) no error
   (3) nevertheless

9. (1) criticism (4) preferably ① ② ③ ④ ⑤
   (2) plagiarism (5) no error
   (3) equiped

10. (1) beatitude (4) succeed   ① ② ③ ④ ⑤
    (2) corruggated (5) no error
    (3) existence

Practice XVIII

Directions: Blacken the circle that corresponds to the number of the incorrectly spelled word in each group. If there is no error, blacken number 5.

1. (1) angle   (4) compel   ① ② ③ ④ ⑤
   (2) conciliatory (5) no error
   (3) exersise

2. (1) description (4) publicity   ① ② ③ ④ ⑤
   (2) hindrence   (5) no error
   (3) memoir

3. (1) belligerent (4) decieve   ① ② ③ ④ ⑤
   (2) dearth   (5) no error
   (3) equator

4. (1) bankruptcy   (4) demurrer   ① ② ③ ④ ⑤
   (2) deliberate   (5) no error
   (3) histrionic

5. (1) crystallized (4) masquerade ① ② ③ ④ ⑤
   (2) mackeral   (5) no error
   (3) maintenance

6. (1) sandwich   (4) scissors   ① ② ③ ④ ⑤
   (2) peculiar   (5) no error
   (3) neumonia

7. (1) temperment   (4) occur   ① ② ③ ④ ⑤
   (2) summarize   (5) no error
   (3) scripture

8. (1) abundence   (4) colossal   ① ② ③ ④ ⑤
   (2) citation   (5) no error
   (3) clamorous

9. (1) acumulation (4) adage   ① ② ③ ④ ⑤
   (2) circumstantial (5) no error
   (3) adoption

10. (1) apparatus   (4) allege   ① ② ③ ④ ⑤
    (2) anceint   (5) no error
    (3) amplify

Practice XIX

Directions: Blacken the circle that corresponds to the number of the incorrectly spelled word in each group. If there is no error, blacken number 5.

1. (1) consumation   (4) emphasis   ① ② ③ ④ ⑤
   (2) anemia   (5) no error
   (3) corporal
2. (1) crucial   (4) asessment   ① ② ③ ④ ⑤
   (2) disappearance   (5) no error
   (3) eminently
3. (1) impartiality   (4) scissors   ① ② ③ ④ ⑤
   (2) impecable   (5) no error
   (3) indictment
4. (1) maneuver   (4) presumptuous   ① ② ③ ④ ⑤
   (2) preparation   (5) no error
   (3) fasinated
5. (1) rythm   (4) interruption   ① ② ③ ④ ⑤
   (2) pamphlet   (5) no error
   (3) panicky
6. (1) controler   (4) scripture   ① ② ③ ④ ⑤
   (2) labyrinth   (5) no error
   (3) judiciary
7. (1) similar   (4) column   ① ② ③ ④ ⑤
   (2) mediocrity   (5) no error
   (3) emphatically
8. (1) commandant   (4) commemorate   ① ② ③ ④ ⑤
   (2) aquaint   (5) no error
   (3) across
9. (1) demurring   (4) laboratory   ① ② ③ ④ ⑤
   (2) detrimental   (5) no error
   (3) conversent
10. (1) liquidate   (4) medieval   ① ② ③ ④ ⑤
    (2) matinee   (5) no error
    (3) mecanical

Practice XX

Directions: Blacken the circle that corresponds to the number of the incorrectly spelled word in each group. If there is no error, blacken number 5.

1. (1) wholly   (4) adjunct   ① ② ③ ④ ⑤
   (2) thorough   (5) no error
   (3) symetrical
2. (1) arouse   (4) proceed   ① ② ③ ④ ⑤
   (2) superceed   (5) no error
   (3) actually

3. (1) accede   (4) arraignment   ① ② ③ ④ ⑤
    (2) succeed   (5) no error
    (3) appellate
4. (1) adjunct   (4) amendment   ① ② ③ ④ ⑤
    (2) advise   (5) no error
    (3) preceed
5. (1) anoyance   (4) actually   ① ② ③ ④ ⑤
    (2) antipathy   (5) no error
    (3) biased

Commonly Misspelled Words

Give special review to all those words that have given you trouble. Do not try to learn more than 10 new words at one time.

abandoned	adopted	apparently	awkward
aberration	adoption	appellate	axle
abeyance	advisable	appetite	
abscess	advise	appreciation	baccalaureate
absence	advising	appropriation	bachelor
absurd	affirmative	apricot	bacteria
abundance	aggravate	aquatic	balance
abutting	aggregate	architecture	banana
academy	agitation	arduous	bankruptcy
accede	agreeable	arguing	barely
accent	agreement	arouse	beaker
accessible	aisle	arraignment	beatitude
acclimate	alcohol	arrest	beleaguered
accommodate	allege	article	belligerent
accumulation	allies	artificial	benefit
accusation	all right	ascertain	biased
achievement	ambassador	aspirations	bigamy
acknowledge	amendment	assassination	bimonthly
acquaint	amplify	assessment	biscuit
acquired	ancient	assigned	blamable
acquisition	anecdote	association	blight
across	anemia	assurance	bookkeeping
actually	angle	athletic	border
acutely	annoyance	attach	bored
adage	annum	attempt	bounteous
addressee	anticipate	attendance	breeding
adequate	antipathy	attendants	brief
adieu	antique	attorneys	bulletin
adjournment	apologetic	authentic	bungalow
adjunct	apparatus	aversion	bureau

burglaries
business

cafeteria
calendar
cameos
campaign
cancel
candidacy
candle
cannon
canon
capital
capitol
  (a building)
carburetor
carnage
carriage
category
caucus
cauldron
cavalier
cavalry
cease
ceiling
cemetery
certain
certified
chagrined
chamois
chancellor
changeable
character
charitable
chauffeur
chef
chisel
Christian
circumstantial
citation
clamorous
classified
clique
clothe
colonel
colossal
column

comedian
commandant
commemorate
commenced
committal
committing
community
comparative
compel
competition
competitors
complacency
conciliatory
conclusively
condemned
confectionery
congenial
congestion
conjunction
connoisseur
conquer
conscript
consequently
conservatory
consistent
consummation
contagious
contemptible
continually
control
controller
convenient
conversant
cooperate
coronation
coroner
corporal
corral
  (an enclosure)
correlation
correspondence
correspondent
corrugated
corset
countenance
courtesies
criticism

crochet
cronies
crowded
crucial
crystallized
currency

death
deceive
decision
declaration
deferred
definite
delegate
deliberate
delicious
delinquent
democrat
demurrage
denunciatory
deodorize
derogatory
description
desecration
desert
desirable
despair
dessert (food)
destruction
detrimental
development
digestible
dilapidated
dining room
diocese
diphtheria
dirigible
disappear
disappearance
disapprove
discipline
discretion
diseases
disgust
dispatch
dispensable
dissatisfied

dissatisfy
dissolution
distillery
distinguished
distributor
dizzy
doctor
dormitory
drastically
dual
duchess
duly
dungarees
duped
dyeing

economical
economy
ecstasy
eczema
effects
efficient
elaborate
electrolysis
embarrass
embassies
emergency
eminently
emolument
emphasis
emphasize
emphatically
endurance
enlargement
enormous
enthusiastic
ephemeral
equilibrium
equinoctial
equipped
error
essential
everlasting
exaggerate
exceed
excel
exercise

exhibition
exhortation
existence
extradite
extraordinary
extravagant

facilitation
faculties
fallibility
falsify
falsity
fascinated
fatal
feudal
filial
finally
financial
financier
finely
fireman
flexible
foggy
foliage
forcible
foreign
foretell
forfeit
fortissimo
forty
fragrance
fraternally
freshman
frightfully
frostbitten
function
fundamental
furl

gallery
galvanized
gelatin
glimpse
gout
government
grammar
grandeur

grapevines
grease
grieve
guaranteed
guardian
guidance
guild
guitar

handicapped
harass
hearth
height
heinous
hence
herald
heritage
hideous
hindrance
histrionic
holly
hosiery
humorists
hybrid
hygienic
hysterics

idiomatic
ignoramus
ignorant
illegitimate
illuminate
illustrative
imminent
impartiality
impeccable
impromptu
incongruity
indecent
indictment
individual
ingenuity
ingenuous
inimitable
innocent
innocuous
insulation

insurance
integrity
intelligence
intercede
interruption
irreparably
itemized

jealous
jeopardy
journal
jovial
judgment
judiciary
jurisdiction

kindergarten
kinsman

label
laboratory
labyrinth
laceration
lacquer
ladies
larceny
latter
leased
legend
leggings
legitimate
leisure
libel
lieutenant
ligament
lightning
likeness
likewise
liquidate
literally
logical
loose
loot
lose
losing
lovable
loveliness

loyalty
lucrative
luxury
lynch

macaroni
mackerel
magnificent
maintain
maintenance
malice
maneuver
mania
manual
marital
marmalade
masquerade
massacre
matinee
matrimony
mattress
maturity
mayonnaise
mechanical
medal
medallion
medicine
medieval
mediocrity
melancholy
memoir
mercantile
mercury
merely
midget
midriff
military
millinery
millionaire
misanthrope
mischievous
misdemeanor
mislaid
misspell
misstep
monarchical
monkeys

morale
moribund
mortgage
movable
murmuring
muscle
museum
myriad

necessity
negligible
negotiate
nervous
nevertheless
nickel
niece
ninety
ninth
notary
notoriety
nowadays
nuisance

obedient
obliged
obstacles
occasionally
occur
occurrence
odyssey
official
omissions
omitted
operated
opportunity
option
ordinance
overwhelming

pacifist
pageant
pamphlet
panel
panicky
papal
parachute
paradoxical

parasite
parliament
parole
partisan
partner
patient
patronize
pattern
peculiar
penitentiary
people's
perilous
perjury
permanent
permissible
persevere
pervade
physical
physician
picnicking
piquancy
pitiful
plagiarism
plague
planned
playwright
pneumonia
policy
politician
portable
portend
portiere
possession
possibilities
post office
postpone
potato
poultry
prairie
preceding
precious
predatory
predilection
preferably
preference
premises
preparation

prestige
presume
presumptuous
previous
primarily
primitive
principal
principalship
prisoner
privilege
probably
proffer
profit
proletarian
promissory
promptness
propaganda
proprietor
psychology
publicity
publicly
punctilious

quantities
quartet
questionnaire
queue
quinine

rabid
raisin
realize
reasonable
receipted
receipts
receptacle
recognizable
recommend
recompense
reconcile
recruit
refrigerator
regrettable
regretted
rehearsal
relevant
relieve

religious
remodel
renaissance
renascence
repetitious
requisition
reservoir
resilience
resonance
resources
response
responsibility
responsible
restaurant
rheostat
rhetorical
rheumatism
rhubarb
rhythm
rickety
ridiculous
righteous
roommate
routine

Sabbath
sacrilegious
salable
salaries
salient
sandwiches
Saturn
saucy
scenes
scissors
screech
scripture
scrutiny
secretary
seize
senior
serenity
series
session
sieges
significant
silhouette

similar	successor	transaction	vague
sincerely	suffrage	transient	valuing
sitting	summarize	transparent	vegetable
sobriquet	superb	treachery	velvet
society	surfeit	tremendous	vengeance
solemn	surgeon	triumph	verbal
soliciting	symmetrical	troupe (theatrical)	villain
sophomore	sympathy	truce	visible
soporific	systematic	tuition	vivisection
source		turkeys	voluntary
sovereign	tableaux	twelfth	voucher
specialized	(or tableaus)	twins	
specific	taciturn	typewriting	warrant
specifically	talcum	typhoid	warranted
speech	tantalizing	tyranny	weather
spiritualist	tariff		Wednesday
squalor	taunt	unanimous	weird
squirrels	technical	unauthorized	welfare
staid	temperament	unbearable	we're
standard	temperature	unconscious	whether
stationary (fixed)	temporarily	undecided	wholly
statistics	tenet	undoubtedly	width
statutes	tennis	undulate	wield
staunch	terse	unfortunately	wiring
steak	tetanus	uniform	witnesses
strengthen	thermometer	unify	woman's
strenuous	thesis	universe	women's
stretch	thorough	unnecessary	worlds
studying	thought	utilize	wrapped
subsidy	together		wretched
suburb	tournament	vacancy	
subversive	tragedy	vacillate	yacht
succeed	traitor	vacuum	yoke

Chapter 18 Spelling

Practice I *Page 173.*

1. reinstate
2. disillusion
3. unnecessary
4. cooperate
5. immortal
6. misspell
7. irreverent
8. illegal
9. acclimate
10. overrate
11. malcontent
12. inaccurate

Practice II *Page 174.*

1. announcement
2. dyeing
3. snappiness
4. association
5. dispensable
6. definitely
7. economical
8. courageous
9. movable
10. necessarily
11. practically
12. portable
13. rudeness
14. guidance
15. truly

Practice III *Page 175.*

1. (4) irrational
2. (2) happiness
3. (4) misspell

4. (1) commencement
5. (1) safety
6. (5) No error
7. (3) accumulate
8. (4) noticeable
9. (2) argument
10. (5) No error

Practice IV *Page 176.*

1. paint´ • er
2. pri´ • vate
3. of´ • fice
4. e • con´ • o • my
5. ad • vise´
6. bal´ • ance
7. dis • sat´ • is • fy
8. de • vel´ • op • ment
9. in • di • vid´ • u • al
10. pre • fer´
11. pref´ • er • ence
12. psy • chol´ • o • gy
13. vac´ • il • late
14. u • nan´ • i • mous
15. wretch´ • ed

Practice V *Page 176.*

1. (2) preference
2. (4) deterred
3. (5) No error
4. (3) deterrent
5. (4) occurrence

Practice VI *Page 177.*

1. niece
2. deceive

3. th<u>ie</u>f
4. rel<u>ie</u>ve
5. n<u>eig</u>h
6. rec<u>ei</u>ve
7. conc<u>ei</u>ve
8. bel<u>ie</u>f
9. n<u>ei</u>ther
10. s<u>ei</u>ze

Practice VII *Page 178.*
1. (2) mouthfuls
2. (1) Chinese
3. (2) sons-in-law
4. (5) No error
5. (1) 8's

Practice VIII *Page 179.*
1. (3) conclusively
2. (2) coronation
3. (1) similar
4. (2) achievement
5. (2) seize
6. (4) duped
7. (3) pertinent
8. (5) No error
9. (3) lovable
10. (5) No error

Practice IX *Page 180.*
1. (5) No error
2. (2) merciful
3. (1) dissolution
4. (5) No error
5. (3) weird
6. (2) government
7. (3) cordially
8. (4) piece
9. (5) No error
10. (5) No error

Practice X *Page 181.*
1. (3) habitually
2. (4) deference
3. (1) candies
4. (2) disappoint
5. (1) potatoes
6. (3) propelling
7. (4) truckfuls
8. (1) truly
9. (5) No error
10. (1) salaries
11. (5) No error
12. (5) No error

Practice XI *Page 182.*
1. (3) niece
2. (4) relief
3. (3) referred
4. (3) assessment
5. (5) No error
6. (4) receipt
7. (1) acquired
8. (4) lieutenant
9. (1) adjournment
10. (1) chef

Practice XII *Page 182.*
1. (2) athletic
2. (3) temperature
3. (3) incessant
4. (1) legitimate
5. (5) No error
6. (5) No error
7. (5) No error
8. (4) tetanus
9. (5) No error
10. (1) fundamental

Practice XIII *Page 183.*
1. **(5)** No error
2. **(1)** absence
3. **(3)** discussion
4. **(2)** athletic
5. **(5)** No error
6. **(1)** Wednesday
7. **(5)** No error
8. **(2)** possession
9. **(5)** No error
10. **(4)** library

Practice XIV *Page 184.*
1. **(2)** aberration
2. **(5)** No error
3. **(1)** ascertain
4. **(2)** resilience
5. **(5)** No error
6. **(3)** lucrative
7. **(4)** surfeit
8. **(1)** wield
9. **(5)** No error
10. **(1)** psychology

Practice XV *Page 185.*
1. **(2)** negligible
2. **(3)** forfeit
3. **(5)** No error
4. **(1)** fallibility
5. **(4)** promissory
6. **(2)** ephemeral
7. **(3)** exhortation
8. **(4)** eczema
9. **(1)** dissatisfied
10. **(1)** deferred

Practice XVI *Page 185.*
1. **(2)** resonance
2. **(3)** patient

3. **(1)** secretary
4. **(2)** distinguished
5. **(5)** No error
6. **(2)** chauffeur
7. **(3)** permissible
8. **(3)** recognizable
9. **(2)** mischievous
10. **(2)** sovereign

Practice XVII *Page 186.*
1. **(2)** carburetor
2. **(1)** biscuit
3. **(5)** No error
4. **(5)** No error
5. **(3)** relevant
6. **(4)** weather
7. **(1)** exceed
8. **(2)** foreign
9. **(3)** equipped
10. **(2)** corrugated

Practice XVIII *Page 187.*
1. **(3)** exercise
2. **(2)** hindrance
3. **(4)** deceive
4. **(5)** No error
5. **(2)** mackerel
6. **(3)** pneumonia
7. **(1)** temperament
8. **(1)** abundance
9. **(1)** accumulation
10. **(2)** ancient

Practice XIX *Page 188.*
1. **(1)** consummation
2. **(4)** assessment
3. **(2)** impeccable
4. **(3)** fascinated

5. **(1)** rhythm
6. **(1)** controller
7. **(5)** No error
8. **(2)** acquaint
9. **(3)** conversant
10. **(3)** mechanical

Practice XX *Page 188.*
1. **(3)** symmetrical
2. **(2)** supersede
3. **(5)** No error
4. **(3)** precede
5. **(1)** annoyance

Chapter 19

BUILDING VOCABULARY

Costard: "O, they have liv'd long on the almsbasket of
words. I marvel thy master hath not eaten
thee for a word; for thou art not so long by
the head as *honorificabilitudinitatibus*; thou
art easier swallowed than a flapdragon."

—William Shakespeare
from *Love's Labour's Lost*, Act V, Scene 1

A Word With You . . .

Costard, a clown in Shakespeare's comedy, uses one of the longest words in the English language (almost as long as *antidisestablishmentarianism*) in his conversation with Holofernes, the schoolmaster. Not only did Shakespeare know that 27-letter word, but he knew thousands upon thousands of other choice vocabulary words. Youngsters in his time were exposed to Latin and Greek in the schools and were able to develop a mastery of English words through their knowledge of prefixes, suffixes, and roots in those languages.

You may not catch up to Shakespeare, but you can get started in a modest way with the hints offered in this chapter.

Some Facts About Vocabulary

We use words to think. A large and precise vocabulary leads to clear thinking.

The words we use "talk" about us. They create an impression of intelligence or dullness, success or failure.

The average person stops collecting new words early in life—probably during the twenties. Only by a conscious effort do we continue to add words to our vocabulary. This chapter will show you how to expand your vocabulary.

There are many ways to increase your vocabulary. If you are an avid reader, you've found the most natural way. But what if you're not? You can choose one or more of the following methods to help you. You may find that certain ways appeal to you more than others.

To increase your vocabulary, take advantage of what you like to do. When we like what we're doing, we learn faster. Building vocabulary may not be your idea of fun, but if you start with a topic you like, you might develop an interest.

Are you interested in history? Learn new words by studying their histories. Many English words include Latin, Greek, and other languages in their histories. One of our most frequently used words is an example of this. The word *television* came to English from the French: *télévision*. But television was not originally a French word. In fact, its journey through history includes both Latin and Greek.

tele from the Greek *tēle*, meaning at a distance, or far off
vision from the Latin *vīsiō*, meaning see

Put the two parts together and you have a good definition of television: pictures taken at a distance that you can see. Let's see how this works with other common words.

Pratice I

Directions: Draw a line from the Latin and Greek word parts in the left-hand column to the English words in the right-hand column.

Note: In the dictionary, histories of words follow definitions and are placed in brackets.

Latin and Greek Word Parts	English Words
1. [Greek *tekne*, skill, art + *logos*, word speech]	video
2. [Latin *alere*, to nourish]	computer
3. [Latin *com*, together, jointly + Latin *dominium*, property]	alimony
4. [Latin *com*, together + Latin *putare*, to think, reckon]	technology
5. [Latin *videre*, to see]	condominium

Practice II

Directions: Use your dictionary to discover the histories of the following words. Notice that a word may have gone through more than one language before it reached English. A word's most recent history is found at the beginning of the bracketed information. Its earliest history is at the end. Copy the earliest history.

1. compress _____
2. vindictive _____
3. pedicure _____
4. manicure _____
5. unique _____

Latin roots are found over and over again in English words. Once you know the meanings of these roots, you can unlock the meanings of many English words. The following are just a few examples:

Common Latin Roots	English Words
bene	well
dicere	to say
facere	to do, to make
volens	wishing
unus	one, single
signum	sign
portare	to carry
manu	by hand

Pratice III

Directions: Can you guess from which Latin root each of the following words was formed? Use the above list to make your decision.

1. united _____
2. factory _____
3. benefit _____
4. insignia _____
5. portable _____
6. dictation _____
7. volunteer _____

Sometimes two roots combine to make another word.

> *bene + dicere* = benediction = a blessing, or "saying well"
> *bene + facere* = benefactor = one who does something good for another
> *bene + volens* = benevolent = wishing others well, kindly

Building Your Vocabulary With Prefixes

Perhaps you are interested in building your vocabulary. You can build words by learning how prefixes add to the meanings of roots. Below is a partial list of common prefixes that will help you build a larger vocabulary.

COMMON PREFIXES

Prefix	Meaning	Example
ab-	away, from	absent, absorb
ad-	to, toward	advice, adhere
ante-	before	antebellum, antecedent
anti-	against	antisocial, antihistamine
auto-	self	autobiography
bi-	two, twice	biannual
bio-	life	biology, biography
com-, con-	with, together	combine, conflict, confederate
contra-	against	contradict, contraband
de-	down from	debase, decamp
dia-	through, around	diagonal, diameter
dis-	not, apart	disapprove
en-	put into, on	engrave
ex-	out of	except, expel
il-	not	illegal
im-, in-	not	impossible, inadequate
in-	in, into	inward, ingest, insert
inter-	between, among	interfere, interject
ir-	not	irrational
mal-	evil, wrong	malicious, malign
mono-	one	monorail, monotone
non-	not	nonfiction
post-	after	postpone, postdate
pre-	before	precede, prescription
pro-	for, forward	promote, provide
re-	again, back	reapply, return
semi-	half	semicircle
sub-	under	submarine
super-	over, above	supervisor
trans-	across	transportation
tri-	three	triangle
un-	not	untied, unbutton

Practice IV

Directions: Think about the meaning each prefix adds to these words. The prefixes are underlined. Answer the questions. If you are in doubt about the meanings, check the list above or your dictionary. Prefixes appear in this way: pre-.

Prefixes	Meanings
predate	1. Which prefixes make root words negative?_____
impossible	_____
disorganize	_____
return	2. Which prefix means "evil"?
extract	_____
untie	3. Which prefix means "self"?_____
malodorous	4. Which prefix means "back" or "again"?
postnatal	_____
amoral	5. Which prefix means "after"?_____
automobile	6. Which prefix means "out"?_____
	7. Which prefix means "before"?_____

Practice V

Directions: Make new words by adding a prefix to each word below. If you need to check the meaning of a prefix, look back at the long list of prefixes on page 201.

dis-	trans-	un-	sub-	re-	auto-	pre-	bio-
post-	ir-	non-	bi-	im-	ab-	anti-	ex-

1. _____view
2. _____agree
3. _____biography
4. _____live
5. _____dress
6. _____contract
7. _____continental
8. _____port

9. _____profit
10. _____sent
11. _____biotic
12. _____script
13. _____sphere
14. _____regular
15. _____mortal
16. _____cycle

Building Your Vocabulary With Action and Descriptive Words

How would you like to enlarge your vocabulary and improve your writing skills—*at the same time?* You can accomplish both by increasing the number of action and descriptive words you know. Begin by using the word *get* less frequently and by using precise words more.

Less Interesting	Precise
1. We should *get* a new computer for the office.	1. We should (*buy, lease*) a new computer for the office.
2. Milton tried to *get* me to take his side in the debate.	2. Milton tried to *persuade* me to take his side in the debate.
3. The first baseman *got* hit by the pitcher's fast ball.	3. The pitcher's fast ball *struck* the first baseman.
4. When he spoke of his war buddies, he *got* sad.	4. When he spoke of his war buddies, he *grew* sad.

Try to avoid overused words. Learn new descriptive words to replace them. Start with the word *very*. *Very* plus an overused word hides a precise word.

Overused Words	Precise Words
very pretty	captivating
very new	novel
very lazy	indolent
very funny	amusing
very slow	languid

Practice VI

Directions: Replace the italicized word in each sentence with a descriptive one chosen from the list below.

ancient   swift   overjoyed   terrified   craves

1. I am *very afraid* of night noises._____
2. We toured a *very old* ruin in Rome._____
3. A *very fast* runner won the marathon._____
4. My friend, Sheila, *really wants* fame._____
5. I was *very glad* to hear of your good fortune._____

This chapter offers only a few techniques for increasing your vocabulary. There are many more. In fact, entire books have been written on the subject. Now that you have completed a sample improvement program, don't stop building your vocabulary. Be aware of new words. Keep a list of them, define them, and write them in sentences. Try to use them in your everyday conversations, letters, or memos. Your personal gains will make it well worth the effort.

Chapter 19   Building Vocabulary

Practice I *Page 199.*

1. technology
2. alimony
3. condominium
4. computer
5. video

Practice II *Page 199.*

1. [Latin: com-, together + premere, to press]
2. [Latin vindicare, to revenge]
3. [French pédicure: pedi + Latin cūrāre, to take care of]
4. [Latin manus, hand + cūra, care]
5. [Latin ūnicus, only]

Practice III *Page 200.*

1. unus—one, single
2. facere—to do
3. bene—well
4. signum—sign
5. portare—to carry
6. dicere—to say
7. volens—wishing

Practice IV *Page 201.*

1. im-, dis-, un-, a-
2. mal-
3. auto-
4. re-
5. post-
6. ex-
7. pre-

Practice V *Page 202.*

1. preview
2. disagree
3. autobiography
4. relive
5. undress
6. subcontract
7. transcontinental
8. import
9. nonprofit
10. absent
11. antibiotic
12. postscript
13. biosphere
14. irregular
15. immortal
16. bicycle

Practice VI *Page 203.*

1. terrified
2. ancient
3. swift
4. craves
5. overjoyed

Chapter 20

WORD USAGE

I was a pretty good student back in Wilberforce in the
1930's but there were a few things that always gave
me trouble. I never felt comfortable with *affect* and
effect, *capital* and *capitol*, *beside* and *besides*—and
hundreds of others like that with which Miss Conway
used to torture us every Friday.
"Now we come to words frequently confused," she
would drool, adjusting wig and lorgnette, her eyes
brightening with anticipation.
I think what really turned me off on that subject
was when old Mr. Wentworth tried to show me the
difference between *principal* and *principle*,
pontificating that "Your princi*pal* is your *pal*," and
spraying me with tobacco juice in the process.
I didn't believe him then, and I still have trouble
with those words, forty years later. Traumatic, I guess.

—Oliver L. Kenworthy
Bluegrass Lawyer

A Word With You . . .

English seems to have so many more words that sound alike and words that are frequently confused than any other language. The same problems young Oliver Kenworthy
found in Wilberforce, Kentucky may have plagued you, too.

In the following pages, you will find some of the more troublesome sets of words. See
how well you can handle them.

Commonly Misused Words

Many words are easily confused. Some words sound the same but are spelled differently
and have different meanings. These are *homophones*.

EXAMPLES:

1. A full moon *shone* brightly last night.
   The film was *shown* on TV.
2. Once we nail up this *board*, the tool shed will be finished.
   I was very *bored* during that long, rainy week.
3. The *pain* in my lower back increases during rainy weather.
   Could you please replace the cracked *pane* of glass?

Other words are confusing because they sound almost the same.

EXAMPLES:

1. The legislators had an angry debate before *adopting* a policy on school funding.
   Since we moved from the West Coast to the Midwest, we've had to *adapt* to colder weather.
2. The politician's *allusions* to his opponent's past errors in judgment were unnecessary.
   In the story *A Christmas Carol*, Scrooge's visitors were *illusions*.
3. How do you think the current job action will *affect* management?
   I think the *effect* will be that management will meet labor's demands.

In order to improve your understanding of easily confused words, study the following list. An example of correct usage is given for each commonly confused word.

accept—except
I *accept* your apology.
Everyone *except* John may leave.

adapt—adopt
When visiting a foreign country, you must *adapt* yourself to the customs practiced there.
The Grays plan to *adopt* several hard-to-place children.

advice—advise
Because of Michael's excellent *advice*, Bob completed a successful business deal.
Michael will *advise* Bob to be daring.

affect—effect
The accident did not *affect* Thomas.
The *effect* on his brother, however, was great.

aggravate—annoy
If you continue to scratch that rash, you will *aggravate* your condition.
Your constant scratching *annoys* me.

all ready—already
Call me when you are *all ready* to go.
By the time Sue arrived, we had *already* finished dinner.

all right
(*Alright* is not an acceptable word.)
Is it *all right* to leave this window open?

all together—altogether
The four of us were *all together* at the coffee shop.
This book is *altogether* too long.

allude—refer
In passing, the speaker *alluded* to the effectiveness of Internet marketing.
The speaker *referred* to statistics that demonstrated the effectiveness of Internet marketing.

allusion—illusion
I resent your *allusion* to my cooking as comparable with MacDonald's.
You have the *illusion* that I enjoy classical music; I don't.

altar—alter
Many a would-be-bride has been left at the *altar*.
Would it be inconvenient for you to *alter* your plans for this weekend?

among—between
The campaign director divided the state *among* his *three* most competent assistants.
In many of today's homes, the care of the children is divided *between* the *two* parents.

amount—number
You would not believe the *amount* of time I have spent on this project.
I wish I could reuse the *number* of hours I have spent on this project.

angry at—angry with
Ira was *angry at* the thought of working overtime.
Ira was *angry with* his boss for insisting that Ira work overtime.

anxious—eager
I am *anxious* about the diagnosis.
I am *eager* to see your new car.

anywhere
(There is no such word as *anywheres*.)
Marlene cannot find her glasses *anywhere*.

as—like
Paula looks very much *like* her sister.
Rosemary swims *as* well as Pam does.
Carl looks *as* if he needs a nap.

ascent—assent
The *ascent* to the tower was frighteningly steep.
Because I value his opinion, I will not go ahead with the project without his *assent*.

awful—very—real
This fish tastes *awful*.
This fish tastes *very* bad.
Are these pearls *real* or imitation?

because of—due to
Because of our tight budget, we're vacationing at home.
We're vacationing at home *due to* our tight budget.

beside—besides
Joto likes to sit *beside* Sam at the table.
Who, *besides* Holly, is taking tai chi lessons?

born—borne
Our youngest child was *born* last month.
John has *borne* the burden by himself for long enough.

borrow from
(*Borrow off* is unacceptable.)
Mickey *borrowed* the book *from* Allen.

borrow—lend—loan
May I *borrow* your pocket calculator?
I can *lend* you my mechanical pencil.
I need a $500 *loan*.

brake—break
I prefer a bicycle with a foot *brake*.
Because he did not *brake* in time, Herman crashed into the tree.
If you are not careful, you will *break* that dish.

can—may
Some fortunate people *can* arrange their time to include work and pleasure.
You *may* hunt deer only during certain seasons.

capital—capitol—Capitol
Ricardo has 90 percent of the necessary *capital* for his new business venture.
Trenton is the *capital* of New Jersey.
New Jersey's *capitol* building is in Trenton.
Did you visit the *Capitol* when you were in Washington, D.C.?

cite—sight—site
An attorney often *cites* previous cases that support his argument.
One of the most beautiful *sights* in the country is the Grand Canyon.
The alternative school will be built on this *site*.

coarse—course
I find this *coarse* fabric to be abrasive.
That is an acceptable *course* of action.

complement—compliment
Rice nicely *complements* a chicken dinner.
I'd like to *compliment* you for doing such a thorough job.

communicate with—contact
I will *communicate with* (call, write, speak) you in May.
Contact (call, write, speak) me when you return.

continually—continuously

Tom is *continually* late.

The river runs *continuously* through several towns.

council—counsel

Our neighbor has just been elected to the town *council*.

The troubled man sought his friend's *counsel*.

credible—creditable—credulous

Because the defendant had a good alibi, his story seemed *credible*.

As a result of many hours of hard work, Joe presented a *creditable* report.

Sally is so *credulous* that one could sell her the Brooklyn Bridge.

currant—current

His unusual recipe called for *currant* jelly.

Because the *current* was swift, the canoe was difficult to maneuver.

desert—dessert

The *desert* is very hot and dry.

More and more young soldiers have been *deserting* the army.

Apple pie is America's favorite *dessert*.

die—dye

Eventually, every living thing *dies*.

I'll never *dye* my hair.

discover—invent

The builders *discovered* oil on our land.

Whitney *invented* the cotton gin.

disinterested—uninterested

The *disinterested* observer of the accident was certain that the driver of the blue car was at fault.

Because Sheila was *uninterested* in the lecture, she paid no attention.

draw—drawer

Marlene *draws* very well.

She keeps her pads and pencils in the top *drawer* of her desk.

emigration—immigration

The Harlows *emigrated* from England.

After *immigrating* to the United States, the Harlows settled in Kansas.

famous—infamous

John Simpson is a *famous* pianist.

Arthur Jones is an *infamous* car thief.

farther—further

My car can run *farther* on this other brand of gasoline.

I cannot continue this discussion any *further*.

fewer—less

Gerry invited *fewer* people to her office party this year.

Since she moved from a house to an apartment, she has *less* space.

formally—formerly
Please dress *formally* for the wedding.
I was *formerly* employed by a jewelry company, but I am now working in a bank.

good—well
Maria performed a *good* job.
Maria performed the job *well*.
Maria doesn't feel *good*.
Maria doesn't feel *well*.

grate—great
The continuous harsh and rasping sound *grated* on my nerves.
A *grate* in the sidewalk covered the opening to the sewer.
Ernest Hemingway was considered a *great* writer in his own lifetime.

healthful—healthy
Orange juice is *healthful*.
If you eat properly and exercise sufficiently, you will be *healthy*.

imply—infer
Although he did not state it directly, the candidate *implied* that his opponent was dishonest.
From the mayor's constructive suggestions, the townsfolk *inferred* that he was trying his best to do a good job.

in—into
Marlene stood *in* the living room.
Wayne came rushing *into* the room.

it's—its
I think *it's* a fine idea!
The dog wagged *its* tail.

kind of—sort of—type of
(These expressions can be used interchangeably. They should never be followed by "a.")
Mrs. Peterson always buys that *kind of* meat.
I like that *sort of* book.
This is my favorite *type of* music.

later—latter
Sue can finish the report *later* this week.
I can meet you Tuesday or Thursday. The *latter* would be more convenient.

lead—led
I'll need one more *lead* pipe to complete this plumbing job.
I only enjoy a race when I am in the *lead*.
John was unfamiliar with that route, so Jules *led* the way.

learn—teach
Harriet is having great difficulty with her efforts to *learn* flowcharting.
Leslie is patiently trying to *teach* Harriet how to flowchart.

leave—let
If the customs officer finds nothing wrong with a traveler's baggage, the officer *lets* the traveler *leave* the area.

loose—lose
Eric was excited about his first *loose* tooth.
If you step out of line, you will *lose* your place.

manor—manner
The *manor*, or landed estate, dates back to feudal times in England.
They don't like the *manner* in which you responded to my sincere question.

miner—minor
The coal *miners* were trapped during the cave-in.
The young man was not allowed to enter the bar because he was a *minor*.

moral—morale
Because of Ed's high *moral* standards, he returned the wallet to its owner.
The story of *The Boy Who Cried Wolf* has a *moral* that applies to everyone.
Because the war was *immoral*, the *morale* of the troops was low.

nauseated—nauseous
When we drove past the skunk, the car was filled with a *nauseous* odor.
The odor of the skunk *nauseated* Sara.

pail—pale
The amount of paint needed to finish the job would fill a one-gallon *pail*.
Because of her long illness, Maria's complexion was very *pale*.

passed—past
We *passed* the Model T on the parkway.
You cannot always try to recapture the *past*.

peace—piece
If we work together, perhaps we can end the war and achieve a truly lasting *peace*.
I could never eat just one *piece* of candy.

persecute—prosecute
Older children frequently *persecute* their younger siblings.
If you do not return the stolen money, you will be *prosecuted*.

personal—personnel
The items written in a young girl's diary are very *personal*.
When applying for a job at a large company, you must go to the *personnel* office.

plain—plane
The meaning is quite *plain* and requires no further explanation.
We rode for miles across the open *plains* of Kansas.
The *plane* landed smoothly.
Please *plane* that wood so that I can build a birdhouse with it.

precede—proceed
A preface always *precedes* the body of a book.
Don't let me interrupt you; *proceed* with your work.

practicable—practical
Studying computer programming is a *practicable* plan in today's job market.
Computerizing payroll is a *practical* business decision.

principal—principle
A school is as good as the teachers and *principal*.
The *principal* actors in the play remained for a final rehearsal of the second act.
The *principle* upon which many simple machines are based is frequently the lever.

quiet—quite
As the campers lay down for the night, *quiet* settled over the campsite.
That is *quite* a strong accusation.

raise—rise
When we *raise* the flag, we'd like everyone in the audience to *rise*.

sit—set
The chairman requested committee members to *sit* down.
The artist *set* his clay on the workbench and began to create a sculpture.

stationary—stationery
Theater seats are most often *stationary*.
When I write letters, I always use my personal *stationery*.

sure—surely
I am *sure* Alice will be at the meeting.
Surely, you don't expect me to take notes.

teach—learn
Miss Smith *teaches* math every Thursday.
Ron Jonas, a student, *learns* math from Miss Smith.

than—then
New York is smaller than Wyoming, but Wyoming has a much smaller population *than* New York.
First the eastern seaboard was colonized, *then* settlers moved westward.

their—there—they're
When leaving *their* war-torn country, most of the refugees left all *their* possessions behind.
There are no easy answers to the problem of worldwide hunger.
As for the members of Congress, *they're* not always responsible for the wisest decisions.

through—threw
The special crew worked *through* the night to repair the damaged wires.
When the Little League pitcher *threw* the ball, her teammates cheered.

to—too—two
United States presidents often travel *to* foreign countries.
Many foreign heads of state visit the United States, *too*.
Two visitors were the late Anwar Sadat and Margaret Thatcher.

vain—vane—vein
The *vain* man peered at his reflection in every window as he strolled down the street.
A rooster is the traditional weather *vane* symbol.
Veins are passageways that carry blood to the heart.

vale—veil
Vale is an uncommonly used synonym for valley.
The mourning woman hid her grief behind her *veil*.

wade—weighed
The smaller children were told to *wade* near the shore.
The clerk *weighed* and priced the fresh vegetables.

waist—waste
If you measure your *waist* before you go to buy a pattern, you will avoid much confusion.
Don't *waste* precious time gossiping on the phone.

weather—whether
Tomorrow morning the general *weather* conditions will determine the distance of our first day's hike.
Whether or not you wish to pay taxes, you must.

who's—whose
The teacher asked, "*Who's* responsible for clean-up today?"
We must determine *whose* turn it is.

writes—rights—rites
Kurt Vonnegut *writes* excellent fiction.
Their attorney explained the family's *rights* in the lawsuit.
Religious *rites* and rituals are at the center of many cultures.

your—you're
Your references are excellent.
You're hired.

Practice I

Directions: Blacken the circle that corresponds to the number of the correct word to complete each sentence.

1. <u>Your</u> <u>You're</u> on the right track.   ① ②
    1   2

2. I enjoy a cold <u>bier</u> <u>beer</u> on a warm day.   ① ②
         1   2

3. Please use the main <u>aisle</u> <u>isle</u> in the theater.   ① ②
         1 2

4. We left early because we were <u>bored</u> <u>board.</u>   ① ②
         1   2

5. The ship traveled through the <u>straight</u> <u>strait.</u>   ① ②
         1   2

6. The _sum_ _some_ collected was not significant.   ① ②
      1   2

7. Please, don't _waist_ _waste_ my time.   ① ②
              1   2

8. The queen sat gracefully on her _thrown_ _throne._   ① ②
                                    1   2

9. Buddy would never _steal_ _steel_ from anyone.   ① ②
                      1   2

10. The wise old Indian knew many interesting _tales_ _tails._   ① ②
                                               1   2

Practice II

Directions: Blacken the circle that corresponds to the number of the sentence in each group that contains an incorrectly used word. If there is no error, blacken number 5.

1. (1) The jewel was shown to the prospective buyer.   ① ② ③ ④ ⑤
   (2) Her hair shown in the bright sunlight.
   (3) The sun shone brightly this morning.
   (4) I have never been shown how to use this machine.
   (5) No error.

2. (1) I would like you to cite at least three examples.   ① ② ③ ④ ⑤
   (2) Her husband was cited for contempt.
   (3) For that sight, we're planning a municipal parking lot.
   (4) When the bridge is within your sight, start looking for our street.
   (5) No error

3. (1) The some of these figures is 182.   ① ② ③ ④ ⑤
   (2) Take some cake with you to the picnic.
   (3) I have some clothes that are no longer useful to me.
   (4) That sum of money is to be labeled petty cash.
   (5) No error

4. (1) Before the development of the tape recorder, Braille was the   ① ② ③ ④ ⑤
       sole method of communicating fine literature to sightless people.
   (2) Lemon sole is one of the many varieties of fish that can enhance
       a meatless diet.
   (3) Sole music is very popular among people of all ages.
   (4) The concept of the soul does not have the same meaning in all
       religions.
   (5) No error

5. (1) Napoleon had a great deal at steak when he decided to   ① ② ③ ④ ⑤
       invade Russia.
   (2) Finally, William hammered the last stake into the ground.
   (3) I would enjoy a steak dinner tonight.
   (4) Sue was upset because her job was at stake.
   (5) No error

6. (1) Please, remain stationary while I draw your picture.   ① ② ③ ④ ⑤
   (2) Irene wrote the letter on her finest stationary.
   (3) I believe you can buy staples at the stationery store.

     (4) This appliance cannot be moved; it is stationary.

     (5) No error

7. (1) Ilene attended a conference there.

     (2) There is the book I've been wanting to read.

     (3) There's is a truly open relationship.

     (4) I have never been to their summer home.

     (5) No error

① ② ③ ④ ⑤

8. (1) Those two stairs make this house bi-level.

     (2) Hers was hardly a friendly stair.

     (3) We've already swept the stairs today.

     (4) Don't stare at me!

     (5) No error

① ② ③ ④ ⑤

9. (1) Karthik rents a suite of offices downtown.

     (2) We've already eaten our portion of sweets for this day.

     (3) The visiting lecturer's hotel suite was paid for by the university.

     (4) Don't make the chocolate pudding overly sweet.

     (5) No error

① ② ③ ④ ⑤

10. (1) The boat was taken in toe after its motor failed.

     (2) We were towed all the way to shore.

     (3) At the football game we had a bad case of frozen toes.

     (4) When you go beyond your own authority, you must step on somebody's toes.

     (5) No error

① ② ③ ④ ⑤

Practice III

Directions: Blacken the circle that corresponds to the number of the incorrect word in each sentence. If there is no error, blacken number 5.

1. The guide *led* us to a *straight* path *through* the
      1   2   3
woods and to a lovely *veil. No error*
              4   5

① ② ③ ④ ⑤

2. My neighbor *dies* her *hair* *two* times every *week. No error*
           1   2   3   4   5

① ② ③ ④ ⑤

3. We had *already* planned our vacation to an unknown
          1
isle when our friends said that they were *all ready* to
 2   3
come along *to. No error*
     4   5

① ② ③ ④ ⑤

4. You are *all together* mistaken about *their* decision
         1   2
to write to the newspaper. *No error*
 3 4   5

① ② ③ ④ ⑤

5. Ira Swanson *writes* about the religious *rights* of the
          1   2
Indians who inhabit the island *right* off the coast *of*
                    3   4
Japan. *No error*
    5

① ② ③ ④ ⑤

6. The _capital_ of each state is the _cite_ of the _capitol building_   ① ② ③ ④ ⑤
       1   2   3
   of that state and main attraction for _sightseers._ _No error_
                                        4   5

7. Because the _currant_ was _strong,_ we had _great_ difficulty   ① ② ③ ④ ⑤
               1   2   3
   reaching _shore._ _No error_
          4   5

8. I, for one, _didn't appreciate_ the _manor_ in _which_ she   ① ② ③ ④ ⑤
              1   2   3   4
   answered. _No error_
            5

9. We _truly_ felt that the _exorbitant_ _expenditure_ was a   ① ② ③ ④ ⑤
         1   2   3
   waist. _No error_
    4   5

10. We _wade_ both _arguments,_ and we decided in _favor_ of   ① ② ③ ④ ⑤
         1   2   3
    the _contract._ _No error_
         4   5

11. The _nutritious_ food, the fine _weather,_ and the _exercise_   ① ② ③ ④ ⑤
         1   2   3
    made us feel _grate._ _No error_
           4   5

12. The _members_ of the _panel_ were asked to leave _their_   ① ② ③ ④ ⑤
         1   2   3
    jackets in the _outer_ office. _No error_
           4   5

13. We _heard_ Pete _moan,_ and we saw that he _had become_   ① ② ③ ④ ⑤
       1   2   3
    deadly _pail._ _No error_
        4   5

Practice IV

Directions: Blacken the circle that corresponds to the number of the incorrect word in each passage. If there is no error, blacken number 5.

1. Because I was _anxious_ to avoid another argument, I   ① ② ③ ④ ⑤
                1
   accepted Roy's apology. His story seemed _credible_ so there
     2   3
   was no point in carrying the argument any _further._ _No error_
                                  4   5

2. Sue left the elevator and _proceeded_ to the _personal_ office.   ① ② ③ ④ ⑤
                           1   2

   The cold, efficient interviewer lowered Sue's _morale,_ but she
                                      3

   was _eager_ to obtain the job. _No error_
      4   5

3. The _effect_ of the unusual visitor on the family was startling.   ① ② ③ ④ ⑤
      1

   Mother _adopted_ Mrs. Chuggley's speech habits; father _altered_
           2   3

   his smoking habits to suit Mrs. Chuggley's allergy; and I
   found myself _continuously_ saying, "Yes, Ma'am." _No error_
              4   5

4. The _course_ of action determined by the city _counsel_ at its last   ① ② ③ ④ ⑤
      1   2

   meeting has _already_ begun to _affect_ us. _No error_
           3   4   5

5. Family gatherings are _always_ interesting. Grandpa is usually   ① ② ③ ④ ⑤
                  1

   angry with Aunt Jean. Rhoda insists upon sitting _besides_
    2   3

   Grandma. Mother tries to divide her attention equally _among_
                                    4

   all of the guests. _No error_
         5

6. I was _altogether_ shocked when Sam returned the ice bucket   ① ② ③ ④ ⑤
        1

   that he had _borrowed from_ us last spring. When I _complemented_
            2   3

   him for returning it so promptly, Sam's red face told me that he
   understood my _implied_ sarcasm. _No error_
          4   5

7. Please put the change _into_ your pocket before you lose it. It's   ① ② ③ ④ ⑤
            1

   hard enough to keep pace with today's prices without carelessly
   losing money. That _kind of_ carelessness makes me _loose_ my
    2   3   4

   temper. _No error_
      5

8. The *minor* *led* his *team* into the shaft. After several hours of   ① ② ③ ④ ⑤
      1   2   3

dangerous work, they *ascended* jubilantly. *No error*
              4   5

9. I am *formally* engaged in a program of good nutrition. I   ① ② ③ ④ ⑤
       1

always eat a *healthy* breakfast. I consume *fewer* sweets and I
            2   3

spend *less* time stalking the refrigerator for snacks. *No error*
      4   5

10. Sue asked if she *might* go swimming at the pool. Although   ① ② ③ ④ ⑤
          1

Sue *can* swim *quite* well, her mother refused permission. Sue
   2   3

was angry and said she was being *prosecuted.* *No error*
                      4   5

Practice V

Directions: Blacken the circle that corresponds to the number of the sentence in each group that contains an incorrectly used word. If there is no error, blacken number 5.

1. (1) The damage has all ready been done.   ① ② ③ ④ ⑤
   (2) Father was altogether too surprised to speak.
   (3) Events have borne out my prediction.
   (4) The altar was adorned with flowers, incense, and a bronze statue of Buddha.
   (5) No error

2. (1) The family was all together for the annual picnic.   ① ② ③ ④ ⑤
   (2) Terry's mother cautioned, "If you break a window, you will have to pay for it."
   (3) Paris is the capital of France.
   (4) My mother was borne in Canada.
   (5) No error

3. (1) Was his work all right?   ① ② ③ ④ ⑤
   (2) I use old shirts as cleaning cloths.
   (3) The dome on the capital is lighted each night.
   (4) Everyone was wearing his best clothes.
   (5) No error

4. (1) I applied the brakes immediately.   ① ② ③ ④ ⑤
   (2) Cars are borne across the river on a ferry.
   (3) Are you feeling all right?
   (4) When you are all ready, I will pick you up.
   (5) No error

5. (1) John is considered an imminent member of congress. ① ② ③ ④ ⑤
   (2) The duke was received formally at the ambassador's home.
   (3) Out of deference to her loss, we did not resume the music.
   (4) We could hear a vigorous discussion of current problems.
   (5) No error

6. (1) When you give your report, be sure to cite as many ① ② ③ ④ ⑤
       concrete examples as possible.
   (2) "I am surely not guilty of excessive spending!" he shouted.
   (3) We are not likely to meet again in the near future.
   (4) Because of several miner disagreements, the discussion came
       to a halt.
   (5) No error

7. (1) The politician was asked to accede to the council's wishes. ① ② ③ ④ ⑤
   (2) I am opposed to the construction of the bridge for two good
       reasons.
   (3) Do not hire anyone whose personality doesn't complement
       the rest of the staff.
   (4) Prospective homeowners are eager for reduction of the
       mortgage interest rate.
   (5) No error

8. (1) The attorney set fourth his ideas and told us all of the ① ② ③ ④ ⑤
       angles of his case.
   (2) Will you sign this senior citizen petition?
   (3) The beauty of the mountains exceeded all our expectations.
   (4) Mike is quite an athlete.
   (5) No error

9. (1) Wayne is likely to be defeated. ① ② ③ ④ ⑤
   (2) There was nothing to do but accept his plan.
   (3) I am opposed too airing family matters in public.
   (4) The crowd was quiet until the rocket ascended.
   (5) No error

10. (1) After listening with great patience, the diplomat listed ① ② ③ ④ ⑤
        his objectives.
    (2) No one knew him as well as I.
    (3) Choose your coarse of action and stick to it.
    (4) I think the skirt is too loose on you.
    (5) No error

Practice VI

Directions: Blacken the circle that corresponds to the number of the incorrect word in each passage. If there is no error, blacken number 5.

1. The <u>principal</u> members of the committee decided to <u>lead</u> a   ① ② ③ ④ ⑤
        1   2

    discussion about the <u>peace</u> movement and the <u>type of a</u> person
                            3   4

    attracted to it. <u>No error</u>
                       5

2. Many of the <u>minors</u> in the audience began to <u>lose</u> <u>there</u> tempers   ① ② ③ ④ ⑤
                    1   2   3

    because the discussion <u>seemed</u> partisan. <u>No error</u>
    3   4   5

3. The chairman <u>tryed</u> <u>to</u> explain that the <u>principle</u> of freedom   ① ② ③ ④ ⑤
                   1   2   3

    to pursue one's beliefs was not the <u>main</u> issue. <u>No error</u>
                                           4   5

4. It was not the committee's intention to <u>persecute</u> anyone but   ① ② ③ ④ ⑤
                                               1

    rather to make <u>plain</u> the <u>already</u> divergent viewpoints and to
                      2   3

    <u>precede</u> to bring them together. <u>No error</u>
       4   5

5. The <u>main</u> effect of the chairman's speech was <u>to</u> <u>quiet</u> the   ① ② ③ ④ ⑤
          1   2   3

    audience so that the discussion could continue <u>farther.</u> <u>No error</u>
                                                      4   5

6. The next speaker <u>waisted</u> more time by expressing anger   ① ② ③ ④ ⑤
                       1

    with the young people <u>present</u> rather than <u>formally</u> addressing
                            2   3

    the <u>issues</u> at hand. <u>No error</u>
          4   5

7. I am certain that the committee <u>learned</u> a lesson about   ① ② ③ ④ ⑤
                                      1

    discussing <u>volatile</u> issues. Next time it will <u>altar</u> <u>its</u> presentation
                 2   3   4

    so that speakers will be more to the point. <u>No error</u>
                                                  5

8. That way, <u>less</u> misunderstandings will occur. The Lakeview   ① ② ③ ④ ⑤
                1

    Town <u>Council</u> had planned a <u>similar</u> discussion, but changed
           2   3

    <u>its</u> program. <u>No error</u>
      4   5

9. It will have a speaker on the new _adoption_ laws. Many people
                                    1
① ② ③ ④ ⑤

   need _advise_ on this topic. It _plainly_ will be less controversial
        2   3

   than the _peace_ movement was. _No error_
            4   5

10. The council has _all ready_ advertised in local papers and
                        1
① ② ③ ④ ⑤

   expects a large _number_ of people to be _eager_ to attend. _No error_
     2   3   4   5

Practice VII

Directions: Circle the error in each incorrect sentence. If there is no error, put a "C" next to the sentence. Write the correct word to replace each error.

1. Ahmed wants to lend your calculator.   _____
2. Please contact me by phone.   _____
3. The book alluded to the Civil War in great depth.   _____
4. Company B's continued dumping into the stream has
   aggravated the pollution problem.   _____
5. His foot-tapping really aggravated me.   _____
6. Please rise your hand if you know the answer.   _____
7. She gives the allusion of being much thinner than she is. _____
8. Bill sure doesn't want to work overtime.   _____
9. John promised to learn Maria English.   _____
10. José felt awful bad about the accident.   _____

Words and Phrases to Avoid

Some incorrect words and phrases are used frequently. Because of their common use, we begin to think they are _correct_. No amount of usage will make the following words acceptable as proper English. Just as Eliza Doolittle's dialect labeled her as "lower class," our use of certain words and phrases can label us "uneducated." This may sound unfair, but most employers are looking for people who can give their businesses the best "image." "Ain't" won't do it.

ain't
We used to be able to say, "Ain't" ain't in the dictionary. Now it is! Most educated people do not accept this word. You would do well to avoid it. _Ain't_ is used incorrectly in place of **am not, is not, isn't, are not, aren't.**

could of
This is incorrect grammar. You mean **could have**. The contraction for **could have** is **could've**, which sounds like **could of** but is not written that way. Example: I _could have_ danced all night.

disregardless, irregardless
There are no such words. The word you want is **regardless**.
Example: *Regardless* of the weather, I plan to wear my new suit.

graduate (high school or college)
You did not *graduate high school*, you **graduated from** *high school*, or any other school.

hisself
There is no such word. Use **himself**. Example: The congressman gave *himself* high marks on his voting record.

nowheres
This is incorrect. Use **nowhere**. Example: This debate is going *nowhere*.

off of
Incorrect usage. The word *of* is to be omitted. Example: He climbed *off* the bleachers.

theirselves
There is no such word. Use **themselves**. Example: The employees, *themselves*, decided on office policy.

you all
This is incorrect grammar. Examples: *All of you* must attend.
You must all attend.

youse
This is not a word. *You* is singular; *you* is plural.

Practice VIII

Directions: Underline the error in each of the following sentences. Rewrite each sentence correctly.

1. This project is going nowheres.

   _____

2. You all are dressed incorrectly.

   _____

3. He ain't a very good businessman.

   _____

4. Wilma could of had the promotion if she had wanted it.

   _____

5. Please take your feet off of my desk.

   _____

6. I graduated high school in 1979.

   _____

7. Irregardless of your opinion, I plan to hire the person I interviewed Tuesday.

   _____

Chapter 20   Word Usage

Practice I *Page 213.*
1. **(2)** you're (you are)
2. **(2)** beer
3. **(1)** aisle
4. **(1)** bored
5. **(2)** strait
6. **(1)** sum
7. **(2)** waste
8. **(2)** throne
9. **(1)** steal
10. **(1)** tales

Practice II *Page 214.*
1. **(2)** shone
2. **(3)** site
3. **(1)** sum
4. **(3)** soul
5. **(1)** stake
6. **(2)** stationery
7. **(3)** Theirs
8. **(2)** stare
9. **(5)** No error
10. **(1)** tow

Practice III *Page 215.*
1. **(4)** vale
2. **(1)** dyes
3. **(4)** too
4. **(1)** altogether
5. **(2)** rites
6. **(2)** site
7. **(1)** current
8. **(3)** manner
9. **(4)** waste
10. **(1)** weighed
11. **(4)** great
12. **(5)** No error
13. **(4)** pale

Practice IV *Page 216.*
1. **(1)** eager
2. **(2)** personnel
3. **(4)** continually
4. **(2)** council
5. **(3)** beside
6. **(3)** complimented
7. **(4)** lose
8. **(1)** miner
9. **(2)** healthful
10. **(4)** persecuted

Practice V *Page 218.*
1. **(1)** already
2. **(4)** born
3. **(3)** Capitol
4. **(5)** No error
5. **(1)** eminent
6. **(4)** minor
7. **(5)** No error
8. **(1)** forth
9. **(3)** to
10. **(3)** course

Practice VI *Page 219.*
1. **(4)** type of
2. **(3)** their
3. **(1)** tried
4. **(4)** proceed
5. **(4)** further
6. **(1)** wasted
7. **(3)** alter
8. **(1)** fewer
9. **(2)** advice
10. **(1)** already

Practice VII *Page 221.*

1. Ahmed wants to *borrow* your calculator.
2. Please *communicate with* me by phone.
3. The book *referred* to the Civil War in great depth.
4. C (correct)
5. His foot-tapping really *annoyed* me.
6. Please *raise* your hand if you know the answer.
7. She gives the *illusion* of being much thinner than she is.
8. Bill *surely* doesn't want to work overtime.
9. John promised to *teach* Maria English.
10. José felt *very* bad about the accident. Or, José felt *really* bad about the accident.

Practice VIII *Page 222.*

1. This project is going *nowhere*.
2. *You* are dressed incorrectly. *You are all* dressed incorrectly.
3. He *isn't* a very good businessman.
4. Wilma *could have* had the promotion if she had wanted it.
5. Please take your feet *off* my desk.
6. I *graduated from* high school in 1979.
7. *Regardless* of your opinion, I plan to hire the person I interviewed Tuesday.

Chapter 21

CUMULATIVE REVIEW

This review covers the following concepts:

- Effectiveness of Expression
- Punctuation
- Capitalization
- Spelling
- Vocabulary
- Word Usage

After completing the Cumulative Review exercises, evaluate your ability on the SUMMARY OF RESULTS chart on page 236. Acceptable scores for each practice are given.

To identify your areas for skill improvement, find the question numbers you answered incorrectly on the SKILLS ANALYSIS table. The table will show which of your skills need improvement and the necessary chapters to review.

Practice Exercises

PRACTICE I

Directions: Blacken the circle that corresponds to the number of the incorrect sentence in each group. If there is no error, blacken number 5.

1. (1) Doctor Smith ordered a mahogany, octagonal-shaped table for
his office.
   (2) I wasn't never told to take this highway to your house.
   (3) My aunt baked that cake for me because I'm giving a party
for my friend Joan.
   (4) The plumber left the job almost immediately because he did
not have the parts he needed.
   (5) No error

   ① ② ③ ④ ⑤

2. (1) After the clerk gave the customer his change, he heard the
store's closing bell ring.
   (2) We went to a concert at City Center and heard an especially
fine pianist, Peter Serkin.
   (3) The best part of our day occurred when we realized we were
seated behind Woody Allen.
   (4) The traveling lecturer hardly ever has time for lunch.
   (5) No error

   ① ② ③ ④ ⑤

3. (1) The lecturer prepared slides to accompany his talk.   ① ② ③ ④ ⑤
   (2) Since the hour was late, the Senate adjourned its session.
   (3) Our weekly discussion club, which meets each week on Thursday, invited Michael Moore to comment on his latest book.
   (4) Although our building was painted last year, it looks as if it needs to be painted again.
   (5) No error

4. (1) Our group, we visited the museum to see a display of mobiles.   ① ② ③ ④ ⑤
   (2) The supplies included colored pencils, erasers, and a sketch pad.
   (3) I have never seen a neater room!
   (4) The president meets with his aides at 11:55 A.M.
   (5) No error

5. (1) I cancelled the meeting because I expected to be too busy to attend.   ① ② ③ ④ ⑤
   (2) Do you ever feel pressured by a too-full schedule?
   (3) Because the plane arrived late, we missed our connecting flight.
   (4) The resettled Cuban refugees, they finally got jobs.
   (5) No error

6. (1) The best part of the book occurs when the brothers meet after a 25-year separation.   ① ② ③ ④ ⑤
   (2) The most exciting event in the movie is the car chase.
   (3) The reason for his absence is because he has the flu.
   (4) Richard Robinson hasn't been seen for weeks.
   (5) No error

7. (1) What the florist wanted to know was what colors the man's wife preferred.   ① ② ③ ④ ⑤
   (2) Because it's Monday, the stores are open late.
   (3) The reason for my confusion is that my notes are incomplete.
   (4) My children left for day camp at 9:00 A.M.
   (5) No error

8. (1) Because the power steering fluid had evaporated, the wheel would not turn.   ① ② ③ ④ ⑤
   (2) An insect, it is difficult to eliminate after it has become established in an area.
   (3) William the Conqueror and the barons of Normandy were not in agreement about the invasion of England.
   (4) His parents said that John was neither too young nor too busy to hold a part-time job.
   (5) No error

9. (1) If history doesn't repeat itself, why is there never an end to war?   ① ② ③ ④ ⑤
    (2) Why is it that nothing never goes smoothly?
    (3) On the subject of the dangerous effects of depletion of the ozone layer, one cannot hope for scientists' accord.
    (4) An automobile accident occurred when two drivers proceeded into the intersection at the same time.
    (5) No error

10. (1) More and more people are eating fruits and vegetables because they are health conscious.   ① ② ③ ④ ⑤
    (2) There are many solutions to the energy crisis.
    (3) A man, carrying a fishing pole and wearing hip boots, stood knee-high in the flooded street.
    (4) The layoffs did not affect Shirley.
    (5) No error

11. (1) The football team played football well yesterday at the football game.   ① ② ③ ④ ⑤
    (2) Mark's hockey team is the best in the league.
    (3) None of the basketball players was at the victory party.
    (4) Lucas rarely plays tennis with a player who isn't a pro.
    (5) No error

12. (1) Sylvester Stallone's latest movie seems to be a variation on his famous *Rocky* movies.   ① ② ③ ④ ⑤
    (2) The novel that the customer requested was out of print.
    (3) Herbert Hoover, a man of humble beginnings, he was the son of a blacksmith.
    (4) Because the restriction on misleading food labels is vague, the consumer must be vigilant.
    (5) No error

13. (1) The reason the ERA was defeated was a lack of understanding of the benefits.   ① ② ③ ④ ⑤
    (2) The reason the primitive people relied on witch doctors was because these people thought they had been attacked by evil spirits.
    (3) Our specialty is good service.
    (4) We feature the finest service in the field.
    (5) No error

14. (1) Although I am exhausted, I plan to rest this afternoon.   ① ② ③ ④ ⑤
    (2) Please don't leave early; we are enjoying your company.
    (3) The world's future population is hardly ever discussed without mention of food and other resources.
    (4) If you continue to smoke, I'll continue to ask you to stop.
    (5) No error

15. (1) Don't you find reality shows boring?   ① ② ③ ④ ⑤
    (2) Are you not Mary Smith's aunt?
    (3) The business manager, who was ranting uncontrollably, lost
        the respect of his colleagues.
    (4) Although it isn't none of my business, I'm concerned about
        your health.
    (5) No error

Practice II

Directions: Blacken the circle that corresponds to the number of the best completion for
each sentence.

1. The mailman slipped on the steps   ① ② ③ ④
   (1) because he was wearing boots.
   (2) even though they were icy.
   (3) because the steps, they were icy.
   (4) because they were icy.
2. Jules continues to smoke   ① ② ③ ④
   (1) because he cannot read the warning.
   (2) since smoking is hazardous to his health.
   (3) although smoking is hazardous to his health.
   (4) when it's hazardous to his health.
3. The camping trip was uncomfortable   ① ② ③ ④
   (1) in spite of the heat and the bugs.
   (2) although it was hot and buggy.
   (3) even though it was hot and buggy.
   (4) because of the heat and the bugs.
4. The Giants played well   ① ② ③ ④
   (1) because they feared the fans.
   (2) because the day was unseasonably hot.
   (3) even though the day was unseasonably hot.
   (4) even though the weather was perfect.
5. That man, who speaks at every public meeting,   ① ② ③ ④
   (1) he is my uncle Joe.
   (2) he is a town nuisance.
   (3) never offers an acceptable suggestion.
   (4) hardly never offers an acceptable suggestion.
6. I'd like draperies made of a transparent fabric   ① ② ③ ④
   (1) that sees through and is durable.
   (2) that is durable.
   (3) that I can see through and is durable.
   (4) that is durable and I can see through.
7. My favorite scene in *Romeo and Juliet*   ① ② ③ ④
   (1) is when Romeo kills himself.
   (2) is the one where Romeo kills himself.
   (3) is because Romeo kills himself.
   (4) is the one in which Romeo kills himself.

8. Bob Rice, my brother's friend,　　　　　　　　　　① ② ③ ④
   (1) he's a male chauvinist.
   (2) is a male chauvinist.
   (3) he is a male chauvinist.
   (4) are male chauvinists.

9. The reason for the meeting　　　　　　　　　　　① ② ③ ④
   (1) was that the principal had resigned.
   (2) was because the principal had resigned.
   (3) was when the principal had resigned.
   (4) was to discuss the principal's resignation.

10. The game was dull　　　　　　　　　　　　　　① ② ③ ④
   (1) because the teams were not evenly matched.
   (2) although the teams were not evenly matched.
   (3) in spite of the fact that the teams were not evenly matched.
   (4) since both the teams played well.

Practice III

Directions: Blacken the circle that corresponds to the number of the error in each sentence. If there is no error, blacken number 5.

1. "Would you like to record the song you wrote? " , the　　① ② ③ ④ ⑤
  1　　　　　　　　　　　　　　　　　2 3 4
  conductor asked the singer. *No error*
  　　　　　　　　　　　　　5

2. If you wish, you may pick some flowers—only those along　　① ② ③ ④ ⑤
  　　　　　　1　　　　　　　　　　　　2
  the side of the house—for your centerpiece." *No error*
  　　　　　　3　　　　　　　　　4　　5

3. "My favorite book," said Melissa "is *Animal Farm.*" *No error*　　① ② ③ ④ ⑤
  1　　　　　　　　　2　　　　　3　　　　　4　　5

4. The show (for which you have tickets) begins promptly at　　① ② ③ ④ ⑤
  　　　　　1　　　　　　　　　　　2
  7:45 and ends (believe it or not at 11:00. *No error*
  3　　　　　　　　　　4　　　　　　5

5. Last Sunday, I met my *ex* roommate (whom I haven't seen　　① ② ③ ④ ⑤
  　　　　　　1　　　　2　　　　3
  for twelve years) in the supermarket. *No error*
  　　　　4　　　　　　　　　　5

6. "After you've practiced writing r's," said Miss Green, go   ① ② ③ ④ ⑤
   1   2   3

   right on to s's." No error
                    4   5

7. The Brownies annual party was at the home of Jane   ① ② ③ ④ ⑤
          1

   Simpson on Friday, at 4:15 P.M. No error
      2   3   4   5

8. Two thirds of the membership voted—despite last year's   ① ② ③ ④ ⑤
      1   2   3

   increase—to increase the dues for the next fiscal year. No error
                          4   5

9. The painter called this morning to say "that he won't be able   ① ② ③ ④ ⑤
                                              1   2

   to begin working until next weekend. No error
   3   4   5

10. Please take that envelope (the one on the hall table) across the   ① ② ③ ④ ⑤
              1   2   3

    street to Mrs. Jones. No error
                   4   5

Practice IV

Directions: Blacken the circle that corresponds to the number of the error in each sentence. If there is no error, blacken number 5.

1. Sue Simpson, the lead in The Glass menagerie, is a really   ① ② ③ ④ ⑤
   1   2   3

   competent actress. No error
             4   5

2. When you leave School today, take a bus and meet me in   ① ② ③ ④ ⑤
   1   2   3

   New York City. No error
            4   5

3. Our course, history IA, will include discussion of the settlement   ① ② ③ ④ ⑤
   1   2   3

   of the American colonies. No error
            4   5

4. _Remember_ that _Ellie_ said we should meet _Her_ for lunch on
     1   2   3
    Tuesday. _No error_
      4   5
    ① ② ③ ④ ⑤

5. _On_ _Twenty-second_ _Street_ there's a charming restaurant called
     1   2   3
    Lou's. _No error_
      4   5
    ① ② ③ ④ ⑤

6. _Mr._ _Goren_ reminded _us,_ _"all_ lights must be turned off in the
     1   2   3 4
    laboratory at the end of the work day." _No error_
                           5
    ① ② ③ ④ ⑤

7. The _lieutenant_ asked _captain_ _John Forbes_ to cut the ribbon
          1   2   3
    at the ceremonies marking the opening of _Fort Titan._ _No error_
                                4   5
    ① ② ③ ④ ⑤

8. _This_ _October,_ _halloween_ falls on a _Tuesday._ _No error_
     1   2   3   4   5
    ① ② ③ ④ ⑤

9. _"We can learn much,"_ said _Edith,_ _"from_ the cultures of the
    1   2   3
    east." _No error_
      4   5
    ① ② ③ ④ ⑤

10. _One_ of the earliest and most significant _British_ _documents_ is
     1   2   3
    the _magna carta._ _No error_
         4   5
    ① ② ③ ④ ⑤

Practice V

Directions: Blacken the circle that corresponds to the number of the incorrectly spelled word in each group. If there is no error, blacken number 5.

1. (1) reinstitute   (4) foxes   ① ② ③ ④ ⑤
   (2) overated   (5) No error
   (3) happily

2. (1) dyeing   (4) dice   ① ② ③ ④ ⑤
   (2) dying   (5) No error
   (3) dies

3. (1) truly   (4) duly   ① ② ③ ④ ⑤
   (2) noticable   (5) No error
   (3) famous

4. (1) guidance   (4) edibles   ① ② ③ ④ ⑤
   (2) necessarily   (5) No error
   (3) mispell

5. (1) safely   (4) recede   ① ② ③ ④ ⑤
   (2) proceed   (5) No error
   (3) preceed

6. (1) merrily   (4) theif   ① ② ③ ④ ⑤
   (2) quickly   (5) No error
   (3) niece

7. (1) succeed   (4) wierd   ① ② ③ ④ ⑤
   (2) willingly   (5) No error
   (3) reference

8. (1) canning   (4) radios   ① ② ③ ④ ⑤
   (2) caning   (5) No error
   (3) confering

9. (1) seize   (4) axes   ① ② ③ ④ ⑤
   (2) secede   (5) No error
   (3) skys

10. (1) recede   (4) hunches   ① ② ③ ④ ⑤
   (2) ilegal   (5) No error
   (3) disillusion

11. (1) sheep   (4) exrays   ① ② ③ ④ ⑤
   (2) data   (5) No error
   (3) datum

12. (1) sevens   (4) loosens   ① ② ③ ④ ⑤
   (2) courtisans   (5) No error
   (3) 9s

13. (1) atheletic   (4) mice   ① ② ③ ④ ⑤
   (2) exceed   (5) No error
   (3) supersede

14. (1) vaccinate   (4) height   ① ② ③ ④ ⑤
   (2) mouthsful   (5) No error
   (3) oxen

15. (1) befitting   (4) leisure   ① ② ③ ④ ⑤
   (2) allegiance   (5) No error
   (3) tonage

16. (1) deceive   (4) heroes   ① ② ③ ④ ⑤
   (2) relieve   (5) No error
   (3) ferret

17. (1) contraltoes   (4) duly   ① ② ③ ④ ⑤
   (2) trout   (5) No error
   (3) brothers-in-law

18. (1) crises   (4) seeing   ① ② ③ ④ ⑤
   (2) knifes   (5) No error
   (3) disappoint

19. (1) colonel   (4) concurred   ① ② ③ ④ ⑤
    (2) interceed   (5) No error
    (3) release
20. (1) rheostat   (4) vacuum   ① ② ③ ④ ⑤
    (2) tariff   (5) No error
    (3) trafic

Practice VI

Directions: Blacken the circle that corresponds to the number of the incorrect sentence in each group. If there is no error, blacken number 5.

1. (1) Once the bill was defeated, it was too late to argue its merits.   ① ② ③ ④ ⑤
   (2) In this decade of shortages, the large-scale waist of paper is outrageous.
   (3) During the 1992 and 1996 elections, Bill Clinton led the Democrats to victory.
   (4) Before Hillary Clinton, most American first ladies were quiet partners.
   (5) No error
2. (1) The headlights of a solitary car shone down the deserted country road.   ① ② ③ ④ ⑤
   (2) All of the museum's newest paintings were shone at the recent exhibition.
   (3) The weather vane is broken again.
   (4) Beneath his unruffled exterior were the falsely arrested gentleman's true feelings of rage.
   (5) No error
3. (1) Napoleon would not settle for a small piece of Europe.   ① ② ③ ④ ⑤
   (2) The judge carefully weighed both arguments.
   (3) Crew is a sport in which races with row boats take place.
   (4) Former senator Bill Bradley was once a principle player on the New York Knicks.
   (5) No error
4. (1) During the summer of 1994, many American families traveled to New England.   ① ② ③ ④ ⑤
   (2) Many immigrants have had difficulty adapting to life in America.
   (3) If you plan to film the entire Thanksgiving Day Parade, you'll need more than one real of film.
   (4) Even an expert fisherman has, on occasion, lost a rod and reel.
   (5) No error

5. (1) The United States had overlooked many acts of aggression
towards other nations, until the Germans sank the *Lusitania*.
  (2) Mark lifts weights every morning.
  (3) My wait has dropped considerably since I've been on that
diet.
  (4) Phil refuses to wait in line for a movie, a show, or dinner.
  (5) No error

                                                 ① ② ③ ④ ⑤

6. (1) Some people enjoy camping.
  (2) The sum of my camping experience is two days.
  (3) Martha is too vane to travel without a mirror.
  (4) All of our efforts were in vain because the project failed.
  (5) No error

                                                 ① ② ③ ④ ⑤

7. (1) A bird flew past the window.
  (2) Ira is home with the flu.
  (3) A squirrel was trapped in the chimney flue.
  (4) Did you bring a flie-swatter?
  (5) No error

                                                 ① ② ③ ④ ⑤

8. (1) A female pig is called a sow.
  (2) Jeannette cannot sew well at all.
  (3) That gift is so nice!
  (4) The ball crashed through the pain of glass.
  (5) No error

                                                 ① ② ③ ④ ⑤

9. (1) The old man could not walk without his cane.
  (2) Sugar comes from sugar cane.
  (3) Queen Elizabeth had a peaceful rein.
  (4) That sprained ankle caused me great pain.
  (5) No error

                                                 ① ② ③ ④ ⑤

10. (1) The bough was full of blossoms.
  (2) Everyone cheered when the pitcher through the third strike.
  (3) I don't like to sit in the bow of the boat.
  (4) Suzy enjoys wearing bows in her hair.
  (5) No error

                                                 ① ② ③ ④ ⑤

11. (1) Do you like to walk in the rain?
  (2) Have you ever seen a ewe?
  (3) The canoe floated silently down the straight.
  (4) Please, straighten your tie.
  (5) No error

                                                 ① ② ③ ④ ⑤

12. (1) Some young women will not marry because they are waiting
for nights in shining armor.
  (2) My favorite fish dinner is baked fillet of sole.
  (3) Many poems have been written about the journeys of the
soul.
  (4) Because I was the sole tennis player in the group, I played a
great deal of golf.
  (5) No error

                                                 ① ② ③ ④ ⑤

13. (1) Do you grate potatoes into that recipe? ① ② ③ ④ ⑤
    (2) No, but I beet the eggs thoroughly.
    (3) Have you tried beet soup?
    (4) Yes, it's delicious.
    (5) No error

14. (1) I am not fond of that newscaster. ① ② ③ ④ ⑤
    (2) His manor is very offensive.
    (3) Did you visit the Manor House at Batsto?
    (4) In what manner would you like the idea presented?
    (5) No error

15. (1) Since the recent stories about meat contamination, I've been ① ② ③ ④ ⑤
    eating less meat.
    (2) Did you see the lovely freeze on the museum wall?
    (3) Please mcct me at Wendy's.
    (4) Lately, loud noises wear on my nerves.
    (5) No error

Practice VII

Directions: Blacken the circle that corresponds to the number of the incorrect word in each sentencc. If there is no error, blacken number 5.

1. Please *leave* Marie go to the movies *with* me because I *may* not ① ② ③ ④ ⑤
        1   2   3
    go to town *alone. No error*
          4   5

2. If you don't *want* to *build* shelves for me, *then* *learn* me how ① ② ③ ④ ⑤
            1   2   3 4
    to build them myself. *No error*
             5

3. Because this is a *real* problem in *our* community, we need a ① ② ③ ④ ⑤
          1   2
    real dedicated group of citizens *to* study possible solutions.
    3   4
    No error
    5

4. Many reports indicate that sugar-coated *serials* are not ① ② ③ ④ ⑤
                       1
    healthful; therefore, more nutritious breakfast foods *are*
      2   3   4
    appearing on the market. *No error*
          5

5. When Stuart gives the signal, _everyone_ must _rise_ to his feet,   ① ② ③ ④ ⑤
                                  1   2

   raise his hands above his head, and _set_ down. _No error_
     3   4   5

6. Because so _many_ campers had cut down trees, _there_ were _less_   ① ② ③ ④ ⑤
                 1   2   3

   trees this year _than_ ever before. _No error_
                    4   5

7. Mrs. Smith _taught_ the science _class_ the _affect_ of radiation _upon_   ① ② ③ ④ ⑤
                1   2   3   4

   cells. _No error_
          5

8. That _author_ carries the _principle_ of free will _farther_ than any   ① ② ③ ④ ⑤
          1   2   3

   previous author. _No error_
     4   5

9. Mrs. Kelly Warren, _formally_ Miss Kelly O'Rourke,   ① ② ③ ④ ⑤
                        1

   emigrated _from_ Ireland this _past_ year. _No error_
       2   3   4   5

10. _Its_ an _illusion_ to expect that _course_ of action to have a positive   ① ② ③ ④ ⑤
      1   2   3

    effect on our long-range plan. _No error_
      4   5

After reviewing the Answer Key on page 238, chart your scores below for each practice exercise.

SUMMARY OF RESULTS

Practice Number	Number Correct	Number Incorrect (Including Omissions)	Acceptable Score
I			11 Correct
II			7 Correct
III			7 Correct
IV			7 Correct
V			15 Correct
VI			11 Correct
VII			10 Correct

To identify your areas for skill improvement, locate the questions you answered incorrectly and circle the numbers on this Skills Analysis Chart. Wherever you have circled errors, review the chapters listed in the last column.

SKILLS ANALYSIS

Skill	Question Number	Review Chapter
Practice I		
Double Negative	1, 9, 15	15
Unclear Pronoun Reference	2	15
Repetition	3, 4, 5, 8, 11, 12	15
Wordiness	6, 7, 13	15
Coordination of Ideas	14	15
Practice II		
Coordination of Ideas	1, 2, 3, 4, 10	15
Repetition	6, 8	15
Wordiness	7, 9	15
Practice III		
Quotation Marks	1, 2, 3, 6, 9	16
Parentheses	4	16
Hyphen	5, 8	16
Apostrophe	7	16
Practice IV		
Capitalization	1 to 10	17
Practice V		
Spelling	1 to 20	18
Practice VI		
Word Usage	1 to 15	20
Practice VII		
Word Usage	1 to 10	20

Chapter 21 Cumulative Review

Practice I *Page 225.*

1. **(2)** I wasn't *ever* told to take this high-way to your house.
   Never use *not* (n't) and *never* together.

2. **(1)** After giving the customer change, *the clerk* heard the store's closing bell ring.
   Substitute *the clerk* for *he* in order to clarify who *heard*.

3. **(3)** *Our discussion club, which meets each Thursday,* invited Michael Moore to comment on his latest book.
   Using *weekly* and *each week* in the same sentence is repetitious.

4. **(1)** *Our group visited* the museum to see a display of mobiles.
   We refers to *our group* and is, therefore, repetitious.

5. **(4)** The resettled Cuban *refugees finally* got jobs.
   They refers to the *Cuban refugees* and is, therefore, repetitious.

6. **(3)** *He is absent* because he has the flu.
   Is because is unacceptable form. The sentence reads more smoothly as corrected.

7. **(1)** *The florist wanted* to know what colors the man's wife preferred.
   What . . . was is poor form. The sentence reads more smoothly as corrected.

8. **(2)** *An insect is difficult* to eliminate after it has become established in an area.
   The first *it* referred to *insect* and was, therefore, repetitious.

9. **(2)** Why is it that nothing *ever* goes smoothly?
   Never use *nothing* and *never* together.

10. **(5)** No error

11. **(1)** *The football team played well yesterday*.
    Football is repetitious.

12. **(3)** Herbert Hoover, a man of humble beginnings, *was* the son of a black-smith.
    He refers to *Herbert Hoover* and is, therefore, repetitious.

13. **(2)** *Primitive people relied on witch doctors because* those people thought they had been attacked by evil spirits.
    Was because is unacceptable form. The sentence reads more smoothly as corrected.

14. **(1)** *Because* I am exhausted, I plan to rest this afternoon.
    Although contradicts the intended meaning of the sentence. *Because* clarifies the meaning.

15. **(4)** Although it isn't *any* of my business, I'm concerned about your health.
    Never use *not* and *none* together.

Practice II *Page 228.*

1. **(4)** The mailman slipped on the steps *because they were icy*.
   Because they were icy explains, simply, why the mailman slipped on the steps. The word *because* makes the connection between the mailman's slipping and the icy steps.

2. **(3)** Jules continues to smoke *although smoking is hazardous to his health.*
Although smoking is hazardous to his health shows that Jules continues to smoke despite the hazards.

3. **(4)** The camping trip was uncomfortable *because of the heat and the bugs.*
Because of the heat and the bugs explains, simply, why the camping trip was uncomfortable. The word *because* makes the connection between the discomfort and the heat and the bugs.

4. **(3)** The Giants played well *even though the day was unseasonably hot.*
Even though the day was unseasonably hot shows that the Giants played well despite the heat.

5. **(3)** That man, who speaks at every meeting, *never offers an acceptable suggestion.*
Never offers an acceptable suggestion is the only grammatically correct completion for this sentence.

6. **(2)** I'd like draperies made of a transparent fabric *that is durable.*
That is durable is the only possible completion for this sentence. All other choices are grammatically incorrect and repetitive.

7. **(4)** My favorite scene in *Romeo and Juliet is the one in which Romeo kills himself.*
Is the one in which Romeo kills himself is the only completion that conforms to correct style.

8. **(2)** Bob Rice, my brother's friend, *is a male chauvinist.*
Is a male chauvinist is the only grammatically and stylistically correct completion for this sentence.

9. **(4)** The reason for the meeting *was to discuss the principal's resignation.*
Was to discuss the principal's resignation is the simplest completion for this sentence. *Was that, was when,* and *was because* are poor style.

10. **(1)** The game was dull *because the teams were not evenly matched.*
Because the teams were not evenly matched explains, simply, why the game was dull. The word *because* makes the connection between the dull game and the unevenly matched teams.

Practice III *Page 229.*

1. **(4)** "Would you like to record the song you wrote?" the conductor asked the singer.
Never place a comma *outside* quotation marks. Never use two marks of punctuation at the end of a sentence.

2. **(4)** If you wish, you may pick some flowers—only those along the side of the house—for your centerpiece.
This sentence is not a quotation; therefore, the quotation mark at the end of the sentence is incorrect.

3. **(3)** "My favorite book," said Melissa, "is *Animal Farm.*"
Use a comma to separate *said Melissa* from the remainder of the quotation.

4. **(4)** The show (for which you have tickets) begins promptly at 7:45 and ends (believe it or not) at 11:00.
The writer shows by the use of parentheses that *believe it or not* is not necessary to the meaning of the sentence. Once opened, parentheses must be closed.

5. **(2)** Last Sunday, I met my _ex_-roommate (whom I haven't seen for twelve years) in the supermarket.
When the prefix _ex-_ means former or previously, as in _ex-roommate,_ it is followed by a hyphen.

6. **(3)** "After you've practiced writing r's," said Miss Green, _"_go right on to s's."
When continuing an interrupted quotation, precede the quoted portion with quotation marks.

7. **(1)** The _Brownies'_ annual party was at the home of Jane Simpson on Friday, at 4:15 P.M.
Use an apostrophe to show possession. The apostrophe follows the _s_ in _Brownies_ to show that the party belonged to them.

8. **(1)** _Two-thirds_ of the membership voted —despite last year's increase—to increase the dues for the next fiscal year.
Two-thirds is an example of two descriptive words brought together to form a new word; therefore, it is hyphenated.

9. **(1)** The painter called this morning to say _that_ he won't be able to begin working until next weekend.
That signals the fact that this is a report, or an indirect quotation, of what the painter said. Therefore, no quotation marks are needed.

10. **(5)** No error

Practice IV _Page 230._

1. **(3)** Sue Simpson, the lead in _The Glass Menagerie,_ is a really competent actress.
Capitalize the complete title of a play, book, or long poem.

2. **(2)** When you leave _school_ today, take a bus and meet me in New York City.
School is not capitalized because it does not refer to a particular school.

3. **(3)** Our course, _History IA_, will include discussion of the settlement of the American colonies.
History IA is the name of a particular course and, therefore, should be capitalized.

4. **(3)** Remember that Ellie said we should meet _her_ for lunch on Tuesday.
Never capitalize a pronoun unless it is the first word of a sentence or a quotation.

5. **(5)** No error

6. **(4)** Mr. Goren reminded us, _"All_ lights must be turned off in the laboratory at the end of the work day."
All is the first word of the quotation and must be capitalized.

7. **(2)** The lieutenant asked _Captain_ John Forbes to cut the ribbon at the ceremonies marking the opening of Fort Titan.
Captain refers to a particular captain, _Captain John Forbes_, and must be capitalized.

8. **(3)** This October, _Halloween_ falls on a Tuesday.
Halloween is the name of a holiday and, therefore, must be capitalized.

9. **(4)** "We can learn much," said Edith, "from the cultures of the _East._"
East refers to a particular section of the world and, therefore, must be capitalized.

10. **(4)** One of the earliest and most significant British documents is the _Magna Carta_.

Magna Carta is the title of a document and, therefore, must be capitalized.

Practice V _Page 231._
For explanations of the following answers, see spelling rules in Chapter 18.

1. **(2)** overrated
2. **(5)** No error
3. **(2)** noticeable
4. **(3)** misspell
5. **(3)** precede
6. **(4)** thief
7. **(4)** weird
8. **(3)** conferring
9. **(3)** skies
10. **(2)** illegal
11. **(4)** x-rays
12. **(3)** 9's
13. **(1)** athletic
14. **(2)** mouthfuls
15. **(3)** tonnage
16. **(5)** No error
17. **(1)** contraltos
18. **(2)** knives
19. **(2)** intercede
20. **(3)** traffic

Practice VI _Page 233._
For explanations of the following answers, see word list and examples in Chapter 20.

1. **(2)** In this decade of shortages, the large-scale _waste_ of paper is outrageous.
2. **(2)** All of the museum's newest paintings were _shown_ at the recent exhibition.
3. **(4)** Former senator Bill Bradley was once a _principal_ player on the New York Knicks.
4. **(3)** If you plan to film the entire Thanksgiving Day Parade, you'll need more than one _reel_ of film.
5. **(3)** My _weight_ has dropped considerably since I've been on that diet.
6. **(3)** Martha is too _vain_ to travel without a mirror.
7. **(4)** Did you bring a _fly_-swatter?
8. **(4)** The ball crashed through the _pane_ of glass.
9. **(3)** Queen Elizabeth had a peaceful _reign_.
10. **(2)** Everyone cheered when the pitcher _threw_ the third strike.
11. **(3)** The canoe floated silently down the _strait_.
12. **(1)** Some young women will not marry because they are waiting for _knights_ in shining armor.
13. **(2)** No, but I _beat_ the eggs thoroughly.
14. **(2)** His _manner_ is very offensive.
15. **(2)** Did you see the lovely _frieze_ on the museum wall?

Practice VII _Page 235._
For explanations of the following answers, see word list and examples in Chapter 20.

1. **(1)** Please _let_ Marie go to the movies with me because I may not go to town alone.
2. **(4)** If you don't want to build shelves for me, then _teach_ me how to build them myself.
3. **(3)** Because this is a real problem in our community, we need a _very_ dedicated group of citizens to study possible solutions.
4. **(1)** Many reports indicate that sugar-coated _cereals_ are not healthful; therefore, more nutritious breakfast foods are appearing on the market.
5. **(4)** When Stuart gives the signal, everyone must rise to his feet, raise his hands above his head, and _sit_ down.

6. **(3)** Because so many campers had cut down trees, there were *fewer* trees this year than ever before.

7. **(3)** Mrs. Smith taught the science class the *effect* of radiation upon cells.

8. **(3)** That author carries the principle of free will *further* than any previous author.

9. **(1)** Mrs. Kelly Warren, *formerly* Miss Kelly O'Rourke, emigrated from Ireland this past year.

10. **(1)** *It's* an illusion to expect that course of action to have a positive effect on our long-range plan.

Chapter 22

WRITING RIGHT

May 13, 2002

Golden Oldie Records
WOR-TV
1440 Broadway
New York City, NY 10019

Dear Dumbbells:

What's the matter with you people? I sent you my
hard-earned money (I'm a construction worker) for the
Lawrence Welk records you advertised, and after
waiting eight weeks I received a Rolling Stones album.
Can't you get anything right? I hate rock'n roll music.
It gives me a splitting headache. I have a good mind to
punch you in the nose!

Boiling mad,

Harry Flowers

Harry Flowers[1]

A Word With You . . .

Harry Flowers' letter is one of the horrible examples presented in the National Association of Retailers' booklet, *How Not to Get Results*. Mr. Flowers has a legitimate complaint, but he should realize that he will not win friends or influence people by abusing them. Furthermore, a letter of complaint should contain all the necessary information needed to help a merchant redress your grievance.

Homework assignment for Mr. Flowers: Study this chapter . . . and clean up your act!

---

1 National Association of Retailers, *How Not to Get Results*.

Thinking Before You Write

Whether you intend to write a letter, memo, report, or essay, one thing is certain. You should make some important decisions before you get started. You could delay making those decisions—as many people do—and end up writing your piece again and again until you hit upon what you want to say. By doing some critical thinking before you write, you could save yourself a great deal of time and frustration. Following are some questions to help you plan your writing.

Should You Write?

If you can accomplish your purpose by talking to someone, then talk! During your work day, if you see an associate three, four, perhaps five times, there may be no need to write a memo regarding a simple matter. Say what you want if the issue can be concluded with that conversation, and save time and paper. Do not, however, expect a busy co-worker to carry your request in his or her head for an hour, a day, or a week. Do yourself and the person with whom you are communicating a favor. Put the question, the information, or the request in writing, if the issue cannot be concluded with a brief conversation. If you don't commit your request or message to paper, the person receiving it will have to remember it or write it down. You risk having your message ignored or forgotten.

If you have a complaint about the dangerous cracks in the sidewalk on your block, your request to the town administrator will get faster attention if it arrives on paper. If you are a student with an assignment to write a term paper, of course you have no choice but to put your thoughts down on paper. When you write, you must make those thoughts clear to your reader. You want your message to be understood.

What Do You Want to Say?

Recognizing what you feel and think can still be worlds apart from understanding the "purpose" of your writing. For example, you may feel angry that the dress you bought shrunk when you had it dry-cleaned, but the purpose of your writing a letter to the store will be to persuade them to refund your money. Consider your basic motivation in writing. Are you going to berate your senator for voting against the Clean Air Bill or will you congratulate him for his veto? Will your term paper support the idea that Hamlet had a tragic flaw or will it show him as a victim of circumstance? Before you write, you must know what you want to say.

Who Is Your Reader?

A first step in writing is determining who will read what you write. Your audience will determine what type of writing you will do. Think of one idea going to two different people. For example, the following two letters describe a job, first to a friend, then to a potential employer. Notice how Jane's tone changes, depending on whether she is writing to someone she knows well or a potential employer.

Dear Judy,

I've finally decided to pack in this dead-end job. I can no longer calmly listen to Mr. B. present my ideas as his accomplishments. He is so convinced they're his, he even brags to me about them. Most recently, I developed a training program for new employees. I sent him a draft. A week later, a manual was circulated with his name on it. He didn't even correct my typing error. I've applied for a comparable position in another company and hope to have good news for you soon.

Love,
Jane

16 Sunset Road
Boise, Idaho 83701
April 3, 2003

Ms. Eunice Munson
General Manager
ABC Corporation
Boise, Idaho 83720

Dear Ms. Munson:

I am writing in response to your ad in Sunday's *Inquirer* for an assistant manager. I believe my experience is directly related to the position offered.

For the past five years, I have assisted the manager of XYZ Corporation. My duties have included drafting speeches, devising company manuals, and providing administrative support. Most recently, we worked together on a training manual for new employees. While I still find my present position challenging, I am seeking employment with greater growth potential.

I enclose a copy of my résumé and look forward to hearing from you at your earliest convenience.

Sincerely,
Jane Brody

How Do You Say It Best?

Writing takes many forms: letters, memos, reports, notes, lists, and books, to name just a few. Depending on your intention, the form you choose will determine the structure of your writing. We discuss letters, memos, reports, and essays in the following pages.

Letters

In the age of audiovisual miracles, letter writing has become a forgotten art. When phones were not available to exchange news or greetings, letters were common. Because people wrote often, they wrote well.

We still need letters on occasion in our personal lives: thank you notes, condolence notes, letters to distant friends or relatives, and greetings of all kinds. Letter writing is also helpful when we want to request information, complain about a product, let our congressmen know our views, or apply for a job.

Another type of letter that has not been eliminated by the telephone is the business letter. Anyone who works for a business, large or small, should be able to write a clear business letter. While modern office technology may somewhat reduce the need for letters, it won't eliminate it. Although computer software—spellchecks and grammarchecks—override human error, the machines continue to be only as good as their operators.

This chapter will not attempt to deal with all the skills necessary to write a perfect letter. Elements such as grammar, spelling, and punctuation, covered earlier, play an important role. This chapter provides you with models and helpful hints for form and style.

Headings

Headings consist of your address, the date, the name and address of the recipient, and the salutation or greeting. Business letters include each of these elements (see Sample Business Letter on page 248). However, when writing to a friend or relative, your address and the recipient's address need not be included. The sample letters later in the chapter will show you the correct formats to use for both informal letters and business letters.

Part of the heading is the salutation or greeting—the "Dear [Somebody]." Changes in language usage and business itself have made "Dear [Somebody]" increasingly complicated. Once upon a time, if you were addressing an unknown group, the term "Gentlemen:" was appropriate. Today, those gentlemen include women who would not take kindly to that greeting. Often, business people sign letters that give no clue to the signator's gender. For example: "T. Warren" or "Terry Smith." "Ladies and Gentlemen:", "Dear T. Warren:", or "Dear XYZ Company:" could replace more conventional salutations. Some sample salutations follow.

Friendly Salutations	Formal Salutations
Dear Aunt Sue,	Dear Mr. Wright:
Dear Rosa,	Dear Ms. Smith:
Dearest William,	Dear Dr. Schwarz:
	Dear Personnel Director:
	Dear Salespeople:
	Dear T. Warren:
	Dear XYZ Company:

Introduction, Body, Conclusion

Since your opening paragraph is like a first meeting with your reader, the impression you make is a lasting one. The reader expects to have your purpose revealed. Whether it is to complain, compliment, or inform, it should be clear immediately.

Throughout the letter, say what you want to say as clearly and as briefly as possible. Your letter may be long, but it should not ramble. Every sentence should be a necessary one.

The traditional interviewer-reporter questions help keep a letter clear and concise. Note which questions apply to your letter: *who, what, when, where, why.* If you answer these questions, you will probably give all the necessary information for situations ranging from a party invitation to a complaint about a broken radio.

Just as your first impression is a lasting one, so is your final one. Make sure your reader knows what you expect. If you plan a follow-up phone call, say so and say when. If you want a written or telephone response, ask for it. If you began the letter by thanking the person, reinforce your appreciation in the final paragraph.

Closings

Closings range from "Love," to "Very truly yours," depending upon the purpose and audience of your letter. The closing should be in the same style as the salutation. A letter would not begin "Dear Sir:" and end with "Love."

Friendly Closings	Formal Closings
Sincerely,	Sincerely,
Warmly,	Very truly yours,
Fondly,	Yours very truly,
Warmest regards,	Yours truly,
With love, (personal)	Sincerely yours,
Love, (personal)	Yours sincerely,
(Any other nice thought	Respectfully yours,
you may want to use)	Very respectfully yours,
	Yours respectfully,

Business Letter Format

Sender's Address:
This is obviously not necessary on printed stationery. If your letter will be on plain paper, place your address in the upper right-hand corner or upper left.

Date:
Spell out the month in a business letter. Date can be right or left, but it must be aligned with the recipient's address and closing. In this age of personal computers many people keep their letters "flush left." Everything lines up with the left margin.

Recipient's Address:
On the left-hand side of the page, include the name (and title or position if you know it) of the person to whom you are writing. Then, put the name of the company or organization and, finally, the complete address of the organization.

Salutation:
See page 246 for examples of formal salutations.

Introduction:
One short paragraph states the subject or purpose of the letter. Make your purpose clear immediately.

Body:

One, two, three, or more paragraphs contain the relevant details. Each paragraph should expand on one main point.

Conclusion:

The conclusion should give direction. One short paragraph finishes the letter with a summary, a recommendation, an instruction, or a thank you.

Closing:

See page 247 for formal closings.

Name and Signature:

Business form dictates typing your name and title beneath your signature. If your title is on your letterhead, do not repeat it. If you are handwriting a business letter as a consumer, print your name beneath your signature. You want the response addressed to you correctly. Name and signature should be aligned with the date and closing.

SAMPLE PERSONAL LETTER

July 15, 2003

Dear Aunt Polly,

Thank you so much for the leather-bound dictionary. It was a perfect graduation gift. I will treasure it always.

My family and I were sorry you couldn't come to Arizona for the graduation and party. We all missed you very much. I'm enclosing some photos for you.

Love,
David

SAMPLE BUSINESS LETTER

ABC Corporation

---

231 West 53 Street, New York, New York 10022

July 10, 2003

Ms. Cary Jeffers
66 Columbus Avenue
Tarrytown, New York 10571

Dear Ms. Jeffers:

Thank you for your résumé and letter (dated June 25, 2003), asking about employment opportunities at the XYZ Corporation. Because we receive so many unsolicited requests each year, we must limit interviews to those with relevant work experience. While your résumé indicates a strong manufacturing background, you have no experience with our specialized product.

Thank you for considering ABC Corporation. We wish you every success in your employment search.

Very truly yours,

David Green

David Green
Personnel Director
DG/sl

SAMPLE COMPLAINT LETTER

106 Goodtree Drive
Columbus, Ohio 43201
March 10, 2004

Mr. William Wellington, President
Cool-It, Inc.
738 Second Avenue
New York, New York 10017

Dear Mr. Wellington:

On February 23, 2004, while a local Cool-It, Inc. representative was servicing my air-conditioner, the tank of freon exploded in my basement. The tank was located next to my clothes dryer, so this explosion caused damage to my dryer as well as some clothing that was in the dryer at the time. This event led to an expensive dryer service call and the need to replace a complete load of laundry. I would appreciate full reimbursement for the items listed on the attached bills.

The serviceman who repaired the dryer suggested that the malfunction was mostly caused by the freon. The spilled freon permanently froze the dryer thermostat, preventing the dryer from cooling down. A full load of towels that were in the dryer at the time became excessively dried out to the point of disintegration. In fact, when I removed the laundry from the dryer, the laundry fell apart in my hands. Prior to the explosion, the load of laundry was fine and the dryer worked perfectly.

I've always had an excellent relationship with your company and look forward to your continuing service. Your representative, by the way, was courteous and thorough in his job of repairing the air-conditioning system. I look forward to your payment within a reasonable amount of time.

Thank you.

Sincerely,

Mary Edwards

Mary Edwards

Practice I

Directions: Read the following facts and write a letter of complaint from Tom Williams based on those facts. You can include your opinion or attitude toward the problem in the letter.

Tom Williams bought a clock radio at Warren's Department Store on May 15, 2002. Tom could not get the alarm to work properly from the start. He brought the clock radio back to the store on May 19, 2002, and was told he would have to mail the item to the manufacturer for repair. Tom lives at 1419 Maple Street, Dayton, Ohio 82050. The clock radio was made by the Wake-Up Corporation located at 2042 Main Street, Chicago, Illinois 60791.

Practice II

Directions: Rewrite Matthew Manager's letter. Remember to write simply and clearly.

February 10, 2003

Ms. Suzanne Jones
1 Willow Way
Edison, New Jersey 08817

Dear Ms. Jones:

I wish to thank you for choosing to inform me about the incident which occurred at MarketRite last Friday. It is important to us in management to know what is going on when salespeople help—or don't help—as the case may be customers.

John Rich is usually a generally friendly person. He has been under very extreme personal pressure even though that should not enter into it. I have taken the liberty of speaking with John and am assured that what happened to you won't happen again at least from him.

Please be kind enough to accept the enclosed herewith gift certificate as a small token of our regret.

Thank you for shopping at MarketRite.

Sincerely,

Matthew Manager

Matthew Manager
Vice President
Customer Relations

Memoranda

A memorandum is commonly used for interoffice communications, such as sharing information, setting procedures, or asking questions within a company or organization. Every business has its preferred style for memos, but the tips that follow can be applied in most situations. Treat a memo as you would any other kind of writing. Plan ahead and then construct clear and concise sentences that convey your intentions. Either write a brief outline or jot down phrases that will help you organize your thinking. Stick to the subject at hand. State your purpose first, then give all the necessary facts. Tell what you want done or request information. If you are informing the reader, do so simply and clearly, keeping your tone friendly and positive. A memo need not be an edict. Simply answer the question, "What do I want to accomplish?" Again, make sure that what you say is accurate because memos, when filed, become records.

Format for Memos

Although a memo is very much like a letter in purpose, its format is different. The memo style sheet that follows is one, common memo format.

MEMO STYLE SHEET

MEMO

TO: The name of the recipient, including the person's title and/or department

FROM: Your name, title, and department

DATE: The date you send the memo

SUBJECT: The subject of the memo

Start with your purpose in writing the memo. Include relevant details, or what the recipient must know, and close with what the recipient must do.

Thank the recipient and offer to answer any questions.

ABC:df

A memo usually is not signed at the bottom the way a letter would be. Instead, the sender initials the memo next to his or her name at the top. Sometimes, for security reasons, companies require full signatures on memos.

Note the structure of the sample memo on page 252. The opening gets right to the point. Helms recalls that he and Sperry have agreed that there is a potential problem. The memo proposes a solution. For emphasis, the solution is set off—highlighted—in its own paragraph. Other ways to visually emphasize ideas include using numbers, letters, headings, or bullets (black dots) at the left-hand margin. The final two sentences tell the reader what to do.

Note also that job titles appear next to the names. These titles can be omitted in very informal memos. However, memos that will be filed for future reference should have the titles included.

SAMPLE MEMO 1

MEMORANDUM

TO: Janice Sperry, Vice President, Marketing
FROM: Rob Helms, Purchasing Agent
DATE: July 10, 2002
SUBJECT: Purchase Agreement #47

When we spoke last Thursday, we agreed that the above purchase agreement #47 was vague and could cause problems with the completed job. I propose the following changes:

1. Delete lines 4–7.
2. Insert the following in place of lines 2–7: "The seller is under no obligation to accept returned merchandise 90 days after delivery."

Let me know by the 15th if you agree with these changes or have another suggestion. Thank you.

RH:cd

The following memo is a very informal one between two co-workers. No last names appear in the heading, and without these names, the memo would be almost useless as a record. Mary gets to the point immediately, however, noting co-responsibility for coordinating the company's calendar and letting Pat know the times during the week that she will be available. Mary then tells Pat what to do—that is, to decide on a convenient time to work together.

SAMPLE MEMO 2

MEMO

TO: Pat
FROM: Mary
DATE: November 3, 2002
SUBJECT: Company Calendar

You and I are responsible for coordinating the company calendar. I'm available any morning next week. Please let me know the day and time convenient for you.

Now read the following memo. Does it meet all the requirements of a well-written memo? Yes. This short memo gets the job done. The subject is clearly stated in the SUBJECT line. In the first sentence, the reader learns the new due date and what has to be done. Sentences 2 and 3 show the writer's concern for Bill Greenway's well-being. There is nothing wrong with a personal touch. One improvement would be to include the job titles and/or department names.

SAMPLE MEMO 3

FROM THE DESK OF ARI GOLDMAN:

TO: Bill Greenway
DATE: December 10, 2002
SUBJECT: Monthly Report

You should be pleased to know that your December monthly report will not be due until January 7, 2003. This extension should make your vacation a little more relaxing. Enjoy the holidays.

Long Memos

Sometimes you will need to write a longer memo. For example, you may want to provide background information related to the subject, as well as give current information. Read the following memo and note how the need dictates form. In this memo, the introduction explains the background of Dr. Taylor's idea. The first part of the memo tells what the writer intends to do. The memo then asks Martin Atkins, the reader, to do three things: read, select, and estimate. The memo concludes with a due date. It is effective and should result in Dr. Taylor's getting what he wants.

SAMPLE MEMO 4

MEMO

TO: Martin Atkins, Director of Rehabilitation Services
FROM: Bruce Taylor, M.D., Hospital Administrator
DATE: June 10, 2004
SUBJECT: Development of a hortitherapy program for patients

At the recent Hospital Directors' Round Table, Dr. Seymour Watson of the New England Hortitherapy Council gave a speech on the positive results achieved with hospitalized patients who had been taking care of plants. He further explained the long-term benefits of hortitherapy, especially its continued use after the patient's discharge.

Dr. Watson gave me some guidelines on raising funds for such a project. I plan to survey the board to see how much money could be made available for our own hortitherapy program.

I've attached Dr. Watson's studies, "The Use of Hortitherapy in Geriatric Settings," "Hortitherapy in a Psychiatric Setting," and "Outpatient Programs in Hortitherapy." Please study these and decide which approach we could use at Sunnycrest.

After you decide which patients would benefit most from the program, estimate what personnel and supplies would cost for 20 patients. I'll need your cost estimates by July 16, 1994, so that I can review them before presenting my report to the Board of Directors on July 30.

BT:sz

Disciplinary Memos

If you find it necessary to write a disciplinary memo, bear in mind that a disciplinary memo must:

- document inappropriate or unacceptable behavior
- focus on the serious effect of such behavior
- establish guidelines for future behavior
- state consequences of continued inappropriate behavior
- schedule a follow up review of progress

Practice III

Directions: Rewrite the memo below to conform with the guidelines for a disciplinary memo.

Memo

TO: Edna Employee
FROM: Sandy Supervisor
DATE: March 25, 2003

We talked today about your being late a lot lately. This is not the way we do things around here. It makes it look like you don't care about your job, and other people complain about it.

The next time you're late it could be serious.

Practice IV

Directions: Write an appropriate memo for each situation below.

1. From a supervisor in the order department to the inventory control manager, noting a shortage in a recent shipment to a key client.
2. From a supervisor, who plans to be away, to an employee designated to cover that supervisor's duties during that time.

Reports and Proposals

A report is a detailed statement of accomplishments or findings. A proposal is a request for funding or support to solve a recognized problem or to implement a new idea.

Since reports and proposals serve different functions, they take on different forms. Regardless of the format, however, the basics of good writing prevail. You should present your information in a clear, concise style. You need to document your facts, and if you are taking facts from another source, you must give credit to those sources. In a formal report for school, you would use footnotes. For a business report, you would include footnotes where appropriate. Your conclusions should be set off from your facts so the reader is able to distinguish fact from opinion.

Reports

Most reports have a set form, similar to an outline. For example, a business report may follow this format:

COVER PAGE:	Title, author, date of report
SUMMARY OR ABSTRACT:	A brief overview of the subject covered and conclusions drawn
INTRODUCTION:	A beginning section in which you set the scene, giving relevant background information and/or explaining terminology used in the report
BODY:	The information you are sharing, which supports the conclusions you have drawn
APPENDIX:	All additional relevant data, such as sources of information, additional charts and graphs, and supporting statistics

In preparing reports for business, check for company style by referring to previous reports. If you ask, you may even find a company manual with clear guidelines for report writing. For school reports, ask your teacher what particulars are important to him or her. No one form is correct, but you should use the form preferred.

A lengthy report should have a cover page indicating the purpose of the report, the person or persons to whom it is submitted, the person or persons by whom it is submitted, and the date. The table of contents indicates the scope of the report and the organization of the body of the report. Lengthy reports include a summary at the beginning so that the reader can know at the start the scope and breadth of the report without having to first read the entire report. In the following sample, note the cover page, table of contents, and excerpt from the introduction of a report.

REPORT

OF THE

JOINT STATEWIDE TASK FORCE ON

SOLID WASTE DISPOSAL SITES

Submitted to:

John Doe

Commissioner of Environmental Protection

by:

The Joint Statewide Task Force on Solid Waste Disposal

March, 2005

TABLE OF CONTENTS

I. INTRODUCTION AND OVERVIEW

This report assesses the condition of existing solid waste disposal sites in New Jersey. While landfills are closing, the amount of solid waste produced continues to rise. Faced with this crisis, government must make hard choices based on an accurate appraisal of those few remaining sites.

At the turn of the century, refuse was taken to a nearby "dump," of which there may have been a thousand. The focus was then on repelling flies, dissipating odor, and avoiding fires. The remedy was the use of a "sanitary landfill," which meant nothing more than regularly covering the refuse with layers of soil or sand.

Over the years, the nature of the waste stream has changed. Toxic materials have entered those landfills. Often, hazardous waste from manufacturers has been accepted along with household waste. This has contaminated rainwater on the site. The tainted water, leachate, has become part of the groundwater and contaminates nearby wells.

Currently, ten landfills accept household waste, and a dozen accept industrial waste. Each presents problems. Their continued use is necessary because we have not yet reduced the waste stream or employed alternative technologies that would neutralize that waste. While an in-depth discussion of those aspects is beyond the scope of this report, they raise questions in the assessment of existing landfills: May existing landfills safely continue in use? If so, for how long and under what conditions? This report provides answers to those questions.

Proposals

Proposals follow the same general approach as reports, although most proposals have their own form. Among different companies or agencies, the requested format will vary; one typical form follows.

TYPICAL PROPOSAL FORMAT

Background:

Describe in one short paragraph the history of the operation you plan to change.

EXAMPLE:

MarketRite has been offering one express lane to customers with ten or fewer items for the past twelve years. The express shopper used to be the exception, but is now the rule. Many working people stop in for three or four items on their way home.

Present Conditions:
What goes on now? Why is it inadequate?

EXAMPLE:

Express lanes defy the term. The lanes are exceptionally long and customers often choose to forego buying the one or two items to avoid the lines. This is demonstrated by the merchandise left on the magazine racks near the express lanes.

Proposed Solution:
What changes will you make? What new equipment will be needed? What personnel changes will be needed? How will other operations be affected?

EXAMPLE:

Open two lanes for express purchases during peak times. In order to maintain regular service in other lines, additional part-time help must be hired. Encourage respecting the item limit for express lanes. Have the store manager periodically check for bottlenecks during assumed "slow times" and reassign someone from a regular line to express. This step will be difficult at first, but will become easier as patterns are noted.

Benefits:
What long- and short-term benefits will result?

EXAMPLE:

MarketRite will attract the new breed of shopper. Working people will find shopping at MarketRite is as convenient, more cost effective, and more versatile than the convenience stores. We will retain the traditional shopper by continuing to provide quality check-out for them while eliminating the disgruntled "fast shopper" who "just has six items" and would like to cut into the regular line.

Alternatives:
What are some possible alternatives?

EXAMPLES:

Do not hire additional part-time help for peak times. This would mean closing a regular register to open the additional express lane and would reduce service to the traditional shopper.

Hire additional full-time help to keep the extra express lane open. This may not be cost effective. Relieving the problem during peak times may be sufficient.

Essays

Essays, written for school, for publication, or for yourself, present your own ideas, views, or conclusions. Essays, as well as other writing, benefit from careful planning. Follow these steps to good essay writing.

EASY WRITING STEPS

Plan

Establish a controlling idea by defining your topic and major points.

Outline

Think through your writing from beginning to end. A perfect, final outline is not necessary; outlining serves to order your thoughts and ideas and to subordinate supporting details to major points.

Draft

Fast and furious. Get it down on paper. Don't agonize over grammar, structure, and word choice.

Edit

Fine tuning. Now is the time to agonize over organization, grammar, structure, and word choice. Begin with the end. If you want your audience to continue reading, say immediately why you are writing; you are not writing a mystery. Don't keep your audience in suspense.

Follow with relevant details. Include facts that support the point you want to make. If you lead your readers down an unrelated side road, they may not return to the main issue.

Rewrite

The final product. Make sure that editing did not destroy the flow of writing. One change often necessitates others. Follow through. Simplify reading with subheadings, capitalization, underlining, bulleting, and spacing.

Editing and Rewriting

As you begin editing, ask yourself some important questions.

1. Does your letter, memo, report, proposal, or essay follow your original plan? If not, why not? You may have followed your plan but find that the ideas could be arranged more effectively now. Move those misplaced paragraphs or sentences. Don't hesitate to change the order, even though, at the beginning, it seemed the right way to arrange

things. On second look, you may have found a better way of saying what you want to get across to the reader.

2. Are your ideas well supported? If not, you may need to expand on an idea and add evidence to your argument. On the other hand, if you've gone beyond the subject matter when you've defended a point, you may need to shorten that paragraph or delete an entire section.

3. Is the tone of your writing appropriate? Some people answer this question by reading the report or letter aloud. You can read to a friend—real or imagined—and ask yourself along the way, "Is this the way I would talk?" "Is my idea stated in a conversational way?" "Is the letter overwritten and stiff?" Remember: informal does not mean substandard, and substandard does not mean informal.

4. Have you accomplished your purpose? Find a friend who is not an expert in the subject at hand. Have that person read your letter or report. If your friend is honest, you'll soon know if you've accomplished your purpose for writing.

Checking Your Language

Wordiness

Have you avoided repeating words or thoughts? You can expect your first draft to suffer from wordiness and repetition. Remember, though, that no reader wants to waste time cutting through sentences filled with repetition. When you force your readers to struggle, you try their patience. As you read the examples below, remember to go back and take two or three more words out of every sentence after you've finished editing your work.

Here are some examples of wordiness and repetition with their corrected forms:

No: Today in our modern world we can offer new products at competitive prices.
Yes: Today we can offer new products at competitive prices.

Note that "today" means the same as "modern world."

No: These are the basic essentials of our plan.
Yes: These are the essentials of our plan.

Note that by definition, "essentials" are "basic."

Practice V

Directions: In the following sentences, eliminate the words that are not necessary to the meaning of the sentence.

1. Even after the machine stopped, smoke was visible to the eye.
2. We'll rent a conference room midway between our two offices.
3. If you don't understand an abbreviation, refer back to the index.
4. Rewrite the introduction again before you go on.
5. First and foremost, I want to commend your department.
6. Our study group reached a consensus of opinion.
7. Advanced planning was credited with saving the company.
8. Our product is totally unique.

9. The reason is because it would cost too much to replace the old equipment.
10. The technology upgrade produced gains that were small in size.

Stilted Phrases

Have you avoided words that writers seem to *save* for letters, memos, and reports? Business letters are frequently filled with legal language as well as archaic words and phrases, even though they add no meaning. Ask yourself, "Would I use this in conversation or at any other time?" If the answer is no, strike that heavy phrase from your work.

Here are some examples of stilted, out-of-date, and overly formal phrases that creep into business and report writing.

Don't Use	Substitute
Due to the fact	Because
Attached herewith	Here is
In receipt of	Have received
In reference to	Concerning
At the present time	Now
Under separate cover	Separately
Thanking you in advance	Thank you

Practice VI

Directions: Substitute plain English for the stilted language used in the following sentences.

1. In the process of checking your account, we have found that your bill is overdue.
2. Attached please find my check for $42.37.
3. I will take your plan under advisement.
4. We beg to advise you that our product will be on sale in May.
5. I am in receipt of your letter and its contents are noted.

The -Ize Words

-Ize words are fine, but too many can make your writing sound stilted.

Don't Use	Substitute
Utilize	Use
Maximize	Increase
Finalize	Finish
Prioritize	Rank
Optimize	Cut the cost, improve

Practice VII

Directions: Substitute a precise word or a simpler word for the underlined word or words in each sentence.

1. We need to <u>systematize</u> our files so that we can <u>utilize</u> them easily.
2. <u>Size-wise,</u> these bookcases are a better choice for our office.
3. The way you <u>prioritize</u> can <u>maximize</u> your productivity.
4. A larger sales force will <u>minimize</u> individual profit margins.
5. Your report <u>legitimizes</u> our need for monthly meetings to <u>optimize</u> information sharing.

Keeping Sexism Out of Your Writing

Follow these guidelines to avoid sexism in your writing.

1. Do not add *ess* to words that do not require that suffix. For example, *actor* means male actor and *actress* means female, *manager* means male or female *manager.*
2. Where the word is comfortably modified to be unisex, modify it. *Chairperson* sounds as legitimate as *chairman.*
3. Try to avoid situations that require a singular pronoun. For example, instead of the following:

> Each member of the management team took his place (or his/her place) at the conference table.

Use:

> Members of the management team took their places at the conference table.

Proofreading

Proofreading is an important part of editing what you have written. It assures you that careless errors in grammar, punctuation, and sense have been caught and corrected. Proofreading must be done in several steps:

1. Read through for content. Do not expect to pick up technical errors. Do expect to pick up missing or transposed words or sentences and errors in information.
2. Read for grammar, spelling, punctuation, and sense. Force yourself to read *each* word.
3. Read one more time to ensure that changes did not alter consistency or sense.
4. Have another person proofread your work after you have proofread it yourself.

Summary of Steps to Simplify and Clarify Your Writing

1. Use action words. Write so that your performers act and are not acted upon. (Unless you do not want to assign responsibility.)

   INSTEAD OF: A new check-cashing policy will be introduced this spring.
   USE: General Markets will introduce a new check-cashing policy this spring.

2. Limit your use of descriptive phrases.

   INSTEAD OF: We scheduled a meeting of supervisors of MIS for January 12.
   USE: We scheduled an MIS supervisors' meeting for January 12.

3. Eliminate unnecessary words and phrases.

   INSTEAD OF: When a new spa opens, all of the spas in the Wonder Woman chain take part in the grand opening of that spa.
   USE: All Wonder Woman spas take part in the grand opening of a new spa in the chain.

4. Use names rather than pronouns as often as possible.

   INSTEAD OF: When he gives the report to him, make sure he understands the ramifications.
   USE: When Tom gives the report to Jason, make sure Jason understands the ramifications.

5. Focus on concrete word choice rather than abstract.

   INSTEAD OF: In order to create a holiday atmosphere, we want to encourage spirit and festivity throughout the store.
   USE: In order to create a holiday atmosphere, we want managers to develop special displays, provide holiday music, and remind cashiers to say, "Happy holidays" to customers.

6. Avoid using performers as action words.

   INSTEAD OF: Roger authored the user manual.
   USE: Roger is the author of the user manual.

7. Use positive words; avoid negative words.

   INSTEAD OF: Only fifty some odd residents turned out for the opening of the Middletown Bank.
   USE: Over fifty residents participated in the opening of the Middletown Bank.

Practice VIII

Directions: Correct each sentence below according to the rules.

1. Use action words.
   The order was placed too late.
2. Limit your use of prepositional phrases.
   We arranged a meeting with the manager of data processing at the location in East Brunswick.
3. Eliminate unnecessary words and phrases.
   There are two possible approaches that we are considering.
4. Use names rather than pronouns as often as possible.
   When he delivers the papers to him, be sure he gets a signature.
5. Focus on concrete word choice rather than abstract.
   Contributions help many people.
6. Avoid using nouns as verbs.
   Please overnight mail the report to Michael.
7. Use positive words.
   If it's not inconvenient for you now, perhaps we could talk.

Writer's Block

Any adult who has ever had reason to write more than three words at a time has experienced writer's block. What is writer's block? Think of it as the empty paper, or blank screen, syndrome—the fight between the need to get something down on a blank piece of paper and the desire to get it down correctly on the first try—an impossible task.

To a great extent, writer's block occurs because we refuse to admit—or we haven't been taught—that no one can produce perfect written work on the first try. Writer's block results from thinking that you can put an idea on paper AND edit it at the same time. This creates unreasonable pressure. You can't. I can't. Well-known writers can't. You say you need proof? Read on.

The editors of *Writer's Digest* asked several authors of fiction to write articles using the title, "How I Write My Books." Their articles revealed different approaches to their craft, but one idea remained constant: there are two aspects to writing—creating and revising.

You may be wondering if this applies to you—after all, you don't write fiction. It does. Whether writing fiction or fact, you are dealing with two things: creating and revising.

What can be done to circumvent writer's block? Without knowing it, you have probably just taken the first step simply by thinking about the idea that creating and revising are two different tasks. If you accept that as a fact, you can go on to attack the first half of the process—creating.

Educators have developed techniques to help the writer get the creator working. Whether called brainstorming, improvisational writing, mapping, or clustering, these techniques have one idea in common: each writer is a combination of creator and editor. Each technique requires that your editor leave the room while your creator writes. The creator must work unhampered by concerns of spelling, word choice, and sentence structure. Each technique asks that, as you think about your subject, you jot down your thoughts in single words, phrases, or brief sentences, no matter how or in what order they occur to you. DON'T JUDGE YOUR THOUGHTS. JUST WRITE THEM DOWN. The result will be many related ideas (and a few unrelated, but that doesn't matter) that are not in logical order. That's fine. That proves you are part of the human race in which minds do not work in outline form.

Once you have your thoughts on paper, you can open the door and let the editor in. The editor will help you put your thoughts in order and polish your grammar, structure, and word choice. Finally, the editor will increase the readability of your essay by adding necessary subheadings, listing points where appropriate, and using white space creatively.

SOME TOOLS FOR BETTER WRITING

A good dictionary and thesaurus online and on the shelf.

English the Easy Way, Harriet Diamond and Phyllis Dutwin. New York: Barron's Educational Series, Inc.

Executive Writing: A Style Manual for the Business World, Harriet Diamond and Marsha Fahey. New Jersey: Prentice Hall Regents.

Style: Toward Clarity and Grace, Joseph M. Williams. Chicago: University of Chicago Press.

The Business Writer's Handbook, Gerald J. Alred, Charles T. Brusaw, and Walter E. Oliu. New York: St. Martin's Press.

The Elements of Style, William Strunk Jr. and E. B. White. New York: Macmillan Publishing Co., Inc.

The Gregg Reference Manual, William A. Sabin. Ohio: Glencoe/McGraw Hill.

Webster's Instant Word Guide. Massachusetts: Merriam-Webster, Inc.

Write to the Top, Deborah Dumain. New York: Random House.

Writing the Easy Way, Phyllis Dutwin and Harriet Diamond. New York: Barron's Educational Series, Inc.

Chapter 22 Writing Right

Practice I *Page 250.*

1419 Maple Street
Dayton, Ohio 82050
May 20, 2002

Service Manager
Wake-Up Corporation
2042 Main Street
Chicago, Illinois 60791

Dear Service Manager:

I bought the enclosed clock radio at Warren's Department Store in Dayton, Ohio, on May 15, 2002. The alarm did not work properly from the start.

On May 19, I brought the clock radio back to Warren's to exchange it for a new model or to have it repaired. The salesman would not accept the clock radio. He insisted that I return it to you. This is a great inconvenience. I never even used this appliance.

Please send me a new clock radio immediately. I also would encourage you to work out a fairer arrangement with your distributors. I know I would never buy a Wake-Up product again because of the inconvenience.

Very truly yours,

Tom Williams
Tom Williams

Practice II *Page 250.*

February 10, 2003

Ms. Suzanne Jones
1 Willow Way
Edison, New Jersey 08817

Dear Ms. Jones:

Thank you for informing me about the unfortunate experience you had at MarketRite last Friday. You clearly understand the importance of sharing such information with management. We do want to make our shopping environment pleasant.

The treatment you received was inexcusable. John Rich surprised and embarrassed himself by yelling at you. Although that behavior was not typical, it never should have occurred at all. Of course, I have spoken with John and extend his personal apology.

Please accept the enclosed gift certificate and my apology. You are our valued customer. When you are in MarketRite again, please ask for me. I would like to thank you personally for helping us improve our service.

Sincerely,

Matthew Manager

Matthew Manager
Vice President
Customer Relations

MM:er
enc.

Practice III *Page 254.*

MEMO

TO: Edna Employee
FROM: Sandy Supervisor
DATE: March 25, 2003

As we discussed in our meeting today, you have been 30 minutes late for work on three occasions in the last two weeks. These incidents follow two earlier discussions we had regarding your tardiness.

In our talk today, we went over the Company's policy on tardiness and agreed that when you are late it creates problems for other employees who must cover for you. It also results in filling orders late, which can affect our customer relations. Repeated tardiness also causes resentment among co-workers who are consistently on time. As we agreed, you will purchase a new alarm clock and get a bus schedule so you have an alternative mode of transportation if your car will not start. As I pointed out, further incidents of tardiness could result in withholding your upcoming wage increase or, if sustained improvement is not seen, termination.

We will meet again in two weeks to review your record.

Practice IV *Page 254.*

1. TO: Jack Barnes, Inventory Control Manager
   FROM: Sally Farmer, Supervisor, Order Department
   DATE: October 10, 2002
   SUBJECT: ORDER #67-8850/October 1, 2002

   Please note that the above order was shipped short of 50 copies of WRITING THE EASY WAY. This customer is one of our key buyers and expects a replacement shipment within 2 days. Can you look into this and assure me that the shipment will go out immediately via Federal Express?

2. TO: William
   FROM: Rita
   DATE: February 16, 2002
   SUBJECT: My upcoming vacation—2/23–2/30

   Please read the attached outline of duties in its entirety before I leave on Tuesday. I will be available to answer any questions you might have regarding materials, personnel, etc. Please maintain a log of messages, and note which ones will not have been answered. John should be available to assist you when necessary. Thank you for taking on the extra load; I'll be available for same when your vacation comes along.

Practice V *Page 261.*
1. Even after the machine stopped, smoke was visible.
2. We'll rent a conference room between our two offices.
3. If you don't understand an abbreviation, refer to the index.
4. Rewrite the introduction before you go on.
5. First, I commend your department.
6. Our study group reached a consensus.
7. Planning was credited with saving the company.
8. Our product is unique.
9. It would cost too much to replace the old equipment.
10. The technology upgrade produced gains that were small.

Practice VI *Page 262.*
1. Checking your account, we have found that your bill is overdue.
2. Here's my check for $42.37.
3. I will consider your plan.
4. We want you to know that our product will be on sale in May.
5. I've received your letter.

Practice VII *Page 263.*
1. We need to <u>organize</u> our files so that we can <u>use</u> them easily.
2. These bookcases are a better <u>size</u> for our office.
3. The way you <u>rank</u> priorities can <u>increase</u> your productivity.

4. A larger sales force will <u>decrease</u> individual profit margins.
5. Your report <u>affirms</u> our need for monthly meetings to <u>improve</u> information sharing.

Practice VIII *Page 265.*
1. Henry placed the order too late.
2. We arranged a meeting in East Brunswick with the data processing manager.
3. We are considering two approaches.
4. When Smith delivers the papers to Caldwell, be sure Smith gets a signature.
5. Contributions provide food and clothing for the homeless.
6. Please send the report to Michael by overnight mail.
7. If it's convenient for you now, let's talk.

Chapter 23

FINAL REVIEW

This review covers all of the concepts presented in *English the Easy Way*, Chapters 1–22.

- Spelling
- Usage
- Effectiveness of Expression
- Punctuation and Capitalization

After completing the Final Review exercises, evaluate your ability on the SUMMARY OF RESULTS chart on page 284. Acceptable scores for each practice are given.

To identify your areas for skill improvement, find the question numbers you answered incorrectly on the SKILLS ANALYSIS table. The table will show which of your skills need improvement and the necessary chapters to review.

Spelling

Directions: Blacken the circle that corresponds to the number of the incorrectly spelled word in each group. If there is no error, blacken number 5.

1. (1) belief
    (2) reference
    (3) caucas
    (4) changeable
    (5) No error
    ① ② ③ ④ ⑤

2. (1) temperture
    (2) exceed
    (3) misspell
    (4) absence
    (5) No error
    ① ② ③ ④ ⑤

3. (1) quantity
    (2) probably
    (3) warrant
    (4) libary
    (5) No error
    ① ② ③ ④ ⑤

4. (1) subversive
    (2) lucritive
    (3) psychology
    (4) queue
    (5) No error
    ① ② ③ ④ ⑤

5. (1) hygenic
    (2) currency
    (3) eczema
    (4) salient
    (5) No error
    ① ② ③ ④ ⑤

6. (1) Wednesday
    (2) biscuit
    (3) efemoral
    (4) contemptible
    (5) No error
    ① ② ③ ④ ⑤

7. (1) corrugated
    (2) diphtheria
    (3) voucher
    (4) unecessary
    (5) No error
    ① ② ③ ④ ⑤

8. (1) wierd   (4) duly   ① ② ③ ④ ⑤
    (2) tuition   (5) No error
    (3) capital
9. (1) illustrative   (4) receits   ① ② ③ ④ ⑤
    (2) laboratory   (5) No error
    (3) judiciary
10. (1) though   (4) voluntary   ① ② ③ ④ ⑤
    (2) simular   (5) No error
    (3) surgeon
11. (1) preference   (4) deterrent   ① ② ③ ④ ⑤
    (2) economical   (5) No error
    (3) prefered
12. (1) psychology   (4) argument   ① ② ③ ④ ⑤
    (2) cooperation   (5) No error
    (3) rationally
13. (1) generally   (4) portable   ① ② ③ ④ ⑤
    (2) improbable   (5) No error
    (3) dispensible
14. (1) truely   (4) occurrence   ① ② ③ ④ ⑤
    (2) niece   (5) No error
    (3) neighbor
15. (1) cunning   (4) crushs   ① ② ③ ④ ⑤
    (2) tomatoes   (5) No error
    (3) mouthfuls
16. (1) sheep   (4) thiefs   ① ② ③ ④ ⑤
    (2) pianos   (5) No error
    (3) Z's
17. (1) men-of-war   (4) precede   ① ② ③ ④ ⑤
    (2) supersede   (5) No error
    (3) succeed
18. (1) misunderstand   (4) cancellation   ① ② ③ ④ ⑤
    (2) achevement   (5) No error
    (3) condemned
19. (1) acquire   (4) character   ① ② ③ ④ ⑤
    (2) assessment   (5) No error
    (3) Thursday
20. (1) churches   (4) realize   ① ② ③ ④ ⑤
    (2) wield   (5) No error
    (3) category

Usage—Part A

Directions: Blacken the circle that corresponds to the number of the error in each sentence. If there is no error, blacken number 5.

1. No <u>two</u> <u>cities</u> in <u>this</u> country <u>is</u> identical. <u>No error</u>   ① ② ③ ④ ⑤
          1   2   3   4   5

2. _Any_ of the local merchants _are_ _willing_ to _support_ the United
    1   2   3   4
    Fund. _No error_
              5   ① ② ③ ④ ⑤

3. This CD _has_ _been_ _laying_ on the table _all_ week. _No error_   ① ② ③ ④ ⑤
              1   2   3   4   5

4. _Either_ of those two congressmen _will_ _vote_ against the   ① ② ③ ④ ⑤
    1   2   3
    President's _proposed_ bill. _No error_
                    4   5

5. _One_ of the _necessary_ prerequisites for change _are_ _open-_   ① ② ③ ④ ⑤
    1   2   3   4
    mindedness. _No error_
              5

6. Manuel and _me_ _travel_ to _work_ together each _weekday_   ① ② ③ ④ ⑤
                    1   2   3   4
    morning. _No error_
                5

7. Taxes and _laughter_ _is_ always _present_ in our _American_ way of   ① ② ③ ④ ⑤
                  1   2   3   4
    life. _No error_
         5

8. Everyone must _realize_ _their_ own potential and _try_ to _achieve_   ① ② ③ ④ ⑤
                       1   2   3   4
    it. _No error_
        5

9. Mario _is_ a much _more_ _efficient_ bartender than _him._ _No error_   ① ② ③ ④ ⑤
             1   2   3   4   5

10. Elissa _types_ _much_ _quicker_ _than_ any _other_ person in the office.   ① ② ③ ④ ⑤
            1   2   3   4
    No error
      5

11. _Each_ of the choices _are_ _equally_ unappealing to _me._ _No error_   ① ② ③ ④ ⑤
    1   2   3   4   5

12. Before the alarm _had stopped_ _ringing,_ Vera _had_ _pulled_ up   ① ② ③ ④ ⑤
                       1   2   3   4
    the shade. _No error_
            5

13. One of _those_ women _speak_ _as_ well _as_ a professional lecturer.   ① ② ③ ④ ⑤
          1   2   3   4
    No error
        5

14. The dishes in the box _is_ _on_ sale this week only _and_ will be   ① ② ③ ④ ⑤
                           1   2   3
    sold for more next week. _No error_
      4   5

15. The Township Committee _had_ not _realized_ that so many   ① ② ③ ④ ⑤
                             1   2
    residents _were_ _concerned_ about the new zoning law. _No error_
               3   4   5

16. _Either_ the subway or the _buses_ _is_ _crowded_ at this time of day.   ① ② ③ ④ ⑤
      1   2   3   4
    No error
        5

17. I _noticed_ that older women _walk_ _more_ _graceful_ than teen-age   ① ② ③ ④ ⑤
         1   2   3   4
    girls. _No error_
              5

18. _Each_ of the contestants _hope_ to _win_ the _grand_ prize. _No error_   ① ② ③ ④ ⑤
      1   2   3   4   5

19. When I must _speak_ to a _large_ group of people, I always speak   ① ② ③ ④ ⑤
                  1   2
    too _soft_. _No error_
      3   4   5

20. The mail carriers _each_ _has_ _their_ own _personal_ gripes. _No error_   ① ② ③ ④ ⑤
                       1   2   3   4   5

21. _Any_ of the women in that office _may_ express _their_ opinion at   ① ② ③ ④ ⑤
      1   2   3
    any time. _No error_
      4   5

22. Either the executive _or_ members of his staff _was_ _responsible_   ① ② ③ ④ ⑤
                          1   2   3
    for _breaking_ the law. _No error_
          4   5

23. Before they _signed_ the treaty, both parties _agreed_ to _uphold_   ① ② ③ ④ ⑤
                  1   2   3
    the terms _provided._ _No error_
                4   5

24. Reagan *was* president before Bush *was,* and Clinton *served*
       1   2   3

    after Bush *had. No error*
           4   5

    ① ② ③ ④ ⑤

25. Either Charlie or *I* will *call* you or *he* when the order *is* ready.
                  1   2   3   4

    No error
     5

    ① ② ③ ④ ⑤

26. *Romeo and Juliet are* one of my favorite plays, but *I've* never
               1   2

    seen it performed. *No error*
     3 4   5

    ① ② ③ ④ ⑤

27. *Was it* Mr. Farrar *whom called* you? *No error*
    1 2   3   4   5

    ① ② ③ ④ ⑤

28. I *am always* at the bus stop *earlier* than *him. No error*
      1   2   3   4   5

    ① ② ③ ④ ⑤

29. Eileen and *me are working* on the night shift with *them.*
            1 2   3   4

    No error
     5

    ① ② ③ ④ ⑤

30. Fifteen minutes *are* all that I *can spare* to listen to *your*
                1   2   3   4

    problems. *No error*
            5

    ① ② ③ ④ ⑤

31. The problem of *too* many people *require immediate* attention
                 1   2   3

    by world leaders *as well as* scientists and environmentalists.
                    4

    No error
     5

    ① ② ③ ④ ⑤

32. After many months *of arguing,* Congress finally *adapted* the
                    1 2   3

    bill *into* law. *No error*
       4   5

    ① ② ③ ④ ⑤

33. Because his lawyer *strongly adviced* him to do *so,*
                 1   2   3

    Mr. Rodriguez *offered* his wife a generous settlement.
                4

    No error
     5

    ① ② ③ ④ ⑤

34. The _principle_ reason for _my_ not borrowing _your_ credit card   ① ② ③ ④ ⑤
        1   2   3

     is that I'm afraid I'll _lose_ it. _No error_
                     4   5

35. _Your_ supervisor _does_ not appreciate _you_ walking in   ① ② ③ ④ ⑤
     1   2   3

     consistently at 9:10. _No error_
       4   5

Usage—Part B

Directions: Blacken the circle that corresponds to the number of the error in each sentence. If there is no error, blacken number 5.

1. My brother _he_ never _calls_ before _visiting_ _us._ _No error_   ① ② ③ ④ ⑤
            1   2   3   4   5

2. Great men _throughout_ history _hardly_ _never_ avoided some   ① ② ③ ④ ⑤
            1   2   3

     minor _scandal._ _No error_
          4   5

3. If you _had_ called ahead _of_ time, I could _of_ _been_ ready when   ① ② ③ ④ ⑤
          1   2   3 4

     you arrived. _No error_
                5

4. George Burns _scarcely_ _never_ _missed_ a _scheduled_ performance.   ① ② ③ ④ ⑤
               1   2   3   4

     No error
       5

5. The _sightseeing_ trip on the sightseeing bus _was_ _one of_ the   ① ② ③ ④ ⑤
           1   2   3

     highlights of our _much_ deserved vacation. _No error_
                 4   5

6. Manny _was_ shocked when Alfred _raised_ his voice; no one had   ① ② ③ ④ ⑤
         1   2

     never _spoken_ to him in that tone of voice. _No error_
       3   4   5

7. The sun _it_ _is_ 865,000 miles in diameter and _has_ a surface   ① ② ③ ④ ⑤
          1 2   3

     temperature of _about_ 10,000°F. _No error_
               4   5

8. A wise consumer <u>*carefully*</u> <u>*reads*</u> the labels and doesn't   ① ② ③ ④ ⑤

                       1   2

    <u>*never*</u> <u>*buy*</u> unmarked products. <u>*No error*</u>

      3   4   5

9. If you really <u>*had*</u> <u>*wanted*</u> to, you could <u>*of*</u> <u>*prevented*</u> that   ① ② ③ ④ ⑤

                          1   2   3   4

    misunderstanding. <u>*No error*</u>

                   5

10. Some scientists <u>*they*</u> believe <u>*that*</u> one of the long-range <u>*effects*</u>   ① ② ③ ④ ⑤

                         1   2   3

    of food additives <u>*is*</u> hyperactivity in children. <u>*No error*</u>

                4   5

Effectiveness of Expression—Part A

Directions: Blacken the circle that corresponds to the number of the correct completion for each sentence below. Choice 1 is always the same as the underlined portion and is sometimes the right answer.

1. <u>*The new sales associate he arrives late*</u> every morning.   ① ② ③ ④ ⑤
   (1) The new sales associate he arrives late
   (2) The new sales associate arrives late
   (3) The new sales associate arriving late
   (4) The new sales associate is arriving late
   (5) The new sales associates they arrive late

2. <u>*The reason that the doctor missed the emergency call is because*</u>   ① ② ③ ④ ⑤
   he forgot his beeper.
   (1) The reason that the doctor missed the emergency call
       is because
   (2) The reason that the doctor missed the emergency call
       because
   (3) The doctor missed the emergency call because
   (4) Being that the doctor missed the emergency call is because
   (5) Because the doctor missed the emergency call is because

3. Mia's new job offers <u>*not only a better salary but also increased*</u>   ① ② ③ ④ ⑤
   <u>*benefits.*</u>
   (1) not only a better salary but also increased benefits.
   (2) not only a better salary and increased benefits.
   (3) not a better salary or increased benefits.
   (4) not only a better salary and, in addition, better benefits.
   (5) not only better salaries and, in addition, increased benefits.

4. Nowadays employers can afford to be choosy _although the period of slow economic growth has increased_ the number and the quality of the applicants.   ① ② ③ ④ ⑤
   (1) although the period of slow economic growth has increased
   (2) despite the period of slow economic growth has increased
   (3) in addition to the period of slow economic growth having increased
   (4) since the period of slow economic growth has increased
   (5) but the period of slow economic growth has increased

5. The dogs get _tough, demanding, and training that is useful_ in obedience school.   ① ② ③ ④ ⑤
   (1) tough, demanding, and training that is useful
   (2) tough, demanding, useful training
   (3) tough, demanding, usefully training
   (4) tough, demanding, and usefully trained
   (5) tough, demanding, and useful in their training

6. Carl Williams is an excellent basketball coach and _he makes friends with the team members._   ① ② ③ ④ ⑤
   (1) he makes friends with the team members.
   (2) a good friend to the team members.
   (3) the team members are his friend.
   (4) the team members liking him.
   (5) liking the team members.

7. Every Thursday night the Morgan family watches TV and _TV dinners are served._   ① ② ③ ④ ⑤
   (1) TV dinners are served.
   (2) they ate TV dinners.
   (3) eats TV dinners.
   (4) eat TV dinners.
   (5) are eating TV dinners.

8. The City Council meets every Wednesday evening in private and _publicly on Thursdays._   ① ② ③ ④ ⑤
   (1) publicly on Thursdays.
   (2) Thursdays meets publicly.
   (3) every Thursday in public.
   (4) also Thursdays in public.
   (5) has public meetings on Thursdays.

9. Carlos Battaglia has a good historical perspective _since he understands_ current events.   ① ② ③ ④ ⑤
   (1) since he understands
   (2) because he understands
   (3) however, he understands
   (4) ; therefore, he understands
   (5) so he doesn't understand

10. I am not in agreement with most of the policies of the present administration, _but I can't change them._   ① ② ③ ④ ⑤
    (1) but I can't change them.
    (2) so I don't want to change them.

(3) so I can't change them.
(4) since I can't change them.
(5) therefore, I can't change them.

Effectiveness of Expression—Part B

Directions: Blacken the circle that corresponds to the number of the correct completion for each sentence below.

1. The boundaries of science have expanded significantly,   ① ② ③ ④ ⑤
   (1) and two distinct fields of science have emerged: pure and applied.
   (2) even though two distinct fields of science have emerged: pure and applied.
   (3) whenever two distinct fields of science have emerged: pure and applied.
   (4) and two fields of science, they have emerged: pure and applied.
   (5) despite two distinct fields of science have emerged: pure and applied.
2. The British pound was devalued   ① ② ③ ④ ⑤
   (1) and the reason was because of an inflationary spiral.
   (2) and the reason was because of inflation.
   (3) and it was because of an inflationary spiral
   (4) because of an inflationary spiral.
   (5) and it was when the inflation spiraled.
3. The revised Food Guide Pyramid provides a guide to daily   ① ② ③ ④ ⑤
   food choices,
   (1) although it will help people build a healthful diet.
   (2) thereby helping people build a healthful diet.
   (3) however they will help people build a healthful diet.
   (4) and in addition it will also help people build a healthful diet.
   (5) and then if you use it it will help people build a healthful diet.
4. Many people believed that the recent dip in the stock market   ① ② ③ ④ ⑤
   (1) were because of rising interest rates.
   (2) resulted from rising interest rates.
   (3) happened because of rising interest rates.
   (4) were because of the rising interest rates.
   (5) resulted from interest rates, they were rising.
5. Viewers find it difficult to reach agreement on whether   ① ② ③ ④ ⑤
   (1) or not television, it encouraged violent behavior.
   (2) or not television, it does or doesn't encourage violent behavior.
   (3) or not television encourages violent behavior.
   (4) television hardly never encourages violent behavior.
   (5) or not television encourages violent behavior by viewing television.

6. One member of the Surgeon General's Scientific Advisory
   Committee on Television and Social Behavior felt that   ① ② ③ ④ ⑤
   (1) there is scarcely no question about whether television
       has a negative effect on its viewers.
   (2) there isn't no question about whether television has a
       negative effect on its viewers.
   (3) there isn't hardly any question about whether television
       has a negative effect on its viewers.
   (4) there is no question about whether television has a negative
       effect on its viewers.
   (5) there really isn't no question about whether television has a
       negative effect on its viewers.

7. Some TV viewers express their resentment toward anyone else   ① ② ③ ④ ⑤
   censoring their viewing choices,
   (1) saying it's their job to censor the TV programs their
       children see.
   (2) saying it's the parents' job to censor the TV programs their
       children see on television programs.
   (3) saying it's the parents' job to censor the TV programs their
       children see.
   (4) saying parents, they should censor the TV programs their
       children see.
   (5) saying TV it should be censored by no one but parents.

8. An environmental protection agency should   ① ② ③ ④ ⑤
   (1) set automobile pollution standards, oversee stripmining,
       and prohibit dumping in public waterways.
   (2) set automobile pollution standards, oversee stripmining, and
       they will prohibit dumping in public waterways.
   (3) set automobile pollution standards, do the overseeing of
       stripmining, and they will prohibit dumping in private
       waterways.
   (4) set automobile pollution standards, overseeing stripmining,
       and prohibiting dumping in private waterways.
   (5) set automobile pollution standards, and they will oversee
       stripmining, and prohibit dumping in private waterways.

9. Many people who formerly drove to work are now taking buses   ① ② ③ ④ ⑤
   (1) in order to conserve gas, preventing air pollution, and saving
       money.
   (2) and by the way, they conserve gas, prevent air pollution, and
       they're saving money.
   (3) in order to conserve gas, and they'll be preventing air
       pollution, and to save money.
   (4) in order to conserve gas, to prevent air pollution, and
       to save money.
   (5) in order to conserve gas, do air pollution prevention, and
       save money.

10. In order to encourage the commuter not to drive to work, some communities have installed park-and-ride facilities ① ② ③ ④ ⑤
    (1) where the commuter can leave his car and board a bus for the trip to work.
    (2) where they can leave his car and board a bus for the trip to work.
    (3) where they can leave their cars and board a bus for the trip to work.
    (4) and then they can leave their car and board a bus for the trip to work.
    (5) so that they can leave their car and board a bus for the trip to work.

11. The new employee is very organized; ① ② ③ ④ ⑤
    (1) even if she is always late.
    (2) so she is always late.
    (3) however, she is always late.
    (4) despite her always being late.
    (5) although she is always late.

12. The end of 2001 showed a marked decline in Americans traveling abroad ① ② ③ ④ ⑤
    (1) in spite of increasing terrorism.
    (2) inasmuch as there were increased incidences of terrorism.
    (3) due to increased terrorism.
    (4) because terrorism decreased.
    (5) even though there were increasing incidences of terrorism.

13. The French Revolution did not occur when the peasants had no rights whatsoever; ① ② ③ ④ ⑤
    (1) rather, the Revolution occurred when the peasants began to taste the better life.
    (2) but it happened when they began to taste the better life.
    (3) so it did when they got some rights.
    (4) rather, the Revolution occurred when the peasants, they began to taste the better life.
    (5) instead they made the Revolution when they became rich.

14. Modern China has eliminated serious contagious diseases ① ② ③ ④ ⑤
    (1) because they use trained nonprofessionals to aid their country's limited number of doctors.
    (2) since using trained nonprofessionals to aid their limited number of doctors.
    (3) therefore it uses trained nonprofessionals to aid the country's limited number of doctors.
    (4) by using trained nonprofessionals to aid the country's limited number of doctors.
    (5) for using trained nonprofessionals to aid the country's limited number of doctors.

15. During the first half of the eighteenth century, the Carter family ① ② ③ ④ ⑤
    built a mansion at Williamsburg where the family
    (1) it grew its own food, rode to hounds on horses from their own
        stables, and shipped its tobacco to England from its private dock.
    (2) they grew their own food, rode to the hounds on horses from
        their own stables, made equipment in their own craft shops, and
        shipped their tobacco to England from their private dock.
    (3) grew its own food, rode to the hounds on horses from its own
        stables, made equipment in its own craft shops, and shipped its
        tobacco to England from its private dock.
    (4) grew its own food, rode to the hounds on horses from their own
        stables, made equipment in its own craft shop, and shipped their
        tobacco to England from its private dock.
    (5) grew their own food, rode to the hounds on horses from their own
        stables, made equipment in their own craft shop, and shipping
        tobacco from their own private dock.

Punctuation and Capitalization

Directions: Blacken the circle that corresponds to the number of the error in each
sentence. If there is no error, blacken number 5.

1. According to historians, when the people in power cannot keep ① ② ③ ④ ⑤
                         1

   the governed_content, revolution is a possibility. *No error*
              2   34   5

2. The *Declaration of Independence* states, "... that all men are ① ② ③ ④ ⑤
                                              1

   created equal, that they are endowed by their Creator with
              2

   certain inalienable rights; that among these are Life, Liberty,
                                                        3

   and the pursuit of Happiness". *No error*
                         4   5

3. Great literature, as well as great art_is a part of the ① ② ③ ④ ⑤
                 1   2

   American tradition. *No error*
   3   4   5

4. The pioneers were a hardy_brave group of people_who
                      1   2

   would look in disbelief on the comforts of today'_s middle
                                                3

   class_. *No error*
      4   5

   ① ② ③ ④ ⑤

5. During their first few years on the American continent_ the
                                          1   2

   pioneers lived off the animals in the woods_ and stole corn
                                      3

   from the_natives. *No error*
         4   5

   ① ② ③ ④ ⑤

6. They traveled with the bare necessities: food_ water_ warm
                                 1   2   3

   clothing, tools_ and weapons. *No error*
             4   5

   ① ② ③ ④ ⑤

7. The _Virginians_ needed their own leader_ Jefferson_ Sam
     1   2   3 4

   Adams was not their type. *No error*
                  5

   ① ② ③ ④ ⑤

8. Many say George Washington was a competent general_ and
                                            1

   a good president: however_ some_historians would disagree.
                    2   3   4

   No error
     5

   ① ② ③ ④ ⑤

9. There are those who would say that "John Kennedy was the
                                       1

   greatest president to date_ and others would say that he has
        2   3

   been idealize_d. *No error*
            4   5

   ① ② ③ ④ ⑤

10. A flower_consists of a calyx_ a corolla_ a stamen _ and pistils.
            1   2   3   4

    No error
      5

    ① ② ③ ④ ⑤

After reviewing the Answer Key on page 286, chart your scores below for each practice exercise.

SUMMARY OF RESULTS

Practice Number	Number Correct	Number Incorrect (Including Omissions)	Acceptable Score
Spelling			15 Correct
Usage—Part A			26 Correct
Usage—Part B			7 Correct
Effectiveness of Expression— Part A			7 Correct
Effectiveness of Expression— Part B			11 Correct
Punctuation and Capitalization			7 Correct

To determine your areas for skill improvement, locate the questions you answered incorrectly and circle the numbers on this Skills Analysis chart. Wherever you have circled errors, review the chapters listed in the last column.

SKILLS ANALYSIS

Skill	Question Number	Review Chapter
Spelling	1 to 20	18
Usage: Part A		
Agreement of Subject and Linking Verb	1, 7, 14, 26, 30	7
Agreement: Special Problems	2, 4, 5, 11, 16, 18, 20, 22	8
Correct Form of Irregular Action Word	3	1
Correct Use of Pronouns	6, 8, 9, 21, 25, 27, 28, 29, 35	10
Time: Special Problems	12, 15, 23, 24	9
Agreement of Performer and Action Word	13, 31	2
Word Usage	32, 33, 34	20
Correct Use of Descriptive Words: -ly ending	10, 17, 19	3

SKILLS ANALYSIS

Skill	Question Number	Review Chapter
Usage: Part B		
Repetition	1, 5, 7, 10	15
Double Negative	2, 4, 6, 8	15
Word Choice	3, 9	20
Effectiveness of Expression: Part A		
Repetition	1	15
Wordiness	2	15
Coordination of Ideas	4, 9, 10	15
Balance	5, 6, 7, 8	12
Effectiveness of Expression: Part B		
Coordination of Ideas	1, 3, 11, 12, 13, 14	15
Wordiness	2, 4, 5	15
Double Negative	6	15
Unclear Pronoun Reference	7, 10	15
Balance	8, 9, 15	12
Punctuation and Capitalization		
Quotation Marks	2, 9	16
Comma	3, 4, 5, 8, 10	13
Semicolon	7	13
Colon	6	16

Chapter 23 Final Review

Spelling *Page 271.*

1. **(3)** caucus
2. **(1)** temperature
3. **(4)** library
4. **(2)** lucrative
5. **(1)** hygienic
6. **(3)** ephemeral
7. **(4)** unnecessary
8. **(1)** weird
9. **(4)** receipts
10. **(2)** similar
11. **(3)** preferred
12. **(5)** No error
13. **(3)** dispensable
14. **(1)** truly
15. **(4)** crushes
16. **(4)** thieves
17. **(5)** No error
18. **(2)** achievement
19. **(5)** No error
20. **(5)** No error

Usage—Part A *Page 272.*

1. **(4)** No two cities in this country *are* identical. See Chapter 7.
2. **(2)** Any of the local merchants *is* willing to support the United Fund. See Chapter 8.
3. **(3)** This CD has been *lying* on the table all week. See Chapter 1.
4. **(5)** No error. See Chapter 8.
5. **(3)** One of the necessary prerequisites for change *is* open-mindedness. See Chapter 8.
6. **(1)** Manuel and *I* travel to work together each weekday morning. See Chapter 10.

7. **(2)** Taxes and laughter *are* always present in our American way of life. See Chapter 7.
8. **(2)** Everyone must realize *his* or *her* own potential and try to achieve it. See Chapter 10.
9. **(4)** Mario is a much more efficient bartender than *he.* See Chapter 10.
10. **(2)** Elissa types much *more quickly* than any other person in the office. See Chapter 4.
11. **(2)** Each of the choices *is* equally unappealing to me. See Chapter 8.
12. **(1)** Before the alarm *stopped* ringing, Vera had pulled up the shade. See Chapter 9.
13. **(2)** One of those women *speaks* as well as a professional lecturer. See Chapter 8.
14. **(1)** The dishes in the box *are* on sale this week only and will be sold for more next week. See Chapter 7.
15. **(5)** No error. See Chapter 9.
16. **(3)** Either the subway or the buses *are* crowded at this time of day. See Chapter 8.
17. **(4)** I noticed that older women walk more *gracefully* than teen-age girls. See Chapter 4.
18. **(2)** Each of the contestants *hopes* to win the grand prize. See Chapter 8.
19. **(4)** When I must speak to a large group of people, I always speak too *softly.* See Chapter 4.
20. **(2)** The mail carriers each *have* their own personal gripes. See Chapter 8.

21. **(3)** Any of the women in that office may express *her* opinion at any time. See Chapter 10.

22. **(2)** Either the executive or members of his staff *were* responsible for breaking the law. See Chapter 8.

23. **(2)** Before they signed the treaty, both parties *had agreed* to uphold the terms provided. See Chapter 9.

24. **(1)** Reagan *had been* president before Bush was, and Clinton served after Bush had. See Chapter 9.

25. **(3)** Either Charlie or I will call you or *him* when the order is ready. See Chapter 10.

26. **(1)** *Romeo and Juliet is* one of my favorite plays, but I've never seen it performed. See Chapter 7.

27. **(3)** Was it Mr. Farrar *who* called you? See Chapter 10.

28. **(4)** I am always at the bus stop earlier than *he*. See Chapter 10.

29. **(1)** Eileen and *I* are working on the night shift with them. See Chapter 10.

30. **(1)** Fifteen minutes *is* all that I can spare to listen to your problems. See Chapter 7.

31. **(2)** The problem of too many people *requires* immediate attention by world leaders as well as scientists and environmentalists. See Chapter 2.

32. **(3)** After many months of arguing, Congress finally *adopted* the bill into law. See Chapter 20.

33. **(2)** Because his lawyer strongly *advised* him to do so, Mr. Rodriguez offered his wife a generous settlement. See Chapter 20.

34. **(1)** The *principal* reason for my not borrowing your credit card is that I'm afraid I'll lose it. See Chapter 20.

35. **(3)** Your supervisor does not appreciate *your* walking in consistently at 9:10. See Chapter 10.

Usage—Part B *Page 276.*

1. **(1)** *My brother never* calls before visiting us.

2. **(3)** Great men throughout history *hardly ever* avoided some minor scandal.

3. **(3)** If you had called ahead of time, I could *have* been ready when you arrived.

4. **(2)** George Burns *scarcely ever* missed a scheduled performance.

5. **(1)** The trip on the *sightseeing* bus was one of the highlights of our much deserved vacation.

6. **(3)** Manny was shocked when Alfred raised his voice; no one had *ever* spoken to him in that tone of voice.

7. **(1)** The *sun is* 865,000 miles in diameter and has a surface temperature of about 10,000°F.

8. **(3)** A wise consumer carefully reads the labels and *doesn't buy* unmarked products.

9. **(3)** If you really had wanted to, you could *have* prevented that misunderstanding.

10. **(1)** Some *scientists believe* that one of the long-range effects of food additives is hyperactivity in children.

Effectiveness of Expression—Part A
Page 277.

1. **(2)** *The new sales associate arrives late* every morning.

2. **(3)** *The doctor missed the emergency call because* he forget his beeper.

3. **(1)** Mia's new job offers *not only a better salary but also increased benefits.*

4. **(4)** Nowadays employers can afford to be choosy *since the period of slow economic growth has increased* the number and the quality of the applicants.

5. **(2)** The dogs get *tough, demanding, useful training* in obedience school.

6. **(2)** Carl Williams is an excellent basketball coach and *a good friend to the team members.*

7. **(3)** Every Thursday night the Morgan family watches TV and *eats TV dinners.*

8. **(3)** The City Council meets every Wednesday evening in private and *every Thursday in public.*

9. **(4)** Carlos Battaglia has a good historical perspective; *therefore, he understands* current events.

10. **(1)** I am not in agreement with most of the policies of the present administration, *but I can't change them.*

Effectiveness of Expression—Part B
Page 279.

1. **(1)** The boundaries of science have expanded significantly, *and two distinct fields of science have emerged: pure and applied.*

2. **(4)** The British pound was devalued *because of an inflationary spiral.*

3. **(2)** The revised Food Guide Pyramid provides a guide to daily food choices, *thereby helping people build a healthful diet.*

4. **(2)** Many people believed that the recent dip in the stock market *resulted from rising interest rates.*

5. **(3)** Viewers find it difficult to reach agreement on whether *or not television encourages violent behavior.*

6. **(4)** One member of the Surgeon General's Scientific Advisory Committee on Television and Social Behavior felt that *there is no question about whether television has a negative effect on its viewers.*

7. **(3)** Some TV viewers express their resentment toward anyone else censoring their viewing choices, *saying it's the parents' job to censor the TV programs their children see.*

8. **(1)** An environmental protection agency should *set automobile pollution standards, oversee stripmining, and prohibit dumping in public waterways.*

9. **(4)** Many people who formerly drove to work are now taking buses *in order to conserve gas, to prevent air pollution, and to save money.*

10. **(1)** In order to encourage the commuter not to drive to work, some communities have installed park-and-ride facilities *where the commuter can leave his car and board a bus for the trip to work.*

11. **(3)** The new employee is very organized; *however, she is always late.*

12. **(3)** The end of 2001 showed a marked decline in Americans traveling abroad *due to increased terrorism.*

13. **(1)** The French Revolution did not occur when the peasants had no rights whatsoever; _rather, the Revolution occurred when the peasants began to taste the better life._

14. **(4)** Modern China has eliminated serious contagious diseases _by using trained nonprofessionals to aid the country's limited number of doctors._

15. **(3)** During the first half of the eighteenth century, the Carter family built a mansion at Williamsburg where the family _grew its own food, rode to the hounds on horses from its own stables, made equipment in its own craft shops, and shipped its tobacco to England from its private dock._

Punctuation and Capitalization
Page 282.

1. **(5)** No error

2. **(4)** The *Declaration of Independence* states "... that all men are created equal, that they are endowed by their Creator with certain inalienable rights; that among these are Life, Liberty, and the pursuit of Happiness."

3. **(2)** Great literature, as well as great art, is a part of the American tradition.

4. **(1)** The pioneers were a hardy, brave group of people who would look in disbelief on the comforts of today's middle class.

5. **(3)** During their first few years on the American continent, the pioneers lived off the animals in the woods and stole corn from the natives.

6. **(1)** They traveled with the bare necessities: food, water, warm clothing, tools, and weapons.

7. **(3)** The Virginians needed their own leader, Jefferson; Sam Adams was not their type.

8. **(1)** Many say George Washington was a competent general and a good president; however, some historians would disagree.

9. **(1)** There are those who would say that John Kennedy was the greatest president to date, and others would say that he has been idealized.

10. **(4)** A flower consists of a calyx, a corolla, a stamen, and pistils.

Index

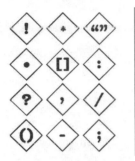

MOVE TO THE HEAD OF YOUR CLASS
THE EASY WAY!

Barron's presents THE EASY WAY SERIES—specially prepared by top educators, it maximizes effective learning while minimizing the time and effort it takes to raise your grades, brush up on the basics, and build your confidence. Comprehensive and full of clear review examples, **THE EASY WAY SERIES** is your best bet for better grades, quickly!

0-8120-9409-3	**Accounting the Easy Way, 3rd Ed.**—$14.95, Can. $21.00
0-8120-9393-3	**Algebra the Easy Way, 3rd Ed.**—$13.95, Can. $19.50
0-8120-1943-1	**American History the Easy Way, 2nd Ed.**—$14.95, Can. $19.95
0-7641-0299-0	**American Sign Language the Easy Way**—$14.95, Can. $21.00
0-8120-9134-5	**Anatomy and Physiology the Easy Way**—$14.95, Can. $19.95
0-8120-9410-7	**Arithmetic the Easy Way, 3rd Ed.**—$13.95, Can. $19.50
0-7641-1358-5	**Biology the Easy Way, 3rd Ed.**—$13.95, Can. $19.50
0-7641-1079-9	**Bookkeeping the Easy Way, 3rd Ed.**—$14.95, Can. $21.00
0-8120-4760-5	**Business Law the Easy Way**—$14.95, Can. $21.00
0-7641-0314-8	**Business Letters the Easy Way, 3rd Ed.**—$13.95, Can. $19.50
0-7641-1359-3	**Business Math the Easy Way, 3rd Ed.**—$14.95, Can. $21.00
0-8120-9141-8	**Calculus the Easy Way, 3rd Ed.**—$14.95, Can. $21.00
0-8120-9138-8	**Chemistry the Easy Way, 3rd Ed.**—$13.95, Can. $18.95
0-7641-0659-7	**Chinese the Easy Way**—$13.95, Can. $18.95
0-7641-1981-8	**Electronics the Easy Way, 4th Ed.**—$14.95, Can. $21.00
0-7641-1975-3	**English the Easy Way, 4th Ed.**—$13.95, Can. $19.50
0-8120-9505-7	**French the Easy Way, 3rd Ed.**—$14.95, Can. $21.00
0-7641-0110-2	**Geometry the Easy Way, 3rd Ed.**—$13.95, Can. $19.50
0-8120-9145-0	**German the Easy Way, 2nd Ed.**—$13.95, Can. $18.95
0-7641-1989-3	**Grammar the Easy Way**—$14.95, Can. $21.00
0-8120-9146-9	**Italian the Easy Way, 2nd Ed.**—$13.95, Can. $19.50
0-8120-9627-4	**Japanese the Easy Way**—$14.95, Can. $21.00
0-7641-0752-6	**Java™ Programming the Easy Way**—$18.95, Can. $25.50
0-8120-9139-6	**Math the Easy Way, 3rd Ed.**—$12.95, Can. $17.95
0-7641-1871-4	**Math Word Problems the Easy Way**—$14.95, Can. $21.00
0-8120-9601-0	**Microeconomics the Easy Way**—$14.95, Can. $21.00
0-7641-0236-2	**Physics the Easy Way, 3rd Ed.**—$14.95, Can. $21.00
0-8120-9412-3	**Spanish the Easy Way, 3rd Ed.**—$13.95, Can. $19.50
0-8120-9852-8	**Speed Reading the Easy Way**—$13.95, Can. $19.50
0-8120-9143-4	**Spelling the Easy Way, 3rd Ed.**—$13.95, Can. $19.50
0-8120-9392-5	**Statistics the Easy Way, 3rd Ed.**—$14.95, Can. $21.00
0-7641-1360-7	**Trigonometry the Easy Way, 3rd Ed.**—$14.95, Can. $21.00
0-8120-9147-7	**Typing the Easy Way, 3rd Ed.**—$18.95, Can. $26.50
0-8120-9765-3	**World History the Easy Way, Vol. One**—$14.95, Can. $19.95
0-8120-9766-1	**World History the Easy Way, Vol. Two**—$14.95, Can. $21.00
0-7641-1206-6	**Writing the Easy Way, 3rd Ed.**—$13.95, Can. $19.50

Barron's Educational Series, Inc.
250 Wireless Boulevard • Hauppauge, New York 11788
In Canada: Georgetown Book Warehouse • 34 Armstrong Avenue, Georgetown, Ontario L7G 4R9
www.barronseduc.com $ = U.S. Dollars   Can. $ = Canadian Dollars

Prices subject to change without notice. Books may be purchased at your local bookstore, or by mail from Barron's. Enclose check or money order for total amount plus sales tax where applicable and 18% for postage and handling (minimum charge $5.95 U.S. and Canada). All books are paperback editions.

(#45) R 9/02